Volume 27, Number 2

differences

Transatlantic Gender Crossings

Guest editors
Anne Emmanuelle Berger and
Éric Fassin

Gender Springtime in Paris:
A Twenty-First-Century Tale of Seasons

Prologue

*I*n the spring of 2014, the Centre d'études féminines et d'études de genre (Center for Women's and Gender Studies) at the University of Paris 8 Vincennes–Saint-Denis celebrated its fortieth anniversary. Among the many events that took place on this occasion, an international conference was convened titled (in French) the International Springtime of Gender: The Scientific and Political Stakes of the Institutionalization and the Internationalization of a Field (Le printemps international du genre).[1] What prompted us at the University of Paris 8 to organize a conference on institutionalization, internationalization, and their vexed relation today was the pressure of a triple context: institutional, indeed, but also more broadly political and intellectual, and inextricably so.

As astonishing as it must always have been for u.s.-based scholars and activists in these areas, given the role that "French thought" played in the intellectual constitution of the field, gender studies in France was only recognized as a legitimate field of study worthy of state support and inclusion in the national curriculum in the last few years. As a result, several new

Volume 27, Number 2   DOI 10.1215/10407391-5621685

programs, new research units, and one CNRS (National Center for Scientific Research)-backed national research network have recently sprung up.[2]

The Centre d'études féminines et d'études de genre (CEFEG) was created at Paris 8 Vincennes in 1974 by Hélène Cixous. At the time, the program was simply named Études féminines; it was the first and oldest doctoral program in women's studies in France and as far as we know in Europe. The Centre soon became internationally renowned, but it had a bumpy and fragile institutional life at both the local and the national levels until the field as a whole received an official stamp. The reasons for the stubborn resistance of the French academy to the inclusion of a women's and/or gender and sexuality studies curriculum are manifold and well known to feminist scholars familiar with France. In a nutshell, the French tradition of state centralism has made it very difficult for local or idiosyncratic initiatives to prosper and gain national acceptance. This same state centralism has always worked to curtail academic institutional and scientific freedom; in particular, it has slowed down efforts to broaden or renew academic curricula unless they are spearheaded from the top down. Finally, the widely shared distrust across the political spectrum toward any initiative—political, intellectual, or institutional—that appears to question the abstract unity of the Republic and the ideal of (French) universalism has meant that any attempt, academic or otherwise, to emphasize the predicament of specific groups or segments of society, be they women, sexual minorities, or so-called ethnic minorities, was met with hostility.

As it celebrated its fortieth anniversary, the CEFEG was in the middle of a local overhaul prompted by the new opportunities afforded by national recognition. While this new state benevolence under the guidance of the center-left government was ushering in an era of unprecedented academic prosperity for the field of gender studies, a battle was raging in the larger public sphere. The center-left government was trying to follow through with its electoral promise to legalize same-sex marriage and to expand homosexual parenting rights. These measures were met with unexpected hostility in a country known for its sexual liberalism. Throughout the year 2013, huge popular demonstrations were organized against the *Mariage pour tous* proposition by a coalition of rightist activists as well as revivified Catholic traditionalists. A counterrevolution seemed to be on the move.[3] In a striking departure from traditional French political discourse, the focus of rightist discontent was cultural rather than economic, recalling the "culture wars" that regularly flare up in the rarefied air of U.S. internal politics. This was due in large part to the fact that the center-left government looked more proactive and more likely to succeed in the realm of what Éric Fassin has called "sexual democracy" than in the area of economic redistribution and other fields of social justice ("Double-Edged"). Calling itself the "Printemps français," the conservative response borrowed the revolutionary rhetoric and appropriated for itself the historical markers of various liberation movements. In particular, such self-naming was meant to suggest a symbolic connection with the "Arab Springs" that had just swept through the Middle East before turning into wintry nightmares. It also evoked ironically the May 1968 uprising,[4] as if the "countersexual" revolution it advocated in 2013 was the belated but pointed answer to the sexual revolution unleashed in 1968. Finally, by calling itself "French," the rightist reaction underlined its nationalist character, thus casting efforts at expanding civil rights for sexual minorities as foreign to the French national ethos. Indeed, soon after the law promulgating same-sex marriage was passed (while attempts to secure legal rights for same-sex parents were stalled by the magnitude of the opposition staged), the focus of this shrewdly engineered political unrest was displaced onto gender theory, as word was spread by a well-crafted propaganda campaign smacking of extreme-right tactics that the government was about to introduce the latter in the national education curriculum. In this instance, gender theory was clearly marked as "American" and understood to be what we might call *queer*. The fear was that such teachings would encourage boys to become girls and would turn innocent little beings into active practitioners of some form of sexuality studies. Thus, no sooner was gender studies fully admitted in the French academy that it became embattled in a public fight.

One has to say that the French media, left and right, had laid the ground for the branding of gender theory as American, since the former had clearly presented the belated development of gender studies in higher education as an effect of the willful Americanization of intellectual life. Gender studies was repeatedly described as "sea landing" (*débarquant*) in France, conjuring up images of the landing of u.s. soldiers come to save Europe in 1944.

All this was also happening in the context of what looked like an inversion of the respective positions held by France and the United States in the realm of academic and more broadly intellectual relations. Between the late sixties and the first years of the twenty-first century, food for thought was massively imported from France by the u.s. academy. As many among the most important representatives of "French thought" died and the intellectual effervescence of the sixties slowly dwindled, France ceased to be the main exporter of ideas worldwide. Plagued by economic recession and self-doubt, suffering the consequences of what postcolonial scholars have called (all the while rightly calling *for* it) the "provincialization of Europe," and engaged, for the first time in the long history of the French academy, in the global race for the market retailing of knowledge and education, France started avidly to import its intellectual nourishment from the United States. It did so not only in the realm of what came to be recognized and accepted exclusively under the heading of "gender studies" (more exactly, in government parlance, *études sur le genre*) but also, more generally, in the realms of the humanities, philosophy (with the spread of analytic philosophy in continental Europe), and cognitive sciences.

True, the work of the U.S.-based feminist and postfeminist thinkers, which, by the end of the first decade of our century, made up the bulk of suggested (or compulsory) reading in gender studies in France as well as in other parts of the world, bore the marks of the forceful inscriptions in French that had helped shape it. True again, the two most widely spoken languages of the so-called feminism of the second wave were French and English, whether they were used alternately or at the same time, ever since Simone de Beauvoir wrote *The Second Sex* in the wake of her stay in "America." But by then, French scholars and activists spoke feminist and postfeminist English more fluently than they did feminist French, with the full acclimation of *gender* and the wide use in French and in some French metropolitan circles of untranslated English terms such as *queer* and its lexical kin or, in another area of lively feminist concern, the word *care.*

It is in this multilayered context that the conference in which the contributors of this issue of *differences* participated took place. It is owing to the political and intellectual ambiance briefly described that we decided to name the event "The International Springtime of Gender."

A number of prominent scholars in the field of gender and sexuality studies attended the conference. They came from different parts of the world (Africa, North America, South America, northern and southern Europe, western Asia); they had different disciplinary training and areas of expertise (anthropology, art history, history, literature, philosophy, sociology, feminist theory); and they belonged to different generations. By different generations, I don't mean only or primarily biological age differences, although whether one had reached adulthood or acquired some form of feminist consciousness in the seventies or later does matter in ways I will address below. More important still, "generations" are a matter of intellectual and affective affiliations, of the nature and depth of the historical experience, of the constitution, transmission (or failure of transmission), and claiming of shared narratives.

Finally, most of the guest participants (only some of whom we were able to include in this issue) had been or were still involved in institution building in major ways and had, therefore, a firsthand experience and role in the shaping and/or handling of the institutionalization of our field. Delphine Gardey has been the director of the young Gender Studies Program at the University of Geneva for the past five years. Miriam Pillar Grossi was, at the time of the conference, the director of the Institute for Gender Studies of the Federal University of Santa Catarina in Brazil. Clare Hemmings had cochaired the Feminist and Women's Studies Association of the United Kingdom and Ireland. Ranjana Khanna directed the Women's Studies Program at Duke University for nine years. Tuija Pulkkinen is president of the Finnish Association for Gender Studies and was then also directing the national Doctoral Program of Gender Studies. Marta Segarra had founded and was the longtime director of the Centre Dona i Literatura of the University of Barcelona. Fatou Sarr Sow is founding director of the first research unit in gender studies (Laboratoire Genre et Recherche Scientifique) of the University Cheikh Anta Diop at Dakkar. Mara Viveros was a founding member of the School of Gender Studies at the National University of Colombia in Bogotá. And Elizabeth Weed is the cofounding editor of *differences* and was a longtime director of the Pembroke Center at Brown University. As for Pinar Selek, a Turkish feminist sociologist involved in both pro-Kurdish and prosexual minorities activities who had to flee her country after being tried and jailed on false grounds, she wasn't given the time or opportunity to contribute to the establishment of women's, feminist, or gender studies in Turkey.

The question of the local forms and effects of the institutionalization of the field of gender studies is a familiar one by now. It has been pondered over time and again, especially in places such as the U.S. and northern Europe where the fields of women's and/or gender studies and, soon after, of sexuality and sexual minorities' studies (LGBTQ+) were allowed to develop and gained wide acceptance relatively quickly and easily compared to most other places. How can it still be of interest today for an anglophone, let alone North American, audience? What more can be argued on the topic since Nancy Miller and Peggy Kamuf debated the effect and import of dragging the signifier *woman* to the center of academic inquiry in the late seventies and Derrida discussed the institutionalization of women's studies at one of its buzzing U.S. locations in the early eighties ("Women")? What else can be said in defense of the academic legitimacy of sexuality studies since the publication of the Routledge *Lesbian and Gay Studies Reader* in 1993? As for the question of the modes and meaning of the internationalization of the field and, more specifically, of the relation between academic recognition and internationalization in the global geopolitical context, it is a major one indeed, which both transnational feminist theorists and postcolonial feminist scholars have attempted to address many times. But why choose to raise it now from the particular site of Paris 8 Vincennes, on the particular occasion of the anniversary of its longtime Centre, when it might be more interesting or at least more truly unsettling to ask it from the vantage point of, say, a Chinese or Indonesian academic institution? To put the question plainly, then, why bother to feature the partial proceedings of this event in an issue of *differences*?

Obviously, I can't answer the question in the place of the journal's editorial board. But here is my guess: in the history of "second-wave" Western feminism and its aftermath(s), the Paris 8 Vincennes Centre functions as a nexus of iconic references, topoi, and issues. I have already, inevitably, named some of them: "French thought," "French feminism(s)," the Anglo-French (or Franco-American) invention of "feminist theory," as well as their postcolonial reinflection or redeployment or sometimes contestation when seen from the u.s. academy.[5]

Then there are the potential intellectual benefits afforded by the celebration of an anniversary. On such occasion, one is invited to look backward in order to look forward in a self-reflexive gesture that is (or appears to be) thoroughly theoretical in the contemporary sense of the term.[6] The mood, in this case, is most often double, at once exhilarated and melancholic: the evocation of beginnings is an ambiguous game, haunted as it always is by the fear or the feeling of an end to come. In a personal exchange we had after the event, Elizabeth Weed cleverly remarked to me on the paradoxical coupling of "old institutional age" (forty-plus years) and springtime, remembrance and emergence, mourning and expecting that characterized the staging of this event. Were we joining the crowd of tired scholars and activists, mainly North American for the time being, who have been announcing the end of feminist theory or gender studies, sometimes even the now cumbersome irrelevance of feminism itself, for almost twenty years now, followed in the last ten years by a sizable number of early practitioners and advocates of queer theory who are now equally worrying about the latter's future? And if so, what internal political and/or intellectual difficulties are prompting this pessimistic outlook and sometimes self-berating attitude on the part of the field(s)' practitioners? Or were we singing a somewhat different tune, owing to the peculiar timing of the blooming of gender studies in France and the particular setting of the University of Paris 8 Vincennes, ensconced as it is in the devastated social landscape of a northern "multicultural" *banlieue* (Saint-Denis) whose social complexities and intellectual yearnings it has been in part trying to address, ever since it was chased out of the semiwild woods of Vincennes?

Anniversaries have become (all too) frequent occurrences in academic and intellectual life in general, whatever the occasion, the field, or the characters involved. Because such rituals are also, today, whether their planners like it or not, advertising tools and exercises in self-promotion, and because they are for that reason unavoidably participating in the commodification of memorialization, they can serve unwittingly to consolidate fictions, adding intellectual commodity fetishism to the inherent risks of forgetfulness, erasure, self-deception, and self-mythologization that threaten the most genuine efforts to do justice to one's past and to further one's self-understanding. But since the Paris 8 Centre underwent many near-deaths and had to reinvent itself several times, both intellectually and institutionally in the course of its eventful and shaky life, and since its life span corresponds roughly to the life span of the field as a whole, then such an occasion might still offer a meaningful opportunity to reflect not only on an already long, multigenerational history, with its own internal waves, shifts, and breaks, but above all, on the ways this history is done, told, passed on, or not.

Finally, I suspect that *differences* was seized by an *unheimlich* feeling of recognition in a place, Paris, that functions somewhat for the field like Rome for Freud or perhaps New York for the inventor of deconstruction. If young women academics in France who were taking part in the MLF (the French Women's Liberation Movement) in the early seventies were inspired at that time by the U.S.-based initiatives to create research and teaching programs in women's studies, the journal *differences*, for its part, was born in the late eighties out of the encounter of "American" academic feminism(s) and more generally U.S.-based humanities with French theory and, more specifically, the so-called French feminism(s). And just as the journal's policy since its inception has been to trace and welcome all the theoretical trends of Western-based feminism and postfeminism in order to foster a dialogue among them, the Centre has always sheltered, sometimes uneasily but enduringly, different theoretical and political positions, even when the emphasis in its midst is clearly (or so it appears to be) on one side or the other of the multilayered divide commonly indexed by references to "sexual difference" or "gender," whether one considers this divide to be time related, epistemological, conceptual, political, idiomatic, or a little bit of all these.

The Resistance of Translation

Starting from the broad question of how institutionalization and internationalization shape and inflect each other and have affected the political and theoretical course of our field, the conference organizers, Éric Fassin and I, asked the participants of the International Springtime of Gender to reflect more precisely on the possible tensions between the demands of institutionalization and the political impetus that prompted the field into existence and that continues to fuel it. Participants were also encouraged to think about the features of the field's internationalization. Did the latter amount to an "Americanization" of the field according to a hegemonic and/ or neocolonial pattern of extension? Or could internationalization enable decentering moves, allowing different ways of conceiving the connection(s) between the local and the global, the center and the periphery, or, even better, between various forms of "locatedness" to emerge? Finally, the organizers asked how the constraints of institutionalization and the course(s) of internationalization might inflect our thinking about such important political and theoretical intersections as the ones between gender and sexuality or between sex and race. Due to sometimes small, sometimes vast differences in geopolitical locations, theoretical orientations, and vocabularies; due also to the nature and depth of historical experience, the answers provided were heterogeneous. But common worries were vented and clusters of issues could be discerned.

As I said, the commemorative dimension of the event prompted retrospective gestures and stirred recapitulative impulses. Past analytical tools and interpretive grids were probed and their continued relevance examined. Several participants expressed some form of anxious concern regarding the possible constitution of a (somewhat) accurate historical narrative and the conditions of its passing down, at least at this point in time. Many founders and witnesses of the beginnings are still around, but memory is fading while history is not yet done, at least not seriously so. Legacy is at stake, whether it is desired or rejected, actively or passively, by reluctant or eager heir(esse)s. What, then, can be transmitted and how? What prevents transmission and what enables it? Or, perhaps more accurately, what makes it at once possible and impossible? The problem of transmission, of making sense across heterogeneous times, is also, to a large degree, a problem of translation, that is, of the conditions and ways in which certain discourses and what one used to call "ideas" are made to cross borders, whether temporal or spatial, internal (intralinguistic and/or within the confines of a seemingly single context) or external (interlinguistic and/or across different contexts), thus fostering connections between heterogeneous spaces and times. All the contributors to this issue wrestled implicitly or explicitly with the question of translation and the nature of its operation(s), hence our decision to make it our framing issue.

Of course, any international scholarly endeavor, and especially one that takes *internationalization* as its explicit theme, is bound to encounter the problem of translation. It is our contention, however, that gender theory and the field of gender and sexuality studies as a whole have been bound up from the beginning with the question of translation in specific and intractable ways. This is so not only because the field initially developed along a transatlantic epistemological and geopolitical axis, or because its current extension is taking place in the context of what one calls globalization, or because it was immediately constituted as an interdisciplinary field requiring and fostering difficult conversations between disciplines that had each developed their own conceptual languages, but also because it is indeed centrally concerned with "crossing(s)," whether crossing(s) functions as a political goal, a metametaphor for the field's variegated theoretical endeavors, or as the name of a multifaceted epistemological problem, and because, in the epistemological and political history of the field, gender has not only functioned as an analytical tool but more precisely as a conversion tool in ways I will try to address shortly.

How Useful Are Dictionaries?

In a twenty-first-century follow-up piece to her famous "Gender: A Useful Category of Analysis," Joan Scott wondered whether the term *gender* "might not have lost its critical edge" for feminist thinking as "its meaning seemed to be able to be taken for granted," at least, she thought, in the English-speaking world (10). Against both the conceptual reifying of gender and the suspiciously easy, if misconceived, generalization of its use beyond the confines of academic feminism, she argued in favor of continuing to put it to the test of translation. In non-English-speaking parts of the world, she wrote, gender still "provided the kind of radical interrogation associated with feminism" because of "the very difficulty of translating [it]" (10). Indeed, she continued, the "language of gender" "cannot be codified in dictionaries, nor can its meanings be easily assumed or translated" (13). Only where gender still feels foreign, then, "because it [falls] outside the national boundaries of 'ordinary usage'" (10), might it still retain its critical power. But, we might ask, isn't the whole world speaking English today anyway, in one form or another? And, conversely, can one assume the easy translatability of gender within the English language itself, such that an English dictionary might provide a satisfactory definition of the term for native or neonative speakers of the language? In fact, Scott makes a somewhat different kind of argument in the last part of her piece. The "language of gender," she warns, "doesn't reduce to some known quantity of masculine or feminine, male or female. It's precisely the particular meanings that need to be teased out of the materials we examine" (13). The "particular meanings" of *gender* we need to tease out of the materials we examine do not derive their particularity from the language in which they are formed and conveyed, so much as they depend on specific or "idiolectic" uses and contextual redeployments and displacements of the term. It is those meanings that a dictionary, whether bilingual or monolingual, can never account for. "When gender is an open question about how those meanings are established, what they signify, and in what contexts, then it remains a useful—because critical—category of analysis," Scott concludes (13). It is not enough, then, to be a native or neonative speaker of a given language, even of English as "the language of gender"; it is not enough, indeed, to be a reliable lexicographer. Only a "translator," that is, somebody who asks her- or himself how meanings are established and what they signify in the particular context or text she or he is dealing with, might be able to trace and convey these meanings.

     I don't have the space and time to tease out the many far-reaching implications of Scott's argument. Let me just stress that, when Scott links the critical fate and force of gender to that of translation, what she means by *translation* is not the ability to provide a proper equivalent based on the most general, that is, generally agreed upon and hence most widely circulating, definition of the term. Quite the contrary. The act of translation, in her view, is what resists the pull or lure of generalization. This pull is certainly reinforced by the combined forces of globalization and *globlishization*, but it doesn't only happen between languages or between English and other languages. It happens within English itself. Translation, conceived here above all as an active task of detection as well as reception of "particular meanings," is thus paradoxically an act of resistance to translatability. And when particular meanings are teased out and stressed over the general use and the unity of meaning such use presumes, the work of (un)translation also becomes inseparable from one of pluralization. Scott's argument here is strikingly consonant with Edward Said's definition of *reading* as an act of both reception and resistance—indeed, the highest form of "resistant reception"—in the service of a reformed humanism. Said calls this practice "democratic criticism," meaning also that such practice has a political import, one that has to do with catering to a plurality of potentially divergent perspectives and especially to those with minoritarian outlooks (61–64).

■

In this issue, Clare Hemmings's and Tuija Pulkkinen's respective arguments about gender are indeed predicated on divergent understandings of the term, relying as they are on different sequences in the history of its becoming-concept. Yet, their different mobilizations of the term lead to convergent assessments, if not of the intended purpose then at least of the effect of its use. In "Is Gender Studies Singular? Stories of Queer/Feminist Difference and Displacement," Hemmings worries about the framing of *gender* (hence, gender studies) as "heterosexual, the property of women, essentialist," and sometimes even racist, by a sizeable portion of queer theorists and/or activists. She questions a certain retrospective view of *gender* as catering only to the political and sexual biases of heterosexual feminists or, worse, women. Finally, she challenges the casting of "gender feminism" as inherently antipleasure(s). According to her, the idea, common among queer theorists and practitioners, that "gender feminists" are stuck dealing with the dangers of sexuality while the queer feminists "have all the fun" doesn't do justice to feminist history. Inherited from the internecine "sex wars" that paved the way for the split between gender studies and sexuality studies, such a view mistakenly presents what happened in a particular time (the eighties) and place (the U.S.) as if it were the whole picture.

Hemmings's argument is very close in thrust and tone to the cautionary warning expressed by Biddy Martin exactly twenty years before in *differences* and republished in *Femininity Played Straight*, a testimony to the endurance of the problem raised. While Martin welcomed the queer turn (within or away from feminism, that is still a question) not only as a self-identified lesbian but as a self-critical feminist, she did question "the tendency to relegate not only femininity, but also feminism to the asexual realm of reproduction" (46). And she suggested that "we stop defining queerness as mobile and fluid in relation to what then gets construed as stagnant and ensnaring, and associated with a maternal, anachronistic, and putatively puritanical feminism" (46).

But queer discourse is in fact as varied and heterogeneous as the feminism(s) it means to question. Martin and Hemmings are aiming at those who want to do away—or believe they can do away—with gender, considered too quickly in their opinion as both a normative social category and a restrictive analytical tool. Other queer thinkers, however, foremost among them, Judith Butler, have taken a stance in favor of keeping gender alive as a descriptive category, an analytical tool, and a political lever. Indeed, a good example of a very different take on gender articulated from a queer perspective is Pulkkinen's hopeful reflection on the pluralization of gender(s) and gender expression allowed and even encouraged by the academic legitimization of gender studies. In her paper, "Feelings of Injustice: The Institutionalization of Gender Studies and the Pluralization of Feminism," Pulkkinen repeatedly emphasizes the role of gender and gender studies in the promotion of "all possible looks, all possible gendered and nongendered bodily expressions" (115). Expressing her faith in the future of feminism(s) thanks to the conceptual work of *gender* defined this time as a queer agent of pluralization, she asserts that "this multiplying of feminist gendered performances and the abundance of genders also signals the pluralization of feminisms" (118).

Both Hemmings and Pulkkinen, then, argue in favor of the pluralization of feminisms, and more specifically "gender feminisms." But Hemmings starts from a definition of *gender* formulated from within the feminism of the seventies and eighties in both Great Britain and the United States, one that latched above all onto power relations between men and women understood as social categories, whereas Pulkkinen relies on the queer reformulation (and radicalization) of gender. Rather than being called upon to designate the social (hence, hierarchical) engineering of sex dualism, *gender*, in this case, becomes the name of what disrupts the neat and dual alignment between sex and "sexual identity." Moreover, it is used as an "affirmative" tool, one that can help free minds and the world from the constraints of sexual binarism. Once gender is analytically severed from sex, there is indeed no reason for it to be bound anymore *by* and *to* sexual duality. In this sense, still, gender hasn't only been a "useful category of analysis": it has been an agent of pluralization. And it remains a conceptual lever, undoubtedly the most important one, for the queer turn taken by feminism and feminist theory, at least within academic programs in the field.

Paradoxically, this more radical (or uprooting) view of gender is also the oldest one from the point of view of a certain epistemological history. The first theorizations of the sex-gender disjunction by John

Money and Robert Stoller in the fifties and sixties were meant precisely to try to account for the breaking of the alignment between sex and gender provoked, or rather revealed, by the double phenomena of intersexualism and transsexualism. And they preceded the feminist critical appropriation of the term that began in the seventies in the Western world. Today, the story of Money's and Stoller's invention of the concept seems to be the preferred tale of origins for gender theory circulating within the field of gender and sexuality studies, at least in the Western world. Isn't this one more sign that gender has operated mainly as a queering agent in the course of its career?

I have emphasized gender's central role as a conversion tool between various competing analytical frameworks and political agendas. If gender exceeds the purview of lexical definitions and conceptual unity, is *sexual difference*, by contrast, the monolithic notion that it is often said to be, whether it is said to constitute the "rock" of mainstream psychoanalytic thinking or the (stumbling) block of thought in all places and ages? Not according to Ranjana Khanna, at least, who, in her contribution, teases out the productive ways in which such a notion has been or could still be put to work. In her talk, Khanna recalled how, as the longtime director of women's studies at Duke University, she had argued in favor of renaming the program "The Program for the Study of Sexual Difference." Such a proposal was bound to be defeated in the present intellectual landscape. For Khanna, though, it was primarily intended as a reminder of the fact that sexual difference, when understood to index the sexual binary, was still either *a* or *the* common problem (or concern) for feminist and queer scholars alike, as well as transgender theorists and activists, busy as they all are trying to figure out what it is, means, or does, coming up against it or going after it. To *study* sexual difference doesn't mean to try and promote one or the other of its meanings, least of all its most conservative ones. As a quasi concept, Khanna reminds us, sexual difference could in fact be put to vastly different, even contradictory, uses and could index opposite psychical and political temporalities: thus, whereas for Derrida sexual difference can never present itself—that is, be simply present—as such and should therefore never be presented as a total, easily recognizable fact of nature or culture; and whereas, in still a different way, it has yet to come through for Irigaray (I would say, in fact, that even more than sexual difference, it is heterosexuality that is "to come" for Irigaray, as preposterous as such a claim may appear to some); to the contrary, for Juliet Mitchell, sexual difference belongs to a past that lives on. According to Mitchell, sexual difference is a matrix of

meaning embedded in generational transmission. The process of its transmission may be unconscious but, Mitchell argues, sexual difference is still
being securely passed down according to a familial and reproductive logic
(xvii–xxii), a view that Judith Butler has forcefully questioned in a recent
issue of *differences* ("Rethinking").

But "sexual difference" as an idiomatic formula doesn't neces
sarily index the sexual binary at all. In Gayle Rubin's vocabulary, and for a
number of other queer thinkers of sexuality, *sexual difference*, spelled most
often in the plural but sometimes also in the singular, designates the whole
gamut of sexual practices, orientations, and outlooks. And although, in the
anglophone world today even more perhaps than in the Francophone one,
sexual difference is largely understood to hark back to the ways in which
psychoanalysis has, or rather is believed to have, conceptualized the sexual
binary, a closer look at the work of Freud himself might spell trouble for this
neat genealogical narrative. For if Freud does write about the *Unterschied
der Geschlecht* or even more simply about *Geschlecht*—a notion that, in any
case, may be closer to "gender" than it is to "sex" in its purview[7]—the bulk
of his efforts lies in uncovering and trying to explain the upsetting nature of
the *sexual*. In most of his writings on sexuality, Freud examines the ways in
which (human) sexuality as such curtails and bypasses the "biological function." And when he uses the phrase *Sexuelle Differenzen*, he actually means
something quite close to what queer thinkers mean, or mean to mean by it:
the different psychical makeups, behaviors, and orientations with regard to
sexuality, the "poly" rather than the "bi."[8]

Each of the contributions I have mentioned so far testifies in one
way or another to the rich and unsteady nature of our fields' conceptual
tools. Such unsteadiness of meaning ensures that "sexual difference" and
"gender" remain first of all as questions, or better as questions *only*—as both
Butler and Scott have suggested each of these notions do in strikingly similar
statements[9]—rather than as securely established analytical tools or, worse,
definitive answers. Each confirms the necessity spelled out by Scott to pay
attention to "particular meanings," that is, to resist the lure of translatability
rather than draw general conclusions.

As for the institutional consequences of this predicament, the
result is a chronic dissatisfaction or uneasiness with the name(s) of the
field(s), an uneasiness that, in my opinion, is better addressed in the United
States than in France. Intellectual wisdom, it seems to me, should consist in
allowing competing vocabularies and issues, ancient or emergent, to do their
work and continue to upset one another, a path that a number of programs

in the United States that started as women's studies programs have taken by renaming themselves, at various points in time, "women's, gender, and sexuality studies," "feminist, gender, and sexuality studies," or whatever set of combinations they deem less unsatisfactory. True, some programs are simply named "gender studies," while others still call themselves "women's studies" and still others "feminist studies," "transnational feminist studies," and so on, but seen from France, one is struck by this ever-changing plurality of options. Meanwhile, the programs of sexuality studies have also adopted an "accretive" strategy, having grown from LGB to LGBTQI. In France, by contrast, only one denomination, *études sur le genre*, has finally been authorized by the state. Such a top-down policy has the felicitous and unintended result of maintaining the institutional and collaborative link between gender and sexuality studies (while, however, subsuming the latter under the former). On the other hand, it produces an illusion of unity or, worse, works to erase the memory of the past, thus hindering the work of transmission. Which brings me to my second point.

Transmission Trouble; or, The Future of Feminist Memory

The performative efficacy of *gender* as a conversion, hence a bridging, tool between feminist and queer theory coupled with the subsequent emergence of sexuality studies in the late twentieth century have rendered the coalition between feminists (that is, women qua feminists and feminists qua women and men) and sexual minorities both possible and necessary. One could also say that queer theory and activism have helped bring back to the fore the core concerns of the feminist struggles of the late sixties and seventies, namely, the various ways in which gender and sexuality, and more precisely gender hierarchy (as well as gender formation) and sexual oppression, are imbricated in one another. As Pulkkinen, eager to refresh our memory and redress the wrongs of partial historiography, reminds us, Sexuality has been a contested issue within the feminist movement and thought from the beginning. Indeed, the women's liberation movements in the West were primarily sexual liberation movements, and they thought of themselves as such. The politicization of the so-called private sphere, the emphasis put on enjoyment (*jouissance*) in both practice and theory, the struggle for the right to a sexuality freed from the reproductive imperative by contraception and abortion, the eager cartography by women activists of their newly discovered bodies, the almost simultaneous formation of women's groups and homosexual (both gay and lesbian) leagues of sort—all point to the early, indeed, founding articulation of the connection between gender and sexuality with its correlative issues, such as sexuality's modes of emergence and disruption or the question of the body as a site of competing political investments.

Yet, as both Griselda Pollock and Clare Hemmings point out with a mixture of worry and regret, the story told about the advent of sexuality studies and queer theory is too often one of epistemological break as well as intellectual supersession, even of axiological (not to say moral) superiority with regard to the feminism(s) of the seventies. This story, which pits queer sexual liberationism against feminist sexual moralism, took shape, as I said, in the wake of the North American sex wars. The divide these feminist wars provoked was compounded by the AIDS crisis, which occurred roughly at the same time. As a result, the early history of the so-called second wave has become illegible and often simply unavailable in many gender and/or sexuality studies programs, at least in the West. According to Pollock, 1968 and its immediate aftermath function at best as a kind of primal scene—mysterious, doubted, and reimagined as such—for those who have heard about it without having witnessed it. As for Hemmings, her concern that gender is being retrospectively misread as catering to heteronormative, essentialist, or, worse, conservative tendencies when cast as the "proper" (and single) object of feminism resonates not only with Butler's and Martin's early warnings against such narrative reordering but also with Annamarie Jagose's more recent criticism of attempts "to typecast feminist theory [. . .] as old-fashioned and passé, temporally quarantined from new-school queer theory" (43). Hemmings notes that the recent cooptation of feminist rhetoric by Western governments at the service of a neocolonialist agenda has thwarted feminism's message and emancipatory thrust, making it all the more vulnerable to queer suspicion. Something similar, though, is now also happening with regard to sexual minorities' claims. Queer forms of kinship are gaining state recognition and support in the West. New possibilities afforded by the development of various biotechnologies of procreation now make the thought of queer parenting quite imaginable, lessening in the process the proclaimed aversion toward reproductive logics and temporalities. Meanwhile, hitherto unthinkable forms of cooptation of gay politics by reactionary political forces with racist overtones have started to emerge. Both feminism and queer activism risk losing their subversive edge in the West, making it difficult for queer theory in particular to maintain "antinormativity" as its central tenet and axis of intervention.[10]

In their respective attempts to account for the reasons why the memory of (early) second-wave feminism has gone bad among the very people who could be expected to keep it alive or rekindle it, Pollock and Hemmings both stress the generational dynamics at work. Hemmings called an earlier version of the piece featured in this volume "From Phallic Feminist Mothers to Polymorphous Queer Children: Institutionalizing Stories of Feminist/Queer Difference," emphasizing the familial configuration of the dispute between young(er) queer theorists and those deemed older feminists. Pollock's plea in favor of transgenerational collaboration aims at fending off what she sees and experiences as a painful generational struggle, which may have ultimately to do less with differing political or theoretical stances than with mother/daughter conflict and rivalry. The very notion of "waves" adopted by feminism to account for the history of its irregular appearances on, and disappearances from, the world stage hurts us, she says, because a wave always rushes to cover up the ground gained and erases past traces. In Pollock's view, the wave allegorizes, perhaps unwittingly but in any case unfortunately, the active and deadly work of forgetting that feminists should precisely strive against. What, then, would the preservation or fostering of a feminist memory look (or sound) like? Pollock calls for a nonlinear and nonteleological understanding of history, which would resist thinking of the future as what comes out of a necessary overcoming of the past by the present, by allowing different temporalities (the lingering, the emergent, the not yet there, etc.) to coexist. She sketches the lineaments of a transgenerational ethics that would involve a double commitment to transmission and education as well as an openness to what is coming on the part of the older generations, while younger generations might cultivate respect for and fidelity (however impious) to both *what* and *who* has come before. In other words, both Hemmings and Pollock look for ways of dealing with legacy, debt, and inheritance that would avoid the double pitfall of dutiful subservience to tradition and received wisdom, on the one hand, and of blindness to (or resentment toward) the specters that continue to haunt, indeed make up, our present, on the other. Both feminist scholars warn, each in their own way, against the at once Hegelian and Oedipal pattern(s) in which intergenerational relations among feminists remain too often caught. It is not enough to deconstruct the Hegelian dialectic and the properly familial dynamics of the power struggle it both stages and enacts, as we might do in our classes. Nor should we content ourselves to question the universal relevance of the Oedipus myth for psychoanalysis. Indeed, it takes more work than words to escape their grip. Of course, such a predicament is not specific to feminism and its history. But this is a reminder that self-proclaimed radicality doesn't suffice to exempt oneself from the most entrenched patterns and ordinary workings of historical processes.

So what can and should be done? At some point, when this whole historical and intellectual sequence recedes into the folds of a remote past, when the current conversation between the recently gone, the still alive, and the future bygones takes place only among the shadows of the dead, when it won't be a question of witnessing, of divergent experiences, and of living or faulty memory, different stories will come out and history will be made all over. It is also worth noting that, in places where gender studies had a late beginning (for instance in Spain, or in Columbia), due to particular political and institutional histories, the feeling may be different: The nineties may not feel like they have superseded the seventies. There may not be older generations left to feel that they have been forgotten or are being misrepresented. Feminist and queer theories may be received and studied at the same time by both scholars and students. As a result, the generational drama might not play itself out and be experienced in the same way. Hence, the decisive importance of location and local temporalities, of what Hemmings calls "the stakes of locatedness" in the consideration of the effects and modalities of the institutionalization and internationalization of the field.

Meanwhile, Hemmings, Pollock, but also Gardey all place their hopes for a feminist act of transmission in what we could call the spatial unraveling of the historical dialectic.[11] Pollock dreams of the (re)constitution of the field of feminist studies as an open space with multiple points of entrance that would enable the peaceful cohabitation rather than the contentious succession of generations. Psychoanalysis teaches us that processes of identification, being predicated on the child/parent bond, are embedded in vertical structures of relations marked by the power differential between generations as well as by rivalry between siblings for the love of the parents. Pollock tries to imagine other patterns of identification between fellow feminists, ones that would make possible the space-sharing she yearns for, whatever the point in time at which a group or an individual might join the cause and/or enter the field. Hemmings questions the Hegelian view of human time as indexing the progress of spirit. This view, still the most commonly held in spite of evidence, tends to construe temporal succession as historical supersession. One should, instead, Hemmings argues, consider "Sedgwick or Rubin not as 'coming after' feminist or gay and lesbian singularity, but as *participating in spaces of debate* about gender and sexuality that are ongoing."[12] As for Gardey, in a striking move for a historian, she also drops the temporal axis in favor of the spatial one and insists, in the wake of Derrida, that feminist transmission can only happen when the paradoxical "territories" of its occurrence are configured as hospitable grounds. The notion of hospitality modifies our understanding of the "home" and "the ground": once it lets the stranger in, the home becomes not only a shelter, an asylum—thus suspending the distinction between private and public, the domestic and the political—but an extraterritorial entity that doesn't obey the law of borders, be they national or otherwise. But the necessarily mutual crossing of borders between the guest and the host in the opening of the space of hospitality—whether these borders are external or internal, recognizable according to political conventions or, on the contrary, difficult to locate, even admit—doesn't mean that all differences are erased. There is in fact no act and no experience of hospitality without the experience and acceptance of difference, sometimes even radical difference. To put it in a different way, the stranger as such always speaks a foreign language, hence Gardey's insistence at several points in the course of her meditation on the disruptive and possibly transformative force of foreign utterances, of linguistic performances that attest to the "absolute" and singular "locatedness" of their site of enunciation. While Gardey, in a move long familiar to postcolonial theorists, advocates hybridization and forcefully demands at one point that feminism(s) speak(s) the Creolized language of truly offered and/or experienced hospitality, she mostly emphasizes the magnitude of the task of translation entailed by the feminist hospitable extraterritoriality she wishes for. And she does this with a form of endearing optimism that is itself as welcoming as it is refreshing, unencumbered as it is in her case by nostalgic remembrance of more joyous times.

As I wrote earlier, transmission is a form of translation and vice versa. Like translation, transmission aims at crossing a gap, at building bridges, at fostering connections. The gap transmission tries to bridge between generations is temporal. Translation, for its part, operates on a horizontal level, even when it strives to make available, in the same time and space, formulations that might belong to different times as well as locations. Between real strangers, however, as Derrida has taught us to consider, translation is both necessary and impossible, and all the more necessary because it is impossible. And because translation stems precisely from the recognition of the unbridgeable gap of difference and the irreducibility of idioms, because the contexts of reception necessarily alter the meaning of the "source" message, translation as transmission can only fail or stray in certain respects. Still, for all the complications Derrida and a number of translation theorists have alerted us to, something happens in and thanks to translation that may open paths and change hearts as well as landscapes, because, as a task taken on deliberately, it involves the act of reading and the active work of reception. Whether it is an individual endeavor or a collective one or both, translation is a responsive act in the most literal sense, an answer to the call of the other that mobilizes subjectivity as responsibility. This may be the reason why Walter Benjamin stressed not the work of translation itself but indeed the (almost moral) task of the *translator*.

But does—or can—translation remain the work of the translator(s) today, that is, the responsive act of a reader (or a group of readers) who at once welcomes and resists, consciously or not, the stranger text's pull? In other words, is there still a future for Said's democratic criticism? Or has translation, that is, the concerted effort to preserve or even mark out differences (that is, "particular meanings") and foster pluralism through multilateral exchanges, merely become a wishful trope, desperately held on to by the humanists' endangered species?

Elizabeth Weed's forceful plea against "The Lure of the Postcritical" does not provide direct answers, but it can help us take the question further.

The Mime, the Meme, and the Market

Weed's essay has many layers. She worries about the forsaking of critical theory that she sees or thinks she sees happening in recent trends in the humanities. Seasoned practitioners of deconstruction are turning against it. Hermeneutical approaches that aim to decipher hidden mechanisms are dropped in favor of "surface reading." One doesn't bother anymore to try and uncover the insidious workings of ideology, presumably because these workings are not dissimulated anymore and there's nothing one can do about them anyway. These reactive trends could be read again as exemplifying the Oedipal pattern of disaffiliation with, and supersession of, previous generations I have already talked about in the light of Pollock's and Hemmings's expressed concerns. But Weed is not interested in tracking the vicissitudes of generational transmission. Rather, she is intent on figuring out what late capitalism and its dominant feature or effect, namely, globalization, are doing to critical thinking. Marx and Freud, the most insightful thinkers of early capitalism, forged analytical tools and offered interpretations that aimed at understanding the world and resisting its course in the same thrust. By contrast, today's thinking, according to Weed, at least in the areas she is dealing with, tends, however unwittingly, to espouse rather than oppose the spirit of (late) capitalism. What might be happening in the realm of the humanities, hence also in feminist theory, is a weakening of what I have called the resistance of translation.

To make her point, Weed focuses on the contemporary theoretical uses and cultural import of a notion that was theorized by both Marx and Freud but has gained ever greater theoretical and cultural currency today: that of fetishism. The word *fetish*, she reminds us, was coined by Portuguese merchants to designate the idols, the fake gods, that some of the exotic people they encountered in their faraway search for new commercial venues worshipped. Indeed, *fetish* (*fetisso*) literally means fake, fictitious, factitious, fabricated, fashioned. Fetishism, in both its Marxian and Freudian senses, is thus a manifestation of what we could call the "prosthetic drive" of modern and contemporary culture, the drive not only to master nature but to replace it with artifacts, fabricated objects, or technological processes. This is precisely what Marx said capitalism was striving to do. Weed alerts us, then, to the potential political and intellectual complications that might arise from the subsequent realization that twentieth-century feminist theory, with its strong antinaturalist bent, and even more queer theory, with its embrace of fetishist practices and fake *godes* ("gode" is the French abbreviated word for dildo) that belie the alleged naturalness of sexuality, might well partake of the very same drive that fuels the capitalistic rush. In other words, late twentieth-century and early twenty-first-century feminist and queer thought may be "framed" by the spirit of capitalism in intractable ways. Not that Weed advocates a (re)turn to nature, a move that would be equally illusionary, if in a different way. Rather, since, as she writes, "we are all practiced fetishists," she advises us to practice a kind of self-reflexive fetishism, one that would be driven (but also perhaps derailed) by the knowing resistance to its own power (170).

Weed shrewdly links the fetish with another metonymic figure for the pervasiveness of late capitalism's processes: the globe. Globalization, that is, market-driven international exchange and enforced interdependency, has turned the world into a globe: a "sphere that forecloses all alternatives and shuts out the horizon by the curve of its arc" (170) in Weed's words. Once again, Weed is interested in the ways globalization shapes symbolic production, hence in the forms it takes in the realm of symbolic exchange. The formidable development of teletechnologies of communication, and particularly of visualization technologies, has rendered irrelevant former reading procedures that painstakingly tried to tease out if not hidden meanings then at least meanings that were said to escape what Derrida qualified in "Plato's Pharmacy" as "anything that could rigorously be called a perception" (63).

At a time when everything is made visible, every move exposed, there is no further need for hermeneutics (which is what Weed, following both Eve Sedgwick and Paul Ricoeur, calls these obsolete reading practices). It comes as no surprise then that the preferred means of exposure today might be the image rather than the text.

Indeed, in the course of her argument about the ways in which globalization and generalized fetishism conspire to inflect, or perhaps deflect, critical theory, Weed quotes *pêle-mêle* Sedgwick's humorous remark on the role played by television in the exposure as well as production of the reign of simulacra ("Paranoid" 141), the unabashed circulation on the World Wide Web of the images of torture at the Abu Ghraib prison and the glossy pictures of alluring transgender figures in fashion magazines. The turning of the transgender figure into a worldwide fashion icon seems to exemplify, in Weed's view, the unwitting convergence of commodity fetishism with its globalizing tendency, the prosthetic drive of capitalism, and a certain course of sexual politics as well as theory that toys with the possibilities afforded by technocapitalism.

But what does this all have to do with the failure of translation? With images, there is no need for dictionaries, or so it appears, not because dictionaries give quick answers rather than raise questions, but because images bypass language differences altogether. Language differences, and more precisely divergences in language usages, point to contextual differences that cannot be erased and should therefore not be overlooked. Images, on the other hand, can be viewed globally without much hindrance. No need to know the context to find them enticing or repellent. Their ability to circulate across borders is thus greatly enhanced. True, an image, any kind of image, can lend itself to something like reading. Conversely, one can choose not to read a text and treat it, as is sometimes the case, particularly with "sacred" texts, as a fetish. The problem, then, doesn't lie with the image in itself. It doesn't lie with the nature of what is being circulated. Rather, the apparent primacy of images tells us something about the mode of circulation itself. The virtual bypassing of borders by symbolic goods and icons (while at the same time material political borders hindering human passage are being re-erected everywhere), their instant availability thanks to the speed and reach of teletechnologies, threaten to change the conditions of intellectual exchange by canceling the time and space of translation, hence of resistant hospitality to the thought of the other(s). We who were raised as humanists, neohumanists, or posthumanists of whatever persuasion are all dismayed at the speed at which "new" propositions today become clichés, mantras, little intellectual fetishes, soon to be dropped like worn-out toys. The unprecedented speed of reification is obviously determined by the mode and speed of circulation. When Jagose, an Australian queer theorist, wonders in her recent piece, "The Trouble with Antinormativity," whether the quasi-automatic antinormative stance of queer theory hasn't "come to prevail as a kind of meme, an easily transmissible conceptual signature the persistence of which is more easily traced to nonepistemological impulses," she draws attention precisely to what the "easy transmissibility" afforded or materialized by current technological modes of information and communication might be doing to critical thinking (32). What happens to queer theory and politics when its claim to subversion appears "automatic" and its surprising moves become predictable in the course of its successful spreading through the (Western) world? The "transmission" of formulas or stances Jagose worries about is a *memetic* transmission, one that occurs without discernable agents of dissemination, without willful actors of reception. The word *meme*, as we know, was coined by Richard Dawkins in the late seventies to designate a genetic replicator of a new kind, one that spreads sameness, as it were, by reproducing itself without differentiation or mutation and that Dawkins characterizes as a "unit of imitation." Dawkins claims to have had in mind the French word *même* (self-same) when he came up with "meme," another example of the attraction of English and French when it comes to theorizing. Unsurprisingly, the meme started to enjoy a "viral" success, spreading across disciplinary and language borders with the development of the Internet precisely because it appeared suited to describe the very ways in which information was being processed and spread across the web. The *meme* is a paradoxical trope. While all metaphors rely on differences (to start with, lexical and semantic differences) to produce similarities or rather semantic encounters, the meme has become a figure for the complete collapse of differences through replication. Thus, while Jagose's invocation of the meme can be said to be twice removed or doubly metaphoric (she borrows it from the field of information theory which borrows it from the field of genetics), the very mention of the meme actually threatens, or marks, the collapse between these fields thanks to the very homogenizing mechanism it designates.

When Jagose wonders if the "memetic" impulse hasn't overcome the epistemological impulse, she is suggesting that replication, that is, repetition without difference, is threatening to replace the work of critical reception (that is, welcoming and hosting with a difference) that inheres in intellectual or scientific pursuit. When Weed notes that the globe, rather than being a figure for the expansiveness and plurality of the world, has become the name for its contraction under the pull of homogenizing forces (while power imbalances remain firmly in place), she is saying something quite similar.

True, globalization and its technologically engineered avatar, the information-driven *memeticism* against which our dreams of infinite hospitality to infinite differences might come crashing, do not threaten only the course of feminist and queer theory or politics. But the stakes are high for an intellectual, political, and social field whose very raison d'être has been and continues to be the excavation of unrecognized and unwanted differences and the promotion of plurality.

Can translation, a neohumanist practice of transnational exchange and now perhaps an ethico-political task of resistant and transformative reception, withstand the trend?

ANNE EMMANUELLE BERGER is a professor of French literature and gender studies at the University of Paris 8 Vincennes–Saint-Denis and the founding director of LEGS (*Laboratoire d'études de genre et de sexualité*), a new CNRS-backed research unit. She has recently published *The Queer Turn in Feminism: Identities, Sexualities, and the Theater of Gender* (Fordham University Press, 2014).

Notes

1   For an overview of the events that took place on this occasion, see the web documentary designed by Barbara Wolman ("Acte V").

2   See the website of the newly founded Institut du genre (*Institut*).

3   This was sadly confirmed by the results of the last regional elections in France as well as by the nationalistic and xenophobic turn taken by almost all political parties, the center-left government included.

4   In the decade following May 1968, demonstrators often chanted in the streets: "Chaud, chaud, chaud, le printemps sera chaud!" ["Hot, hot, hot, the spring's going to be hot!"].

5   Vincennes was committed intellectually and politically to anti-colonialism and "third worldism" in the seventies, welcoming more students from decolonizing and "developing" countries than any other university in Europe at that time. "French feminism," on the other hand, was conflated with first-world metropolitan views by some U.S.-based feminist and postcolonial scholars, in spite of the fact that most of these same French feminists were no more (and no less) "French" than the U.S. scholars calling them to task were "(North) American," and they were for the most part no less virulently opposed to colonialism.

6   Recall how, in his "very short introduction" to *Literary Theory*, Jonathan Culler mentioned self-reflexivity or "thinking about thinking," that is, inquiring "into the categories we use in making sense of things" as one of the defining features of theory (14).

7 On the meaning of the Freudian *Geschlecht* and the difficulty
of translating it into English or
French, see Berger, "La psychanalyse" 126–30; Fraisse; and
Laplanche 188.

8 On this issue, see Berger, "Ends"
and "La psychanalyse."

9 See Butler, "End" 191–92; and Scott
12–13.

10 On this topic, see *differences*'
recent issue on queer antinormativity, edited by Robyn Wiegman
and Elizabeth Wilson.

11 Again, a similar move is made by
Said in *Humanism and Democratic
Criticism* 82.

12 This is from an earlier version of
Hemming's essay included in this
issue.

Works Cited

"Acte V: Le printemps international du genre." Video. 26–27 May 2013. *Les quarante vies du Centre d'études féminines et d'études de genre.* http://teledebout.org/webdocu/40vies/#accueil_.

Berger, Anne Emmanuelle. "The Ends of an Idiom, or Sexual Difference in Translation." *The Queer Turn in Feminism: Identities, Sexualities, and the Theater of Gender.* Trans. Catherine Porter. New York: Fordham UP, 2014. 107–25.

——————. "La psychanalyse comme 'théorie du genre.'" *Subversion lacanienne des théories du genre.* Ed. Fabian Fajnwaks and Clotilde Leguil. Paris: Éditions Michèle, 2015. 107–32.

Berger, Anne Emmanuelle, and Éric Fassin, eds. *Transatlantic Gender Crossings.* Spec. issue of *differences* 27.2 (2016).

Butler, Judith. "The End of Sexual Difference?" *Undoing Gender.* New York: Routledge, 2004. 174–203.

——————. "Rethinking Sexual Difference and Kinship in Juliet Mitchell's *Psychoanalysis and Feminism.*" *differences* 23.2 (2012): 1–19.

Culler, Jonathan. *Literary Theory: A Very Short Introduction.* Oxford: Oxford UP, 1997.

Derrida, Jacques. "Plato's Pharmacy." *Dissemination.* Trans. Barbara Johnson. Chicago: U of Chicago P, 1981. 61–171.

Derrida, Jacques, et al. "Women in the Beehive: A Seminar with Jacques Derrida." *differences* 16.3 (2005): 139–57.

Fassin, Éric. "A Double-Edged Sword: Sexual Democracy, Gender Norms, and Racialized Rhetoric." *The Question of Gender: Joan W. Scott's Critical Feminism.* Ed. Judith Butler and Elizabeth Weed. Bloomington: Indiana UP, 2011. 143–58.

Fraisse, Geneviève. "La contradiction comme lieu du féminisme." *Les Rencontres de Bellepierre.* http://www.lrdb.fr/articles.php?lng=fr&pg=1074 (accessed 1 Jan. 2016).

Gardey, Delphine. "'Territory Trouble': Feminist Studies and (the Question of) Hospitality." Berger and Fassin 125–52.

Hemmings, Clare. "Is Gender Studies Singular? Stories of Queer/Feminist Difference and Displacement." Berger and Fassin 79–102.

Hirsch, Marianne, and Evelyn Fox Keller, eds. *Conflicts in Feminism.* New York: Routledge, 1990.

Institut du Genre. http://institut-du-genre.fr/ (accessed 7 Feb. 2016).

Jagose, Annamarie. "The Trouble with Antinormativity." Wiegman and Wilson 26–47.

Kamuf, Peggy. "Replacing Feminist Criticism." Hirsch and Fox Keller 105–11.

Khanna, Ranjana. "On the Name, Ideation, and Sexual Difference." Berger and Fassin 62–78

Laplanche, Jean. "Psychanalyse et sexualité." Conversation with Francis Martens. *Psychanalyse: que reste t-il de nos amours?* Ed. Francis Martens. Paris: Éditions Complexe, 2000. 187–91.

Martin, Biddy. "Extraordinary Homosexuals and the Fear of Being Ordinary." *Femininity Played Straight: The Significance of Being Lesbian.* New York: Routledge, 1996. 45–70.

Miller, Nancy, K. "The Text's Heroine: A Feminist Critic and Her Fictions." Hirsch and Fox Keller 112–20.

Mitchell, Juliet. New Introduction. *Psychoanalysis and Feminism.* London: Penguin, 2000. xv–xxxviii.

Pollock, Griselda. "Is Feminism a Trauma, a Bad Memory, or a Virtual Future?" Berger and Fassin 27–61.

Pulkkinen, Tuija. "Feelings of Injustice: The Institutionalization of Gender Studies and the Pluralization of Feminism." Berger and Fassin 103–24.

Said, Edward W. *Humanism and Democratic Criticism.* New York: Columbia UP, 2004.

Scott, Joan. "Gender: Still a Useful Category of Analysis?" *Diogenes* 57.1 (2010). 7–14.

Sedgwick, Eve Kosofsky. "Paranoid Reading and Reparative Reading, or, You're So Paranoid, You Probably Think This Essay Is about You." *Touching Feeling.* Durham: Duke UP, 2003. 123–51.

Weed, Elizabeth. "Gender and the Lure of the Postcritical." Berger and Fassin 153–77.

Wiegman, Robyn, and Elizabeth Wilson, eds. *Queer Theory without Antinormativity.* Spec. issue of *differences* 26.1 (2015).

Is Feminism a Trauma, a Bad Memory, or a Virtual Future?

*F*eminism is, I suggest, to be grasped as trauma to the societies in which it emerges. Feminism is trauma because it emerges repeatedly as a contestation of the entire symbolic and imaginary orders of meaning and subjectivity. Feminism is, however, and for this reason profoundly *traumatic* to its own core subjects, or rather potential subjects—women summoned by this movement in thought and action to a political and cultural collectivity. By engaging with feminism, women are called upon to become a new kind of subject: a feminist subject and the "subject of feminism" (de Lauretis 30).

As we understand it, trauma happens. But those to whom trauma happens have no mechanism through which to digest or metabolize the excessive event. The process of the event's becoming a memory involves our testifying to its constitutive absence as known experience as well as its relentless presence reshaping experience. It requires, therefore, the witnessing of this testimony and the forging of a narrative in mediated doses that may generate the terms through which we come to figure (image and fantasy) and to symbolize (word and thought) the unprocessed affect of the

Volume 27, Number 2 DOI 10.1215/10407391-3621697

© 2016 by Brown University and d i f f e r e n c e s : A Journal of Feminist Cultural Studies

unthinkable event. This process is dialogical and provisional, always leaving a residue or a trace as well as resistance and miscomprehension.

The struggle for the entry of the feminist event as memory into representation places the traumatic challenge to a phallocentric order and its complex and varied sociohistorical forms and temporalities, therefore, between remembrance and iconography. Remembrance is an action, collective in some form, effective in its own moment—a collective performance that binds its participants. It secures the presence of what is no longer immediate as part of a continuous process of living. Iconography teaches us how an image is forged for a remembered affect that was once an action, a gesture freighted by its own embodied affectivity (Pollock, *After-affects*).

Thus to write as a feminist, I need to construct a ground for that term in order for it to produce a feminist, that is to say, critical-political, effect. I am arguing that such ground lies between trauma and cultural memory and between remembrance and iconography. It also falls, however, between memory and virtuality. In setting up such pairs, I am seeking to evoke a thinking space suspended between certain poles, an oscillation not an opposition, a spiral not a slash.

The images we create of our past and the stories we tell matter (Hemmings, Scott). They have powerful effects. We need to examine critically the effects of imagining and then narrating the event of the twentieth century we name *feminism* as a succession of waves and as the conflict between generations. I would argue that both figures inflect destructively the historical imagination of feminism and the place of the feminist intervention in the historical imagination.

In my own field of art history/cultural analysis, the historiographical mapping of u.s.-European feminist art history as geographical-generational difference was posited in an influential survey of the state of the discipline published in *Art Bulletin* in 1987 by the distinguished art historians Thalia Gouma-Peterson and Patricia Mathews. Immediately contested from both sides of the Atlantic that formed an intellectual-political divide in this narrative (Broude and Garrard), the authority of the article has nonetheless ensured a consolidation of this representation, while my own challenge to the model disappeared into the unread archive (Pollock, "Generations" and "Politics"). This itself is a continuing question for feminist historiography and cultural memory: what are the memory politics at work when certain framings of the past or theoretical initiatives achieve canonical status while nonbenign amnesia is inflicted on equally coherent possibilities?

Having failed to stem the tide of this discourse and its dominant tropes, I have changed my tactics from irritation to analysis. Thus I want to probe this discourse with psychoanalytic questions about what we might name *feminist desire* (Pollock, *Differencing*).[1] Why have waves and generations become the accepted and tenacious ways of imagining the feminist past? What do they tell us about the unfinished business of the feminist revolt? With what might we work to open up this now institutionalized, iterated, circulated metaphorization of a recent feminist past so that we can move from this bad (poor and disadvantageous) memory to a virtual future?

Falling into an intellectual depression in the face of the repeated declaration during the 1990s that feminism was over, dead, done with, or at best no longer interesting or relevant, I decided to argue the inverse. I suggested that, far from being ready for the dustbin of history, feminism had not yet arrived. Borrowing freely from a Deleuzian trend in feminist theory that I did not philosophically inhabit, I declared feminism to be *virtual*. Not already known, feminism is becoming. As a methodology for confronting the issues of history, time, and cultural memory, I devised what I named the *virtual feminist museum*, in which the qualifier "virtual" is attached to feminism (*Encounters*). Not a cybernetic museum, the production of *differencing* spaces of encounter for artworks and cultural history resisted any unifying retrospective narrative and solicited unanticipated readings of visual inscriptions in an archive that generated a virtuality for the contestation and transformation of the dominant imaginary and symbolic orders of meaning and subjectivity (Pollock, *Differencing*). This freed me from the burden of defending a past that was, of course, itself already being carved up and periodized, treated like a bone to be fought over by contentious generations, or drowned in waves of erasing novelty.

This article is a preliminary elaboration of the questions that form around this tension between feminism as a known event rendered intelligible through our narratives of its generations and waves and feminism as a future not yet arrived because it stakes a claim to what literary theorist Ewa Plonowska Ziarek discerns as the radicality of the underestimated and banalized suffragette moment, namely, the suffragettes' claim to the right to revolt. This is not, however, to replace a dismal sense of melancholic exhaustion with mere utopian gesturing. Virtuality posits something that exceeds the varied actualizations of elements of that virtuality, each of which becomes heterogeneous to it in actualization. This means that each episode of the feminist revolt against phallocentrism and patriarchy is but a contingent actualization of the unharvested virtuality of feminism that is never exhausted or fully known by any of these moments, each of which is to be grasped within its specificity and understood for what it has introduced into cultural and political possibility. Writing a history of feminism as waves and generations inflicts a false sequentiality, deceptive consistency, and obligatory ruptures along a line of time, rather than holding us to moments, flashes, constellations of unexhausted and unpredictable feminist potentiality.

In the generationally titled *Undutiful Daughters*, a volume in the Breaking Feminist Waves series, Australian philosopher Elizabeth Grosz writes of dreaming new knowledge by explaining the relation of concepts and thinking itself to the world we inhabit and to the future of feminist theory.

> *We need concepts in order to think our way in a world of forces we do not control. Concepts are not a means of control, but forms of address that carve out for us a space and time in which we may become capable of responding to the indeterminate particularity of events. Concepts are thus a way of addressing the future, and in this sense are the conditions under which a future different from the present—the very goal of every radical politics—becomes possible. Concepts are not premonitions, ways of predicting what will be; on the contrary, they are modes of enactment of new forces; they are themselves the making of the new. (16)*

If we wish to imagine and initiate a world beyond the present, a movement as it were, we need, in addition to percept and affect, concepts. Grosz turns to explain theory as virtual.

> *In short, theory is never about us, about who we are. It affirms only what we can become, extracted as it is from the events that move us beyond ourselves. If theory is conceptual in this Deleuzian sense, it is freed from representation—from representing the silent minorities that ideology inhibited (subjects), and from representing the real through the truth which it affirms (objects)—and it is opened up to the virtual, to the future that does not yet exist. Feminist theory is essential, not as a plan or an anticipation of action to come, but as the addition of ideality or incorporeality to the horrifying materiality of the present as patriarchal, racist, ethnocentric, a ballast to enable the present to be transformed. (15)*

Rather than posing theory as abstraction from the substance of real lived lives, stranding thought as the opposite of action, for instance, or activism, or politics, or making a difference in the real world, Grosz is reminding us of the politics of theory, the potential and the necessity for conceptual innovation as part and parcel of the project of transformation not only of the world but of our subjectivities as agents of and subjects in the world. This opens on to the key question I want to pose around *political subjectivity* as a combination of concepts from different traditions.

Rebecca Walker and the Third Wave

In an article in the North American feminist *Ms.* magazine in 1992, a twenty-two-year-old African American writer contributed to the creation of what is now widely known as the third wave of feminism by writing on the Senate hearings on the appointment of an African American judge to the Supreme Court, during the course of which Clarence Thomas was accused of sexual harassment by Anita Hill on October 11, 1991.[2] The campaign against Anita Hill became a cause célèbre articulating the complex doubling of violence under race-gender and gender-race politics. Rebecca Walker was moved to articulate her position in the face of this event:

> *I am ready to decide, as my mother decided before me, to devote much of my energy to the history, health, and healing of women. Each of my choices will have to hold to my feminist standard of justice. To be a feminist is to integrate an ideology of equality and female empowerment into the very fiber of my life. It is to search for personal clarity in the midst of systemic destruction, to join in sisterhood with women when often we are divided, to understand power structures with the intention of challenging them. While this may sound simple, it is exactly the kind of stand that many of my peers are unwilling to take. So I write this as a plea to all women, especially the women of my generation: Let Thomas' confirmation serve to remind you, as it did me, that the fight is far from over. Let this dismissal of a woman's experience move you to anger. Turn that outrage into political power. Do not vote for them unless they work for us. Do not have sex with them, do not break bread with them, do not nurture them if they don't prioritize our freedom to control our bodies and our lives.*
>
> *I am not a postfeminism feminist. I am the Third Wave.*

("Becoming")

In this first declaration, the additional wave, the third, marks affirmed solidarity with a history of Black feminist struggle. It asserts continuity and identification. In 1994, Walker published an edited collection under the title *To Be Real: Telling the Truth and Changing the Face of Feminism*. The book's introduction takes a different direction, however. It offers a heartfelt indictment of the pressures Walker experienced in the presence of her feminist mother, aunts, and community. Walker felt herself to be constantly judged against what emerged from the writer's representation as an authoritarian feminism that adjudicated on what was politically acceptable and what undermined the feminist project. "A year before I started this book my life was like a feminist ghetto. Every decision I made, person I spent time with, word I uttered, had to measure up to the image I had in my mind of what was morally and politically right according to my vision of female empowerment. Everything had a gendered explanation and what did not fit into my concept of feminist was 'bad, patriarchal and problematic'" ("Being" xxix).

Attracted to a range of personal, work, and sexual experiences that did not seem to fit into the feminist mold offered to her by her elders, and seemingly policed by silent judgment of the older generation as "unfeminist," Walker, the daughter of a white Jewish lawyer and the African American novelist and human rights activist Alice Walker, tells us that she felt stunted and controlled in relation to what she personally desired to explore, while being obliged to mirror this older generation as the price of winning their love and approval. Seeking other women with similar feelings of profound contradiction between feminist loyalty and new urgencies, Walker invited them to write with her a book about a new wave in feminism that established a division and a reaction (Gillis, Howie, and Munford).

In itself, this is important. The claiming of a "new wave" in feminism is at once an act of solidarity with feminism and a revolt against the embodiment of feminism in an older generation when the lived experience and the vocabulary to hand will link this generational conflict as daughter against mother (Henry; and Gunkel, Nigianni, and Söderback). The impulse to the new as renewal is, therefore, figured as the conflict between feminist generations, between women and their mothers and aunts. Furthermore, it represents the feminist moment of the 1960s and 1970s in specific terms: through the psychological figure of the daughter struggling to separate, to become herself, *to be real*, in the face of an overpowering presence of the "mothers," both the moral judges and the source of love and approval that might be withheld if the child transgresses.

Initiating generational reaction against—and to a certain extent, an excoriating indictment of a new representation of—a second wave of feminism by its successors, Walker's gesture has consolidated into a repeated historiographical and political fact.

I want to relate Walker's important and moving collection of essays to a text written in 1974 by the French writer Hélène Cixous, founder of the first university center for feminist studies, Centre d'études féminines at Paris 8 Vincennes in 1974. Cixous starts by reading stories about women, like *Sleeping Beauty* (why are women always in bed?) and *Little Red Riding Hood*, both of which stage complex relations of sexual difference and generations of women. Cixous identifies "Little Red Riding Hood" as a little clitoris "getting up to some mischief": "Little Red Riding Hood leaves one house, mommy's house, not to go out into the big wide world but to go from one house to another by the shortest route possible: to make haste, in other words, from the mother to the other" (43). Cixous, however, offers an interesting reading of the figure of the grandmother in this tale, since it is her house that stands as the other.

> *And grandmothers are always wicked: she is the bad mother who always shuts the daughter in whenever the daughter might by chance want to live or take pleasure. Grandmother [. . .] is there as jealousy [. . .] the jealousy of the woman who can't let her daughter go [. . .]. The Wolf is grandmother, and all women recognize the Big Bad Wolf [. . .]. The Big Bad Wolf represents, with his big teeth, his big eyes, and his grandmother's looks, that great Superego that threatens all the little female red riding hoods who try to go out and explore their forest without the psychoanalyst's permission. So, between two houses, between two beds, she is laid, ever caught in her chain of metaphors, metaphors that organize culture. (43–44)*

Different from, yet echoing at the level of some deeper tropes in culture, the testimony of Walker, one individual who speaks for a generation summoned into self-awareness through the space she created with words and her book, Cixous offers a feminist reading of the structural logic that is implicated in creating mother hatred, mother fear, and hence self-hatred in women. Cixous's reading exposes the authority of the masculine through the figuration of the monstrous and overly controlling mother/grandmother who is repeatedly imagined as the instrument of prohibition and containment.[3] Is this a trope that was always already waiting for the discontented and differently situated feminists of the 1990s?

There can be no doubt that the conditions each new generation experiences are politically, socially, economically different and newly chal lenging. History happens. Yet, despite different ages, we exist side by side with our overlapping but also very different experiences in and encounters with the world. How do we make sense of the overlaying of the different temporalities of experience, as generations not only succeed each other but coexist in some of the same time zones? What constitutes a "generation" historically may be what Mary Kelly names a formative primal moment, one that occurred to those who came before but remains the enigma to be belatedly deciphered ("On Fidelity"). Each political generation is thus shaped by its inevitable late coming, coming after some other event that was formative for the generation that preceded it, filling the space with its own fantasies and resentments. These historical experiences are, therefore, inevitably inflected by the myths and metaphors indicative of structural and psychodynamic formations in which subjectivities, including political subjectivities, are shaped.

Generally speaking, the succession of generations and historical time have been managed by two different discourses and their practices. The first is the historical imaginary that sets the sequence of many generations into narratives and creates systems of intelligibility for their succession. As an institutionalized discourse, art history, for instance, prototypically narrates the story of art and artists to create a sequence of unbroken human creativity. That this story is at once a story of nations and ethnicities and a story of men is not coincidental. By virtue of the narratives shaping the succession of culture as that of men, it appears that the smooth passing of the creative torch down the generations of men is not only possible; it is indeed synonymous with the narrative of history and with culture itself. Such a concept of culture logically can only exclude recognition of women's creativity because the structural logic of historical time, progress, and activity is written in the masculine pronoun in the shadow of the Oedipal fantasy that manages productively the inevitable patricidal and filiocidal conflict.

This fantasmatic organization leaks into the second model of the psychosymbolic imaginary, which has a longer temporality reaching deep into the past of human cultures and into our individual unconscious. It concerns the monumental time of myth, legend, and deals with the psychic dimensions of human subjectivities, its antecedent enigmas and traumas (Kristeva). It uses figurative language, metaphor, and storytelling. This model installs a logic of hierarchical and asymmetrical sexual difference that those positioned as "women" are forced to live out, and even embody. It was against the hierarchies of both the historical-political-cultural and the psycho-symbolic orders that women have revolted. That revolt is called *feminism.*

To substantiate this assertion, I need to take a short digression into Freud's self-reflexive theory of the foundations of culture in his essay *Totem and Taboo.* Abandoned by his own sons and in conflict with his professional sons, such as Carl Jung, Freud theoretically postulated the origins of culture and religion as the scene of an omnipotent father against whose selfish authority the disenfranchised sons band together. The sons murder the father, burdening themselves thereafter with an idolatrous guilt. Under its effect, the sons (representing the social formation of men) then, paradoxically, set up the symbolic paternal position that no son/man will ever inherit. This move enables the lateral bonding between men that becomes the binding of a social and political sphere of sons defined by the guarantor now provided by the symbolic father of all who are men.

My question is this: Is there any way to imagine and constitute the political sphere that is not based on such a conflicted legend of family as murderous sons and murdered but symbolically resurrected father, writ large? Can it be configured without the violent, murderous revolt and the attendant guilt that creates the solidarity among sons, acted out generation after generation in ways that sustain the masculinist genealogy of symbolic father and the space for the son (and, as we shall see later, for the cross gender–identifying envious daughter)? Do we as women have, or can we as feminists imagine, any form of comparable founding myth for the creation of a political sphere out of a nonviolent, nonmurderous mother/daughter partnership through time? Is there any comparable symbolization that can work to relieve the generational tension between women in time, when the current formations of feminine subjects are trapped in a structurally Oedipal-masculine symbolic, for lack of other narratives?

Feminist philosopher Luce Irigaray has argued for the rediscovery of a mother/daughter genealogy as much as she has proposed a transversal sociality among women in opposition to their distribution as commodities in a phallocentric economy ("Bodily" and "Commodities"). Yet neither of these proposals articulate psychoanalytically a fantasmatic structure to relieve the girl-child of her inevitable small person's anxiety of influence as she enters an already existing world of big persons in ways that do not lead to a mimicry of filial patricide as the only imaginative route to self-realization. Is there, furthermore, any way, for those of us who once revolted as the dissident daughters of a patriarchal order we rejected and who now find ourselves cast as the lupine (grand)mothers, to escape the projected pain of that unrelieved anxiety of the daughter who, in this same patriarchal-Oedipal formation, can only "blame" the Mother either for being too much or having offered too little?

Feminist Arendtian philosopher Adriana Cavarero points out that the counter myth to Laius-Oedipus inherited from the Greeks is not a narrative of daughterly matricide. In the figure of Medea, it is, rather, the myth of maternal infanticide. Mothers are mythically represented as deadly (Cavarero 25–28). The complex myth of Medea plays into our field as both a story and an image in which the devouring or abandoning mother, the too little or the too much mother, leaves no routes for the woman-thinker except through envious cross-identification with the son/father pair. Remember Walker's extraordinary testimony to feminist mothers as mental jailers. Yet, while the Oedipal model allows for the son in fantasy to kill the father and to imagine inheriting/sharing the phallic position, and thus facilitates symbolically the succession of sons and sustains the generations of men, the creation of canons, the sequence of leaders, the archiving and transmitting of culture, this model does not work for the daughter. For in that symbolic order, no value, no meaning, no symbolically enviable possession/position is attributed to the maternal other, nothing to envy for which she might be killed in fantasy and then set up among the political community of revolting daughters as their guarantee of a perpetual inheritance of feminine potency/creativity/difference.

Thus the mother/daughter model of generational envy and succession in the case of the current narratives or memory of feminism is profoundly misplaced because it is skewed by the phallocentric Oedipal frame. What is being acted out, in fact, is not mother/daughter relations so much as the Oedipal formation of the envious daughter. The only model offered in phallocentric society encourages the daughter to repeat the disowning and deforming representation of the maternal feminine as overpresent, cloying, claustrophobic, or as abandoning and insufficient, repressive and denying, what Bracha Ettinger identifies in psychoanalytic discourse as "the ready-made mother-monster." Ettinger explains that the accepted primal fantasies—seduction, castration, and Oedipus—"are reconstructed or redesigned to regulate smoothly male subjectivizing processes vis-à-vis a paternal loving figure with regard to primordial sourceless enigmas." She argues:

The lack of recognition of the three phantasies of Not-enoughness, Abandonment and Devouring as primal destroys mainly the mother/daughter relationship since it systematically rechannels hatred toward the mother and destroys the daughter's desire for identification with the parent of her own sex, with catastrophic results for women, whereas the paternal figure of originary repression constituted as a figure of identificatory love, regulates, together with the establishment of Seduction, Castration and Oedipus as phantasmatic primal complexes, the parallel same-sex father/son identification problem, for the actual son/father relationship. ("From Proto-Ethical" 107)

She further explains:

[T]he failure to recognize these three unconscious threads as primal Mother-phantasies is, in my view, the reason for a flagrant damage to the feminine-maternal dimension and to the mother/daughter matrix caused during the process of psychoanalysis itself encouraged by their defaulting counter-transferential misrecognition of them. This misrecognition accounts for the endless search after non-existing "causes" resulting in the "reply" in terms of a mother-monster readymade that leads to a devastation of the psyche of daughters, to the ruining the daughter/mother relationship in the real, as well as to the fragmentation of the Matrixial web itself and to the destruction of the Eros of compassion. (108)

It is not only authority or primacy that, shall we say, older or senior feminists might ask of those who carry feminism forward in new times and new ways; rather, it is also valuing that which has been done in the name of, and perhaps even for the love of, women and the love of a common world transformed by revolutionary women. Following Ettinger's argument, what we might need is a structure that sustains admiration and respect for the "mother," but not understood as my mother, or the Mother of early psychic life and fantasy. Rather, termed by Ettinger as "m/Other," this is a figuration of the feminine through, across, and down time that could function as an Other-partner "in the feminine" for the becoming and self-transforming political subjectivity of "women." It is that feature of respect that is psychically eradicated for the currently formed feminine subject by the dominance of the Oedipal and phallocentric logic that underpins it.

You may be perplexed by this turn and wonder if this is all a plea for absolution from the new generations and third and fourth waves. I must repeatedly stress that I am not *maternalizing* feminism. It is important to say that I think the constant worry that it might be so indicates how profound this anxiety is within feminism. I am, therefore, interrogating a reaction akin to phobia attendant on any suggestion that feminism might "think with the maternal" or seek in the differently theorized maternal feminine a counter-logic for the feminist subject to the Oedipal and the phallocentric. The negative response within feminism indicates a profound and disabling ambivalence. What I am suggesting is not mythic idealization as we have already seen in feminist, reactive hypervaluation of the divine feminine, a trend Kristeva urgently critiqued as a risk of relegating feminism to religion (208).

The dominant metaphors of waves and generations now claim to be the *story* of feminism, which is, therefore, mythicized and troped negatively. Metaphors such as waves and generations register the problem of time, history, change, and newness. But they are entangled in myth. They remain trapped in the psychosymbolic imaginary and the unresolved trauma of mother/daughter relations created in phallocentric culture and the Oedipal account of subjectivity as the sole account. Waves suggest the endless coming of the new to wash over and erase what preceded. Waves might also evoke the orgasmic rhythms of feminine sexuality. I will come back to waves later. Generations could otherwise suggest continuity and inheritance, love and difference. But the idea of a sequence of waves washing over generational contestation imprisons us in the tortured place of the daughter determined by phallocentric culture.

A Case of Archive Fever

In *Archive Fever*, Derrida examined the psychopathology of disciplinary memory and its institutionalization. Derrida critiqued historian Yerushalmi's project to discover the truth of psychoanalysis by pointing out that, in seeking to establish a "history of psychoanalysis," Yerushalmi had ignored the lessons of psychoanalysis.

> *To want to speak about psychoanalysis, to claim to do the history of psychoanalysis from a purely apsychoanalytic point of view, purified of all psychoanalysis, to the point of believing one could erase the traces of any Freudian impression, is like claiming the right to speak without knowing what one is speaking about,*

without even wanting to hear anything about it. This structure is not only valid for the history of psychoanalysis [. . .], it is at least valid for all the so-called social or human sciences, but it receives a singular inflection here. (54–55)

Let me put feminism in the place of psychoanalysis. To want to know the truth of feminism, that is, to write its history, *without understanding that feminism itself seeks to change how we understand history, memory, and subjectivity,* is to efface the effect of feminism from the writing of its own histories. What I learn from Derrida's comment is that we have to ask about our own desires in writing about pasts in which we are invested, or from which we derive our sense of who we are. What do nonfeminist desires do to our histories? What phobias and paranoias are revealed in the stories that have been written in narratives of feminist history? What *unconscious* forces shape the memory we are fabulating? If the event, feminism, is traumatic, what of it could I/we know? To what might I/we testify, bear witness? Who will or wants to hear that testimony? What of its meaning escapes my or our narratives? What do our narratives do? What can they not do?

Waves and generations formulate the bad memory of feminism by betraying, symptomatically, the traumatic dimensions of the event that is feminism. Our thinking and our self-analysis have not yet been able to meet what has been incited or released by the event of feminism. Academics have played a powerful role in shaping this memory form because our will to knowledge and our desire to make sense of the event and indeed our places in its histories have sought to integrate the traumatic event through existing models of knowledge. These are prey to existing psychological tendencies within the historical imaginary and the protocols of our historical disciplines. *Thus, I want to suggest that feminist memory is not yet sufficiently feminist.* We have used non- or even prefeminist concepts of linear time and relied on Oedipal familial metaphors to emplot our own histories. The stories we have told have not registered fully the implications of our own theoretical and analytical work as feminists that sought to critique the very symbolic and imaginary systems in which we now tell the story of feminism. We create and then fight against continuities that have plots as old as recorded civilization.

Memory work has also been done in the visual arts, though much less visibly, as part of the feminist project than the social sciences studied by Clare Hemmings or the literary studies scholars who have been conferencing on the generations of feminism for a decade or two (Looser

Fig.1
Mary Kelly (b. 1941)
Circa 1968 (2004).
Compressed lint and
projected light noise.
100 × 105 × 1.25 ins.

Courtesy of the artist

and Kaplan; Hemmings; Henry). Let me now introduce a recent artwork by an artist who belongs to the generation of Hélène Cixous and still teaches and works with students entering the field of art in the second decade of the twenty-first century.

In 2004, Mary Kelly (b. 1941) exhibited a work at the Whitney Biennial exhibition in New York titled *Circa 1968* (fig. 1). This was part of her aesthetic reflections on her experience as a professor of fine art known for her involvement in the women's movement in the 1970s and for explorations of feminist issues through a long-term conceptual art practice. She was fascinated by the curiosity expressed by her current students about a historical event they had missed—in a sense, her history.

Let me describe the piece first. You enter a darkened room. On one wall is a single work that, from a distance, looks like a blow-up of a somewhat blurry news photograph. If you move in closer, you discover that the image is, in fact, very material. It is composed of rectangles of lint, compressed cotton fibers that have been culled from the fiber filter of a domestic tumble dryer. This detritus of domestic labor is not a standard artistic material. It has been appropriated by Kelly to serve as the material means of translating the traces of a photograph, divided into rectangular elements on graph paper and thus rebuilt wash by wash into this new materially supported assemblage. But across the surface of the blown-up, fractured, and reassembled image plays electronic noise in the form of light pulses. Bringing up associations with painting, photography, and cinema, the work speaks back to the hours of domestic labor through which this materialization of a historical or archive image has been made. Flickering light also evokes the silent cinema while this pulse animates the effect of encountering a past just out of reach, what curator Debra Singer named "an effect akin to an after-image imprinted on one's memory" (see Kelly, *Circa*).

What is the image that is thus being remade and replayed? It is a reworking of an infamous and iconic image of the student movement in Paris in 1968 that was published in *Life* magazine on May 24, 1968, as well as in *Paris Match*. It represents a demonstration on May 3, one day before the general strike. A young woman, Caroline de Benden, tired of walking, mounts the shoulders of the artist Jean Jacques Lebel and is given a flag to wave. She refuses the communist and anarchist flags but chooses the Vietnamese flag. She is a model. She sees the photographers around her. Stiffening her back, she raises her flag in knowing re-enactment of a famous French painting from the revolution of 1830, *Liberty Leading the People* (1830 Musée du Louvre) by Eugène Delacroix (1798–1863). The image is snapped by Jean-Pierre Rey and becomes the iconic image of *Marianne* (the figure of the Republic) for 1968.[4]

Circa 1968 asks: when is the event that is apparently rendered iconic? Juli Carson comments on this issue:

> *Indeed there is a mystery at the heart of Kelly's* Circa 1968, *a mystery unfolding in the "scene" between the date Rey took the photograph and the date the depicted event returns to us. The scene constitutes an ellipsis of cultural legacy—the productive space between one generation and the next through which historical memory is made. And since history is always a question of that*

> *un-traversable divide between an event that happened "then" and*
> *our recollection of it "now," history is at once a question of* long-
> ing to be where we are not. *It is precisely this question of desire*
> *in the space of critical analysis that's at stake in* Circa 1968. *(194)*

At the time of making this work, Mary Kelly's thinking was deeply engaged
with the work of philosopher Alain Badiou on the event—events are things
like love, science, art, and politics—as that which only comes to be through
subsequent fidelity enacted by its subjects. The event comes to exist performatively, through its aftereffects, that is to say, insofar as fidelity on the
part of those affected or inspired by it iterate it, live it, become its location
and its actors. Badiou is proposing that the event becomes what it is through
the constant work of "not-forgetting." Of Kelly's visual sculptures, including
Love Songs (2007), Rosalyn Deutsche thus writes: "In her theatre of not-
forgetting Kelly used a material that serves the philosopher as a metaphor
for the event: light. The event says Badiou is a kind of 'flashing supplement
that happens to the situation'; it bursts forth as if into flame and gives off
light, which disappears, leaving a 'trace' in the situation, a kind of afterimage that refers back to the vanished event and guides the subject's fidelity"
(30). The flash of the event leaves traces that create an afterimage to guide
she who would remain faithful to the event but who becomes the "she," the
subject, through the continuous work that makes the event become whatever
it becomes.

> *Both fidelity to the event and left melancholy remember the past*
> *and write history. But unlike triumphalist historical narratives,*
> *in which emancipation leads to resolution, Kelly's history is writ-*
> *ten in the tense of the future anterior, an order of time in which*
> *[. . .] reimagining never ends. Theorizing the future anterior as*
> *the time of personal history, Jacques Lacan wrote, "What is real-*
> *ized in my history is not the past definite of what was, since it is*
> *no more, or even the present perfect of what has been in what I*
> *am, but the future anterior of what I shall have been for what I*
> *am in the process of becoming. (35–36)*

This psychoanalytic proposition resists the banal reductionism of the many
misinterpretations of Freudian time. For Freud, the significance of formative infancy lies in its unconscious archiving and its potential for traumatic
return, flashing up in secondary instances that become the only actualized
and always belated sites of the formative events that happened too early to do

more than leave affective after-images. Far from endlessly locating the present in causes locked in the past, the force of the past enters into the present as its moment, linking instances in conjunctions that are potentially regressive or potentially and unpredictably transformative. Deutsche continues:

> *Lacan's description of personal history recalls Walter Benjamin's philosophy of political history. The historian, as Benjamin famously wrote, does not reconstruct the past "as it really was" but, bringing past and present into a* constellation, *"seize[s] hold of a memory as it flashes up at a moment of danger." Kelly mixes Badiou and Benjamin—two philosophers of the flash and of revolutionary not-forgetting. For* Love Songs *the Women's Liberation Movement cannot be distinguished from the transformations it undergoes in the hands of a new generation and, perhaps most important, in* both generations' fantasies. *(36)*

Those who claim to have known the past cannot claim its truth for themselves: its being is in the hands of those who make something of it afterward in a movement of fidelity and deferral. Yet there is some traffic between different spots in time, a mingling of fantasies, projective and retrospective. Far from instituting the familial model of generations here, we need to have a historical sense of colliding temporalities and coinhabited fantasies, for both are alive at the same time, although starting from different places and experiences.

The past is in part framed by fantasies of the past. These fantasies are inter- as well transgenerational. They may be in conflict. But they are also always doubled, for each generation is already fantasizing another's past. In discussing a series of works in the mid-2000s about historical memory, Kelly drew on Freudian theory of the primal scene to suggest an analogy, so that, for instance, 1968 might be said to function as a primal scene not for those who were there, but for those who were not. She tells a young curator:

> *In terms of returning to this moment for those born between 1963 and 1973, May 1968 was what I would call the political primal scene—the mystery of conception in the social and historical sense. [. . .] My generation [remember she was born in 1941] was preoccupied with our parents in the context of WWII [. . .] I might say, well how could my parents have allowed something like the Holocaust to happen, and your generation might think why was not the Cultural Revolution realized? (Carson 195)*

Fig. 2
Mary Kelly (b. 1941)
Interim (1984–89
installation in four
parts).
Part 3: *Historia*
(1989).
Oxidized steel, silk-
screen, stainless
steel on wood base.
4 units, 61 × 36 × 29
ins. each

Collection,
Mackenzie Art
Gallery, Regina.
Courtesy of the artist

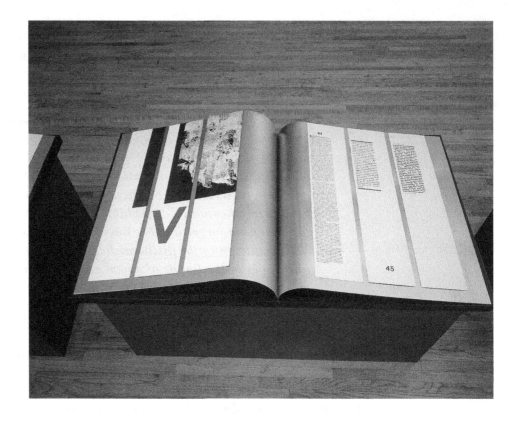

So the present may include a curiosity about a missed event but also a reproach about the failed promise of the event. Inviting conversation, this model mobilizes affects other than those associated with endlessly new waves rolling in to wash away the past or with generational matricide.

In 1990, Kelly completed a four-part artwork titled *Interim* that explored the lack of representational support for the woman of middle age: infant, girl, virgin, bride, wife, mother, and . . . crone or old bag. Where in this clearly heteronormative styling of the life stages of femininity do we find representational support for the woman refusing these kinship sites: could she only register as the sister, the unmarried? No greeting cards to mark her life events. What images do we lack for the very kinds of feminine subjects that feminism engendered: the artist, the thinker, the theorist, the woman loving women? Moreover, Kelly was seeking to pose the question of that uncharted project of the feminist subject (de Lauretis) in relation to time, to history, as changing and shifting, altering the frameworks for political subjectivity and altering the very forms of subjectivity that are historical, cultural, and shifting.

Part 3 of *Interim*, titled *Historia*, took the minimalist form of
opened books in steel, recalling the way archives used to store newspapers
in large, bound volumes (see fig. 2). Her sculptural object references the
storage of history in its transient everyday inscriptions as news. On her
spreads Kelly placed four narratives, each composed of three elements of
oral history or overheard conversation. In addition, one spectral image
haunted the printed columns, moving through the prison-like bars of each
spread, which collectively bore red letters composing the ancient political
slogan VIVA. The image was a negative print of a news photograph from 1905
representing the rough arrest of an elderly bespectacled suffragette by two
British police officers. Transgressing class and gender codes at many levels,
the image does not illustrate a curious past; it indexes a moment of feminist
revolt and the violence of the state's response to that revolt.

Made on the cusp of the decade that generated "postfeminism"
and the declaration of a third wave, this iconic remembrance is evoked
as the ghost haunting a set of narratives, each of which begins with a
significant date: "In 1968, I was twenty-six; [. . .] I was twenty [. . .] I was
fourteen [. . .] I was four." As each woman tells the story of her encounter with the women's movement, with feminism, with queer activism, a
multileveled picture is being painted of a common field or space in which
there is movement. Each individual enters this landscape from a specific
point—carrying into that space the varying personal histories and shifting
configurations of politics and debates about gender, sexuality, class, race.
Thus by the fourth story, the narrator can report encountering feminism
through an academic women's studies course, while the third comes to it
through ACT UP and queer activism, the second witnesses the foundation
of women's groups, and the first arrives at feminist politics from socialism,
the New Left, and political struggle in the Middle East. These four points
of entry are not hierarchically ordered as beginning and late-coming, or
as generations or waves. They represent feminism as an open field of entry
points and shifting priorities.

The work of Mary Kelly on feminist memory and change is affectively affectionate. In 2007 she titled her return to the collision of memory
and otherness across time in relation to being an educator *Love Songs*,
based on Sylvia Plath's poem written in 1960 on the birth of her daughter.
The poem is an elegy to the change, to the poet, wrought by the arriving
child. Like Plath's poem, Kelly's work proposes a space of opened hospitality to the other who comes to bring change. Transformation occurs at the
shared borderspace between becoming subjects in coemergence, the central

Fig. 3
Bracha L. Ettinger
(b. 1948).
Drawing no. 3,
*Mamalangue–
Borderline
Conditions and Path-
ological Narcissism,*
Series no. 5, 1989–90

Courtesy © Bracha
Studio

proposition of Ettinger's theoretical-aesthetic intervention in both feminist
and psychoanalytic theory. Elsewhere I have offered a detailed reading of
Plath's poetics through the prism of matrixial theories of transsubjectivity
proposed by Ettinger ("[M]Other") in order to elaborate on what Ettinger
names as an aesthetic process associated with the Matrixial: *metramorphosis,* which is a logic for the production of meaning that is nonphallic (phallic
being a logic of +/−) that shifts our dominant phallic linguistic figures of
metamorphosis and metonymy. Instead of the classic I and not-I of psychoanalytic thought, Ettinger invites us to consider a coexisting dimension
in subjectivity of I and non-I sharing events across a borderspace that can
become a threshold for trauma or transformation (fig. 3).

Metramorphosis is the process of change in borderlines and thresholds between *being and absence, memory and oblivion, I and non-I, a process of transgression and fading away. The metramorphic consciousness has no center, cannot hold a fixed gaze—or, if it has a center, it constantly slides to the borderline, to the margin. Its gaze escapes the margins and returns to the margins. Through this process the limits, borderlines, and thresholds conceived are continually transgressed or dissolved, thus allowing the creation of new ones. ("Matrix" 201)*

My question is how can difference and time in the histories of feminism be figured? The movement that named itself a second wave did so as an act of fidelity (Bailey 18). To claim a relation to an earlier moment of militant political and cultural revolt by women was to reconnect a broken thread, a thread smashed by mid-twentieth-century fascism that murderously effaced both the earlier socialist-feminist and women's movements for radical democratizing change. The reemergence of the question of gender circa 1968 was not another phase or wave, but an active resumption of a shattered twentieth century, and, we could say, modern history. But in the interim, much that was significant about the moment of feminist militancy circa 1900 or circa 1920–30 had been erased from cultural memory along with the traces of the cultural forms of feminist modernism. We need now to understand it, as it is intimately connected with the kinds of histories we might write, understanding the repressed and disappeared legacies of radical thought and creativity over the twentieth century and into the present one.

The Right to Revolt

In her recent study *Feminist Aesthetics and the Politics of Modernism*, writing from the vantage point of the intellectual revolution that characterized the phase of feminism from the last quarter of the twentieth century, Ziarek identifies a twin legacy within feminism as an opposition between revolt and melancholia. This reveals the "unresolved political contradictions between particular struggles for freedom coexisting with multiple forms of domination—what feminist theory has theorized as race, class, gender, sexuality" (19). If we focus only on domination, we become melancholy and forgetful of the revolutionary tradition. If we focus on the latter, we may disregard both loss and domination. To counter this opposition, Ziarek specifies a feminist aesthetics of potentiality.

Ziarek reconnects the moment of modernist aesthetic innovation with the revolutionary force of militant suffragettism, a force that is belittled in political history and ignored in feminist cultural self-representations.[5] Ziarek's intervention hangs on the following claim: "I want to raise a new question, one that has not yet been addressed by feminist critics of modernity—namely the political and aesthetic implications of the suffragettes' redefinition of *the right to vote as the right to revolt*. In other words, what is at stake in my analysis is the conflicting relation between women's political and literary discourses of revolution and the inaugural force of innovation" (21). It is at this point that we can see the convergence between cultural innovation—the experimental forms of modernist art and literature—and political transformation of an equally radical imaginative order. The suffragette demand is not only for a place in the polis as it was currently defined. They asserted a much more ambitious claim: the right to revolt. The claim was not only directed *against* the then current political and symbolic order. It declared the right to imagine, without having to specify, radically new orders of social relations, social subjectivities, and symbolic systems. "Such a redefinition means that suffragettes' contributions to political modernity and modernist aesthetics are not limited to the enfranchisement of women, although this has been an enormous victory. Equally significant is the suffragettes' discourse on revolution, which to paraphrase Hannah Arendt's insights, reveals the inextricable connection between freedom, the emergence of women's political and artistic subjectivities, and the creation of new forms of political life" (21). In Kelly's *Historia*, the ghost of the militant feminist revolutionary—the suffragette—does not stand for a first wave; she represents an initiating gesture, a founding gesture of modern feminism that remains our future. Not the claim for the right to vote, necessary as that was, if only to participate in existing political formations, the suffragette instates the unfinished, still virtual claim for the right to revolt and to create the new.

By rereading the political aesthetics of a militant feminist moment ca. 1900–1920, Ziarek provides a vantage point in which the melancholic/revolutionary opposition is replaced with a dynamic in which the energy and effectiveness of either the aesthetic or the political depend on coemergence psychodynamically echoing the Matrixial formulation of co-emergence and coaffection that allows each its specificity and both their partnership in difference, and which enables us to hold the intellectual or aesthetic and the political in constant relay.

In her *Impious Fidelity: Anna Freud, Psychoanalysis, and Politics*, about the political theory of Anna Freud and her role in the institutionalization and hence preservation of psychoanalysis—a source for some of my thinking about the questions of institutionalization and transmission in terms of an overdetermined family situation of father and daughter—Suzanne Stewart-Steinberg quotes a passage from Hannah Arendt on education: "We have become accustomed in our tradition of political thought to regard the authority of parents over children, of teachers over pupils, as the *model* by which to understand political authority" (1). Stewart-Steinberg uses Arendt to introduce her discussion of the institutionalization of psychoanalysis: how it moved from its founding generation through the work of the *impious fidelity* of Anna Freud, Freud's only child to follow in his footsteps. She does this in order to tease out from psychoanalysis Freud's theories of both politics and culture, namely, the relevance of what seemed like the study of the private sphere for understanding "the wider stage" (14–49).

Stewart-Steinberg's book seeks to reconnect political theory about the democratic subject and the democratic polity with the understanding of affect that arises through psychoanalysis, affect that is typically exiled from the political and in the same gesture considered feminine in contrast to the objective neutral-masculine space of the political social contract. She asks: what are the psychic processes involved in enabling us to perform as or even to think about a democratic polity as much more than just a consensual arrangement in favor of the existing exploitative relations?

Affectively, the models we have to think about authority derive from the child-adult (extended to teachers and pupils), and indeed one might have to specify this model as one of the son-father relations that involved rivalry, identification, aggression, and the trauma of submission, as I suggested earlier in my discussion of *Totem and Taboo*. Against this model, a clearly Oedipal one, we might set what Anna Freud called the "war in the nursery," which, in a different manner, Juliet Mitchell has more recently theorized as the overlooked psychic dimensions of lateral relations between children, sibling rivalry for the attention and love of the parental figures, negotiating various psychological modes of dealing with *envy*. Stewart-Steinberg thus reconsiders the politics of affect and the affects of politics that are not only central to any thinking about feminism as a political event but are also vital to understanding feminism's own institutionalization as an affective structure, which, over time, will find itself subject to these same issues of authority and rivalry, identification and envy laterally and across generations. Indeed, it is the issue of the creative and destructive dimensions of envy laterally and generationally that seem so fruitful.

Stewart-Steinberg refers to the conclusion of Freud's essay on terminable and interminable analysis, where he admits that he was never able to persuade any woman *not* to want to be a man (the troubling but profoundly important issue of penis envy), and equally, that he was never able to persuade any man *to want* to be a woman (the issue being castration anxiety). The contrary affects of envy versus anxiety can thus be seen to underpin the formations of femininity and masculinity.

Envy can be destructive; it can, however, also be productive and creative. We might paradoxically argue that it is envy that enables the dissident feminine subject to resist the status quo, to be perpetually unhappy with it, to want to be what she is told she is not, and to use the potentialities of cross-identification to have or even be what she wants. A certain kind of psychic flexibility in transgendered imagination becomes possible in the envious feminine subject. The masculine subject is, on the other hand, frozen by anxiety. Becoming other than he imagines himself to be would involve loss, or worse, mutilation by becoming something less, that is, feminine. Freud remarks that this anxiety limits the masculine subject in that "adopting a feminine attitude in men is indispensable for many relations" in terms of education, for instance (Stewart-Steinberg 55). Such insights clash with classic political theory that links affect with the feminine and excludes both. Stewart-Steinberg counterargues that the feminine can be understood paradoxically as the very condition of modern democratic subjectivity:

> *Freud's great contribution to political theory is to have reintroduced affect into the mechanisms of power, not simply as that which must be contained but as the site where social and political relations originate. Freud posits at the origins of democratic subjecthood—which for him is consonant with modern subjecthood—one affect that he views as crucial for the social contract: envy. Envy lies at the root of both Freud's theory of democracy and of this theory of gender construction [. . .]. Envy "engenders" political subjectivity through a series of cross-identifications. In the Freudian fantasy of the social contract, the male democratic subject, I will argue, is a woman who acts like a man. (55)*

Into this complex argument comes Anna Freud's own contribution to political theory. She is positioned as she who comes after the founding gestures of the creation of new ways of thinking subjectivity and the political. She is also she who must negotiate affectively and intellectually some of the contradictions and anxieties that arise from the challenge of fidelity and continuation of the spirit of the creative gesture when it becomes institutionalized not as her father's work but as psychoanalysis, an event in the world.

This historical case study of politics, affect, institutionalization, and continuation resonates with the as-yet-unthought memory or unwritten history of feminism in which I find myself complexly placed as a woman-thinker of a certain age and historical formation. How has feminism been institutionalized by its "daughters" (a condition of us all as inevitable late-comers to histories that always precede us)? What has been the fate of its fantasized now mothers? Why do we write our stories in disabling agonism? Did feminists in effect/affect want to be neither mothers nor daughters, but sons and fathers—or neither of these familial positions? How might we imagine ways of relating laterally and generationally beyond the familial paradigm that at once rehearses the heteronormative modeling of sexual difference but also theoretically and psychically denies any politicizing or creative space to both the maternal and the filial feminine as imaginary and symbolic positions rather than entrapments in descent? Is all affect Oedipal in the last instance or are there other resources in psychic life that we could mobilize for a politics not modeled on the Oedipal figurations of authority and sexual difference, on envy or anxiety, in which women's political subjectivity involves willful transgendering or failed idealization? Is the only way out the queering of feminism or is that also ultimately a symptom of our having no way to love our mothers and to understand what the feminine as it operates as the "seduction into life" (Ettinger, "[M]Other"; Giffney et al.) might actually offer to humankind?

I need to introduce one more resource to think it with, deriving from Stewart-Steinberg's work on Anna Freud. "One way into the nexus of politics, sexual difference and affect is through Freud's relation to his daughter. Anna Freud, who became her father's (contested) successor, did so by becoming the carrier of a node of problems and anxieties within the psychoanalytic movement itself: gender and feminine sexuality, authority and law, the transformation of the envious child into a democratic subject but, above all the handing down of authority and knowledge from one generation to the next" (56). I hear extraordinary parallels between the knot of tensions within the psychoanalytic movement and the knot of tensions within the feminist movement, which, with psychoanalysis, I would position as two related and warring events of significance of the twentieth century.

Let me finally reintroduce Anna Freud's younger contemporary and fellow exile, Hannah Arendt, on the transmission and institutionalization of knowledge:

> *Education is the point at which we decide whether we love the world enough to assume responsibility for it and by the same token to save it from the ruin which, except for renewal, except for the coming of the new and young, would be inevitable. And education, too is where we decide whether we love our children enough not to expel them from our world, and leave them to their own devices, nor to strike from their hands their chance of undertaking something new, something unforeseen by us, but to prepare them in advance for the task of renewing our common world. (193)*

Education is not outside the time and space of the political. In the context of the loss of what Arendt understands as the political, the collective space of our being together to work on our common world, education might be one of its residual sites. It is the site of encounter and exchange. Both occur between two groups situated at different points in time and even space, in different relations of memory. One group takes responsibility for its world that is also the world, which exists before and after this moment. But its continuation requires the coming of the new. The "we" of Arendt's statement as a woman born in 1906 must be oriented to the materiality of the present and the virtuality of the future. Out of "love"—a crucial term for Arendt based on friendship and respect, not passion or eroticism—for those who will come and assume responsibility for renewal, the older group shares its world with the newer, helping and supporting their coming of age through such sharing, while fostering the creation of what is utterly unforeseeable by the older group. Thus the nature of exchange between the two groups in time involves a complex set of psychological operations: responsibility and awareness of limitation, open sharing and active fostering of newness, while passing on the nature of the responsibility assumed for "a common world" with a new group of women who also need the work of their prede-cessors, whom they will not replace but from whom they will continue even in renewal and transformation.

Arendt's key concept for a post-totalitarian politics is the concept of *natality*. For Arendt, we are required to refound a human condition that was revealed to us in its fragility in the wake of its attempted annihilation by the totalitarian experiment. That is the lesson of the concentrationary:

a laboratory for the destruction of the human within a living being and a model for rendering human life superfluous *qua* human life, that is, outside of utility. Arendt defines the fundamental quality of the human condition discovered in the aftermath of such a terrifying almost-reality as plurality. *Plurality* is not just another term for diversity in the sense of multiculturalism. It is the effect of natality: each new life is a new beginning for humanity itself, unpredictable, offering the promise of a creative continuity that is not repetition but poiesis.

The promise is sustained, however, in ethical and political action, being together, throughout life. The creativity of education, its relation to life, spontaneity, and the renewing of the common world, involves what in affective, psychoanalytic terms Ettinger will formulate as the Matrixial pairing of hospitality and compassion ("[M]Other"). Education can be the locus of negotiating such a frame to describe the relations between the generations that are often institutionalized by the modern state for its own less lively and ethical purposes.

Hannah Arendt was no more a mother than Anna Freud was. This makes what they say about relations between the generations interesting, since it is disinterested and structural and speaks of generations beyond familial terms. They were, however, both involved with children, with transmission, and with the issues of the trauma that befalls children in their formative relations to broken connections and terrifying worlds. Arendt was a teacher, one of the key instances that Kristeva identifies as the maternal when it functions as an ethical position in the double relation to love of the world and love for the worlds to come through the otherness one assists in coming into thinking-being or creative-being while instituting the space of sharing difference. The maternal is, according to Kristeva, an instance of remarkable psychological work of ethical self-transformation in which the intensity of one's own eroticism is deflected into the tenderness that lets the other live (qtd. in Pollock, ed., *Aesthetics* 41).

Taking further this philosophical-psychoanalytic rethinking of the maternal in feminist theory, Ettinger will qualify Levinas's parallel argument that the maternal represents the primary ethical instance (*Time*). Levinas, however, renders the maternal-ethical instance sacrificial insofar as the maternal is, for this philosopher, the nonsubjective instance in which a subject produces a life that will outlive it. Ettinger refutes such a sacrificial view of the feminine-maternal by suggesting that the maternal is precisely *that which seduces us into life while desiring to live beside this newness* ("Proto-Ethical" 103–4). The maternal cannot be understood in isolation but as an effect within a coemergence of coaffected subjectivities. First, Ettinger argues that in classical psychoanalytic therapies, "Any kind of unremembered early painful material may lead to the construction of the archaic mother as a cause of pain—this is a therapeutical ready made 'object'—*a ready-made mother-monster*" ("[M]Other" 10). This has serious repercussions:

> *If her part in being a major subjective-object of early affective fascination, awe and compassion, and finally her active participation in the aesthetical and ethical (non-sexual) seduction into life, is re-repressed and diverted (toward the analyst) while splitting the maternal instance from the Matrixial web, hate will result. Such a mother-hating is also, and more deeply, a self-hate, because the (m)Othernal non-I intended by it is not only another subject in inter-subjective relationality and is not even a mere internal object, but is—first of all, on the feminine-matrixial level— a transject that is transconnected to the I, and therefore, also, a psychic continuity of the subject itself (and of the non-I itself) in their transubjective Matrixial web. ("[M]Other" 10–11)[6]*

Ignorance, on the part of analysts and indeed of culture as a whole of any other mode of alleviating the existential anguish of the born subject, creates this mother-trouble that can furthermore enact the betrayal of the daughter. We must remember that every mother has also been a daughter, and that all of us are daughters in this sense "of being subjected to these mechanisms" ("[M]Other" 10).

Moreover, I want additionally to insist that the maternal feminine is significant for all who later acquire and transform their Oedipal genders. Postnatally, we can be mothered and fathered by people not aligned in masculine and feminine or any gender positions. Nonetheless, in the traumatically imprinted late prenatal process of human becoming, we all encounter a sexual difference *before gendering*, indifferent to any Oedipal version of masculine/feminine. This sexual difference is, however, "feminine beyond the phallus." "Only the prematernal figure of archaic pregnancy is always a female, and so, each one of us, male or female, has to deal with its difference-in-jointness with/from a female corpo-real figure. It is on that level of difference-jointness that we first encounter sexual difference, a difference that cannot be abolished" (Ettinger, "[M]Other" 10–11). Turning her attention to *postnatal* existential needs that address their urgency and blame to the postnatal mother, Ettinger argues that the betrayal of the daughter in us all is effected "by the search for an imaginary cause for existential anxieties and anguish and for total understanding of [the] unremembered past and for perfect parenthood that compensates for existential troubles arising from being alive" (10–11).

Ettinger thus profoundly challenges the psychoanalytic and endemic blaming-the-mother culture. Instead she invites our compassion toward the complexity of maternal trauma in sharing this process of human co-becoming. This partnership also effects a transformation of becoming-maternal subjectivity and its changed place in time. From her political theory, Arendt asks that the parental generation demonstrate sufficient love for the children by sharing its own world with them and leaving open spaces for their creativity in the name of renewing a common world. This might be understood Matrixially as hospitality combined with the self- and other-respect for which Ettinger calls. This raises one final question: what is asked of the new, the newly arrived, the potential future created in sharing with those who come before? Are we all free to give rein to affects of mutual rivalry and a murderous need to dethrone the mother-monster blamed for what we have to recognize are in fact the existential lacks inherent in postnatal (hence post-Matrixial) life? Should we allow ourselves to destroy authority in the name of natality's unqualified freedom? Or should the newly arriving demonstrate compassion for its own preceding generators in the knowledge that in turn it, too, will become a before to the new new? Is there a pathway that avoids the Oedipal drive to replace or destroy, and deflects that pressure in order to recognize, and be shifted by acknowledging, a humanizing co-becoming in and across time as a condition of culture and which is not only archontic? What kind of common world can we create if we cannot hold past and future in a creative covenant passing as life through us? The future does not need to be burdened with the authority of the past; it can allow the continuous coinhabiting creativity of the past to animate and share in the potentialities of unknown futures yet to be created. This is one critical means to avoid the compulsive search for the new as the driver of contemporary cultural capitalism. Compassion is the gesture on the part of the new that is becoming in the hospitable presence of the already-but-still-co-becoming (M)Other (this change of case refers to postnatal relations to the prenatal [M]Other). Linear time is thus qualified by coinhabited space-time.

A Matrixial reading already inflects my formulation of the Arendtian model. It speaks the impious fidelity of Ettinger to her psychoanalytic "family" and to the war in the theoretical nursery of contemporary feminist thought and aesthetics. Speaking on *Mother Trouble* in 2010, Ettinger made the case for respect by countering Freud's death drive with her radical reconceptualization of our human becoming as a *seduction into life*. In what I will name a *Matrixial natality*, "we are being interpellated by the continuity of life itself, in us, through us, unconsciously, for the time of without-us, involved in the prolongation of life for which we are only a passage-lane. The prolongation of the living being traverses us; we are a station on this path" ("[M]Other" 23). She continues:

> *It is this prolongation of life that in my view is concerned with the elaboration of the primary affect of awe into respect in the passage from the proto-ethical to the ethical. If human beings are to survive beyond the personal self, respect needs to be re-spected. This begins with the re-spect of the (m)Other. The respect for the mother is required not in order to satisfy her or for getting something from her in return. It is inherent, like awe and compassion, to the futurality of life itself in its continual re-passage to the ethical.*

Ettinger situates this problematic—what in the formations of subjectivity provides the psychological resources for our capacity to move from proto-ethical to ethical response-ability (another Ettingerian neologism) to the other, in time as much as in space—through a reflection on the Mosaic injunction to respect the progenitors to which is attached the reward of long life. Is there, then, "some measure of exchange here, and some measure of a beyond-exchange, and even of a beyond relationality?" From her proposition that dimensions of proto-ethical and aesthetic subjectivity are engendered, archaically and matrixially in the time-space of the late prenatal-prematernal proximity of becoming-infant with becoming-mother, the latter being the archaic (m)Other of all intimations of difference, Ettinger then asks:

> *How are we to understand this* beyond *in the present context of mother trouble and psychoanalysis? Honour and Respect are bred upon awe that is primary and unconditional. In the beginning there was awe [a wondering in the face of intimated but unknown otherness, difference, beyondness]. In the beginning of a certain knowledge, a certain wisdom, there is awe. When awe turns into respect and honour—and not into fear and horror—the [biblical] promise of a long life does not intend a personal reward. It indicates the possibility of life, of an-other-beyond (my) life that*

is, that in the future there will be a life towards which your past participation in the living would already be contributing by this kind of respect which makes the parental [as either a position, a bodily act, or a psychological practice] a possibility for the subject. By respect your very participation in a Matrixially intuned human atmosphere is distinguished. By respecting you reach the domain of Ethics. (23)

I have sought to bring this theorization from feminist psychoanalysis together with Arendt's beautiful image of transgenerational cooperation for thinkers making a common world, with Ziarek's historical analysis of the feminist-modernist claim to the right to revolt and to imagine radical possibilities not yet known through a relation to formal and aesthetic innovation, and with Anna Freud's insights into the psychic obstacles to creating a scene of intellectual practice that is not imprisoned in the war in the nursery, but is enabled by the companionship and excitement of a shared space not imprinted with the figures of older and younger, authority and submission. In anticipation of Ettinger's theoretical gift of the Matrixial supplementary dimension in subjectivity, Anna Freud enjoined us to de-Oedipalize our institutional and imaginary relations while taking responsibility for managing our fantasies. To create transgenerational democratic space for the continuing virtuality of feminism, we need historical understanding of feminism itself that is different from the currently fracturing caricature of generations at war and waves of novelty. We may need to escape the psychologically infused narratives of heroic women or the sensation of a melancholic loss of our heroines. I am proposing that we seek to take charge of and tame the blame and contempt, the anxiety and the resentment playing out in waves and generations (Detloff). In our involvement with feminism we are the bearers of our histories but equally the sites of our historical traumas. Both can be worked through in compassionate hospitality, respect, and awe for what we have undertaken, together and in difference, in partnerships and agonism, with desire to share and enable the creatively new in a transformed world. The words we use as signs of the affective and even unconscious pressures shaping our actions matter enough to be seriously challenged and reconsidered. Otherwise, we performatively instate our own death drive in a figuration of mother-hate, which is, in effect, self-hate, and ultimately forms itself as feminism hating.

This article is a part of a book-length study of the same title scheduled for completion in 2016 to be published by Verso.

GRISELDA POLLOCK is professor of social and critical histories of art and director of the Centre for Cultural Analysis, Theory, and History (CENTRECATH) at the University of Leeds. Her most recent publications include *Concentrationary Imaginaries: Tracing Totalitarian Violence in Popular Culture*, with Max Silverman (I. B. Tauris, 2015); *After-affects / After-images: Trauma and Aesthetic Transformation* (Manchester University Press, 2013); *Art in the Time-Space of Memory and Migration* (Freud Museum and Wild Pansy Press, 2013); *Concentrationary Memories: Totalitarian Terror and Cultural Resistance*, with Max Silverman (I. B. Tauris, 2013); *Visual Politics of Psychoanalysis: Art and the Image in Post-traumatic Cultures* (I. B. Tauris, 2013); and *Bracha Ettinger: Art as Compassion*, with Catherine de Zegher (Exhibitions International, 2011). She has two forthcoming books, *The Nameless Artist in the Theatre of Memory: Analyzing Charlotte Salomon's Leben? oder Theater?* (Yale University Press, 2016) and *Is Feminism a Bad Memory or a Virtual Future?* (Verso, 2017), while her current writing projects include two book-length studies, "From Trauma to Cultural Memory: Representation and the Holocaust" and "Marilyn's Mov(i)es: A Cultural Analysis."

Notes

1   This is a catachresis I created in 1999 as part of an analysis of the structures of desire that keep in place the masculinist canon. I wish to subject feminist theory and practice to a comparable analytics of the psychic passions that shape our narratives, idealizations, and fantasies (Pollock, *Differencing*).

2   Other contemporary articulations of the origins of the term "third wave" include Rosenfelt and Stacey (359). Earlier instances are referenced by Henry (23–24).

3   Remember the story of Rapunzel, where again a young woman is confined in a tower by an ugly old woman who wants to keep her for herself and from going into the world, into a man's bed.

4   This image on the cover of *Paris Match* destroyed the life of Caroline de Benden, the scion of an immensely rich family ennobled by Queen Victoria. When her grandfather saw the image in his newspaper, he disinherited his granddaughter of her 7.5-million-pound legacy while all U.S. modeling agencies dropped a woman thus associated with America's communist enemy, the Viet Cong. Today, de Benden lives in retirement on a small holding in Normandy.

5   Even Lisa Tickner's magisterial study *The Spectacle of Women* focuses on the representational politics of the suffragists, not the performativity of the suffragettes.

6   *Transject* is a formulation of Ettinger's theory that adds to our vocabulary for thinking about further dimensions within subjectivity. We are accustomed to subject/object relations and their relative or opposing positions. For the proto-subjective moment of the becoming-infant and the imaginary regressive dimensions of the becoming-mother reliving her becoming-infant partnership in the Matrixial time-space, Ettinger's terms *transject* and *transjective* highlight moments of partial sharing that characterize this protosubjectivity that is not yet within the subject/object relation and the separations into which birth and a long series of separations precipitate the subject. Because the Matrixial sphere is not an alternative to the postnatal phallic sphere of subjectivity that traumatically produces us as sexed-speaking subjects, but is a

supplement that moves beneath the surface of our necessary formation as sexed and speaking subjects, archaically generated *transjects* and *transjective* elements

refer, postnatally, to moments and partial encounters or threshold instances working largely on the aesthetic and proto-ethical level.

Works Cited

Arendt, Hannah. "The Crisis in Education." *Between Past and Future: Eight Exercises in Political Thought.* 1961. London: Penguin, 2006. 170–93.

Bailey, Cathryn. "Making Waves and Drawing Lines: The Politics of Defining the Vicissitudes of Feminism." *Third Wave Feminisms.* Spec. issue of *Hypatia* 12.3 (1997): 17–28.

Broude, Norma, and Mary Garrard. "An Exchange on the Feminist Critique of Art History." *Art Bulletin* 71.1 (1989): 124–27.

Carson, Juli. "Legacies of Resistance." *Digital and Other Virtualities: Renegotiating the Image.* Ed. Antony Bryant and Griselda Pollock. London: Tauris, 2010. 194–98.

Cavarero, Adriana. *Horrorism: Naming Contemporary Violence.* Trans. William McCuaig. New York: Columbia UP, 2008.

Cixous, Hélène. "Castration or Decapitation?" Trans. Annette Kuhn. *Signs* 7.1 (1981): 41–55.

de Lauretis, Teresa. "The Technology of Gender." *Technologies of Gender: Essays on Theory, Film, and Fiction.* Basingstoke: Macmillan, 1987. 1–30.

Derrida, Jacques. *Archive Fever: A Freudian Impression.* Trans. Eric Prenowitz. Chicago: U of Chicago P, 1995.

Detloff, Madelyn. "Mean Spirits: The Politics of Contempt between Feminist Generations." *Third Wave Feminisms.* Spec. issue of *Hypatia* 12.3 (1997): 76–99.

Deutsche, Roslyn. "Not-Forgetting: Mary Kelly's Love Songs." *Grey Room* 24 (2006): 26–37.

Ettinger, Bracha. "From Proto-Ethical Compassion to Responsibility: Besidedness and the Three Primal Mother Fantasies of Not Enoughness, Devouring, and Abandonment." *Athena* 2 (2006): 100–134.

————————. "Matrix and Metramorphosis." *Trouble in the Archives.* Spec. issue of *differences* 4.3 (1992): 176–208.

————————. "(M)Other Re-spect: Maternal Subjectivity, the Ready-Made Mother Monster and the Ethics of Respecting." *Studies in the Maternal* 2.1–2 (2010): 1–24.

————————, and Emmanuel Levinas. *Time Is the Breath of Spirit.* Trans. Joseph Simas and Carolyn Ducker. Oxford: Museum of Modern Art, 1993.

Freud, Sigmund. *Totem and Taboo.* 1913. *The Standard Edition of the Complete Psychological Works of Sigmund Freud.* Trans. and ed. James Strachey. Vol. 13. London: Hogarth, 1913–14. 1–161. 24 vols. 1953–74.

Giffney, Noreen, Anne Mulhall, and Michael O'Rourke. "Seduction into Reading: Bracha L. Ettinger's Matrixial Borderspace." *Studies in the Maternal* 1.2 (2009): 1–15.

Gillis, Stacey, Rebecca Howie, and Rebecca Munford. *Third Wave Feminism: A Critical Exploration.* 2nd ed. Basingstoke: Palgrave Macmillan, 2007.

Gouma Peterson, Thalia, and Patricia Mathews. "The Feminist Critique of Art History." *Art Bulletin* 69.3 (1987): 326–57.

Grosz, Elizabeth. "The Future of Feminist Theory: Dreams for New Knowledges." Gunkel, Nigianni, and Söderback 13–22.

Gunkel, Henriette, Chrysanthi Nigianni, and Fanny Söderback, eds. *Undutiful Daughters: New Directions in Feminist Thought and Practice.* Basingstoke: Palgrave Macmillan, 2012.

Hemmings, Clare. *Why Stories Matter: The Political Grammar of Feminist Theory.* Durham: Duke UP, 2011. 31–130.

Henry, Astrid. *Not My Mother's Sister: Generational Conflict and Third Wave Feminism.* Bloomington: Indiana UP, 2004.

Irigaray, Luce. "The Bodily Encounter with the Mother." *The Irigaray Reader.* Ed. Margaret Whitford. Oxford: Blackwell, 1991. 34–46.

—————. "Commodities among Themselves." *This Sex Which Is Not One.* 1977. Trans. Catherine Porter. Ithaca: Cornell UP, 1985. 192–97.

Kelly, Mary. *Circa 1968.* 2004. University Art Galleries. UCLA. http://uag.arts.uci.edu/exhibit /circa-1968.

—————. "On Fidelity: Art, Politics, Passion, and the Event." *Feminisms Is Still Our Name: Seven Essays on Historiography and Curatorial Practices.* Ed. Malin Heldin Hayden and Jessica Sjöholm Skrubbe. Newcastle: Cambridge Scholars, 2010. 1–11.

Kristeva, Julia. "Women's Time." 1979. *The Kristeva Reader.* Ed. Toril Moi. Trans. Alice Jardine and Harry Blake. Oxford: Blackwell, 1986. 187–213.

Levinas, Emmanuel. *Humanisme de l'autre homme.* Montpellier: Fata Morgana, 1972.

Looser, Devoney, and E. Ann Kaplan, eds. *Generations: Academic Feminists in Dialogue.* Minneapolis: U of Minnesota P, 1997.

Mitchell, Juliet. *Siblings.* Cambridge: Polity, 2003.

Pollock, Griselda. *After-affects | After-images: Trauma and Aesthetic Transformation in the Virtual Feminist Museum.* Manchester: Manchester UP, 2013.

—————. *Differencing the Canon: Feminism and the Writing of Art's Histories.* London: Routledge, 1999.

—————. *Encounters in the Virtual Feminist Museum: Time, Space, and the Archive.* London: Routledge, 2007.

—————. "Generations and Geographies." *Genders* 17 (1993): 97–120.

—————. "The Politics of Theory: Generations and Geographies in Feminist Theory and the Histories of Art Histories." Pollock, *Generations* 2–38.

—————, ed. *Aesthetics.Politics.Ethics: Julia Kristeva 1966–1996.* Spec. issue of *Parallax* 4.3 (1998).

—————, ed. *Generations and Geographies in the Visual Arts: Feminist Perspectives.* London: Routledge, 1996.

Rey, Jean-Pierre. "Un regard sur Mai '68." *Codhos: Collectif des centres de documentation en histoire ouvrière et sociale.* http://www.codhos.org/exposition/un-regard-sur-mai-68/ (accessed 25 Feb. 2016).

Rosenfelt, Deborah, and Judith Stacey. "Second Thoughts on the Second Wave." *Feminist Studies* 13.2 (1987): 341–61.

Scott, Joan Wallach. *The Fantasy of Feminist History.* Durham: Duke UP, 2011.

Stewart-Steinberg, Suzanne. *Impious Fidelity: Anna Freud, Psychoanalysis, and Politics.* Ithaca: Cornell UP, 2011.

Tickner, Lisa. *The Spectacle of Women: Imagery of the Suffrage Campaigns 1907–14.* Chicago: U of Chicago P, 1988.

Walker, Rebecca. "Becoming the Third Wave." *Ms.* 11.2 (1992). http://www.msmagazine.com /spring2002/BecomingThirdWaveRebeccaWalker.pdf.

—————. "Being Real: An Introduction." *To Be Real: Telling the Truth and Changing the Face of Feminism.* New York: Anchor, 1995. xxix–xl.

Ziarek, Ewa Plonowska. *Feminist Aesthetics and the Politics of Modernism.* New York: Columbia UP, 2012.

On the Name, Ideation, and Sexual Difference

I have often thought that the naming of our programs has been wrong. On one level, it is tedious to think about such institutional questions as the naming of a program, and yet in terms of students' interests in studying within the programs, it is not a trivial issue. At Duke where I directed the Women's Studies program for seven years, we, the faculty, always found our name anachronistic, even as we would acknowledge that some of the original work intended by the project that named itself women's studies is yet to be completed. In addition, a program named Sexuality Studies, which was housed in Women's Studies but was not "of it," was being absorbed by Women's Studies, but we have been striving over the last few years to think about how to mark its different institutional history, the different history of the field, and now the proximate though conceptual distinction of queer theory and feminist theory—because in some ways, it is a department of feminist and queer thought with cross-listed courses that make us something more than that, and perhaps something less. A name like "The Program in Feminist and Queer Thought," which would best describe us, would in all likelihood no longer be a draw for undergraduates even if it would be

Volume 27, Number 2   DOI 10.1215/10407391-3621709

© 2016 by Brown University and d i f f e r e n c e s : A Journal of Feminist Cultural Studies

entirely satisfying for graduate students. And my ideal title (which I'd like to think about today) would be too elusive, apparently: The Program for the Study of Sexual Difference. That name would reach back to its intellectual origins in psychoanalysis with its formulation of the problem of the subject-in-difference-with-the-advance-of-modernity (a modernity that we must understand as coterminous with, indeed depend on, and perhaps synonymous with the advance of capitalism and colonialism). The name would also reach forward to psychoanalysis's understanding that woman does not exist, or perhaps, put better by Derrida in his reformulation of the psychoanalytic understanding of sexual difference, that sexual differences are yet to exist ("Geschlecht"). Indeed, they come into play as the spectral demand from the future (or, more accurately, from what is yet to come). *Sexual difference* is a term with transitional content, yet to be fully conceived, and indeed perhaps intellectually hospitable in ways that resist content as justification, conceptualization as closure, or thought as merely aspirational.

The institutional questions concerning a name are not unrelated to questions of the name and the proper name more generally—those of genealogy, kinship, the patrilineal and matrilineal, and, with the term *Woman* or *Women*, the quandaries that afflicted Marx on the Jewish Question. On the one hand, the naming of a group is necessary in the striving for civic or political emancipation in terms of right. On the other hand, right itself is a compromised political formation, and perhaps a limitation when seeking "human" emancipation, given that the group designated by a name may contribute to its own servitude through embracing that very political emancipation. Does one form of emancipation obliterate the possibility of the other? And is human emancipation the only way to imagine a form of justice that is not premised on the need for protection from other people? In naming a group, the members of which have nothing in common other than the need of liberal freedom from interference, what possibility lies ahead? For Marx, it would be human freedom; for us, perhaps it could be some other form of futurity, or justice to come.

But where does the question of gender fit in here? In principle, gender, as a form of iteration, was supposed, at some point, to solve many of the problems with the category of *woman* as naming something with apparently common characteristics of social positioning: the apparent commonality suggested by the term, the erasure of difference of all kinds, the illusion or perhaps the delusion of metaphysical presence, the "threat" of the biological, the assumption of "two" sexes, of which woman was the second, and indeed the problem posed by psychoanalysis as to woman not existing. *Gender* as a category of analysis also apparently gave the possibility of disidentification (Judith Butler writes of this most forcefully in *The Psychic Life of Power*), whether this manifested itself as melancholia (a response to a loss of something one never knew one had or even imagined to have) or disavowal (the understanding of the nonexistence of something but the subsequent acting as if it were—Octave Mannoni's figuration, *je sais bien, mais quand-même*). Whether these two things could exist simultaneously is also a question worth pursuing. Is the inability to know what one has lost in melancholia contradicted by the knowing that is a part of disavowal? And is it possible to "know," for example, a foundational violence but fail to know one's affect associated with it such that disidentification may occur and manifest itself in disavowal? Another way of posing this question would be: does the category of gender lead us to an understanding of desubjectification, that is, an epistemological and phenomenological category, or does it lead us to desubjectivation, the undoing of the subject itself as a challenge to the neutral subject as Being, that is, an ontological question, or at least one in which the ontic reaches out toward the ontological, as Gayatri Chakravorty Spivak would describe a certain deconstruction in opposition to Foucault and Heidegger in the contexts of madness and sexual difference.

Joan Wallach Scott, when she questioned whether gender was a useful category of analysis, of course pointed out the diversity of problems encountered when the full potential of the challenge of *gender* was not taken on such that there was more continuity rather than more difference between the study of woman and women and that of gender—erasing or avoiding, therefore, the problem of sexual difference. And when Butler wrote *Gender Trouble*, she was, after all, thinking of the trouble with gender and not only how gender "troubles" and has the potential to trouble. The debates between Gayle Rubin and Judith Butler also demonstrated another by-product wherein gender posed a problem for the study of sexuality, again at least partly because in many ways it failed to take on the challenge of sexual difference. In the lists that are produced as the ticks and gestures of feminist discourse—the analogized sense of however separate discourses of race, class, gender, sexuality, national origin, and so on and so forth (listed partly because of their analogization, partly because they cannot, through intersectional analysis, be thought together because, for example, of their separate treatment legally)—we see that *gender* is not a term itself that is open to otherness. Equally, it has often seemed that the philosophical questions that sexual difference sought to pose around translation, especially in Derrida's essay "Geschlecht: Sexual Difference, Ontological Difference," questions that were equally designed to pose institutional questions, have often split the field, such that "third world" women or poor women, for example, were addressed as *women* and seemed to be open to the more traditional feminism and feminist thought in European and u.s. contexts, while questions concerning the philosophical issues raised by gender and sexual difference were focused on those in the "West," a problem that postcolonial theory has tried to undo given the ideational projections of colonial thought that exist at the expense of material factors that go into the constitution of any one figure.

With this question in mind concerning the relationships among the proper noun, the proper name, and the nominal, I want to re-engage with the question of gender and its related cognates that always inhabit it and in principle cannot be thought in isolation from each other—race, family, generation, lineage, species, gender/*genre*—connoted in Derrida's essay. The term *gender* has, for many years and for at least the last twenty-five years through the work of Butler, been invoked as if it solved all the problems inherent in the category of *sex*. But has *gender*—as term and as concept—created another set of problems and problematic analogies? Is it the red herring of current work in our field? And does it have implications for futurity in the sense of what is to come in the field? Is there room within gender for an understanding of materiality, or must that be disavowed along with the problem of the apparent neutrality of being? And if it is disavowed, then does that manifest as an embrace of capitalist performativity that is also highly gendered in the most conventional ways—as someone like Leo Bersani might show us? Is gender a category that really troubles the different arenas and temporalities of the discourses of foundational violence that go into the constitution of the subject—whether androcentric, anthropomorphic, or colonial-national in constitution? Does it, in effect, confirm the mischaracterization, repeated obsessively in the u.s. academy especially, of women's studies as an identity formation rather than as a field that questions the presence—through what Sarah Kofman would identify as the oscillation between presence and absence—or possibility of sexual difference to come?

The question of the *to come* and of futurity has of course been a constant issue in our field, not least because it began with an idea of whether success as a field would imply its demise (that is, the lack of necessity of the field) or its flourishing (a new and yet to be thought area of thought).

Futurity itself has often been a contentious idea and one bound, like the name, to genealogies, whether patrilinear or not. Symbolically, the future is often presented as pregnancy or birth in both feminist and nonfeminist contexts, and theoretically we see that even Hannah Arendt would put forward a theory of natality to explain how novelty appears in the world through *throwing* in a way that articulates something somewhat distinct from Heidegger's being-toward-death. Many in both feminist studies (think of the radical feminism of the 1970s most evident in Shulamith Firestone's work) and more recently in queer studies (most obviously in the work of Lee Edelman) have quite rightly taken a stand against the implicit ideology that imagines temporality through a reproductive logic, even if the notion of reproduction involved is sometimes rather mechanical in this writing and does not engage at all with the idea of the stranger within the body, or indeed the stranger—that is, difference—that a child may be imagined to be.

Feminist utopias often imagine a rethinking of birth; the separatist logic of Charlotte Perkins Gilman's *Herland* imagines a feminist parthenogenesis, and the significant feminist literary utopias of the 1970s often took this on also (Marge Piercy, Joanna Russ, Ursula Le Guin, and so on). Firestone considered artificial wombs as the way forward so women would not be biologically bound, and the idea of fertility—even as the fertile imagination—often moves beyond the human to other species or representations of life itself. Emancipation from reproduction, or at least from its form as part of a heterosexual or bodily dynamic, was then a way to imagine a different feminist future and certainly, in a meeting of time and space, in feminist utopian fiction in which a different future is projected from the present, specifically in terms of a *topos*. The thinking of the future is often architecturally or geographically conceived, but it is also implicated within ideas or retreats from future notions of production and reproduction—in biological, technological, or species-being terms—as a way of trying to understand how we get from this side of the future to that side of it.

As we see, in this formulation, futurity reaches backward and forward simultaneously. It is presented as, on the one hand, a banalized formation (sexual difference as existing solely in the thwarted relation of inequality and binary definition as we have in the current form of relations between men and women, an androcentric formation that actually is productive of a logic of sameness rather than one of difference) and, on the other, a future of justice to come. From this side of the future, we have to understand what is to come as the impossibility of this relation: the material conditions that force us to understand sexual difference as both here and archival, and also yet to come.

But life ultimately is not necessarily sought as productive or even reproductive. Sometimes, the trace of life in the waste products of the modern world may even be the source of possibility. The filmmaker Agnès Varda has explored this idea beautifully in relation to the practice of gleaning, the French law that allows people to take the remains from commercially harvested land. She sees this as the model for making use and finding hope in waste, whether it is the wasted piece of footage in filmmaking, a fragment that proves to be a pearl (as Arendt describes Benjamin's writings, or the rejected materials from supermarkets that can feed populations of vagrants. In Giorgio Agamben, being waste could be a source of redemption. Or, in less heavily Christian language, for Derrida, it could be the beginning point of thinking afresh from the site of loss and disposability. Sexual difference, then, rather than the child or forms of lineage, could be the name of futurity.

■

In "Geschlecht," Derrida offers us a notion of sexual difference (conceived with psychoanalysis) that calls attention to sexual difference in relation to translation and supplement—something further explored by Peggy Kamuf in her magnificent reading of the essay that turns on the practical problem of how to translate a term like *gender* into French when *genre* carries different meanings that have all to be challenged together for their foundational fantasy and their resistances to the division between the ontic and the ontological. Sexual difference is still yet to be thought, and versions of it that we have belong to the anthropological rendering whereby sexes are imagined as existing when one might say they are material conditions formulated within an economy of the same.

This problem of translation as it relates to ontology and desubjectivation leads inevitably to the issue of feminist internationalism, postcoloniality, and, indeed, globalization. This is certainly what is at stake in "Geschlecht" and in much of Derrida's work beyond that essay, and in Hélène Cixous's work, even, perhaps especially, in the early work, for example in *Vivre l'orange* or *Dedans.* We see there the necessity of understanding sexual difference in relation to colonialism and its forms of subjectivation and anthropomorphism. Similarly, in Barbara Johnson's work *The Feminist Difference: Literature, Psychoanalysis, Race, and Gender,* we see sexual difference and race understood as emerging with and through the lyric and the law. These neglected early instantiations of sexual difference as always already constituted with processes of subjectivation in colonial histories and other forms of state racism are often forgotten in the moment that we make the more obvious point—that feminism has often been entirely complicit with colonial gestures and racism and that it continues to be. But it is also in these writers and critics in which, precisely, one sees the past and future of sexual difference operate as a function of such inscription and also emergence of the yet to be conceived.

In the introduction to her 2008 book *Persons and Things*, Barbara Johnson writes of rhetorical figures of emergence of various sorts, something she had done in her earlier work such as her essay "My Monster/My Self" in *Diacritics* from 1982. The continuities in Johnson's work are in many ways marked by the repetition of the word *difference* in her titles and her steady resistance to the category of identity and self she negotiated through her work on literature, things, and feminism. In *Persons and Things*, she writes,

> *Both capitalism and colonization (which are tied closely together) tend to turn persons into things so that everything serves the needs and centrality of commodities. Here, colonized man loses his humanity and becomes a thing to extend the reach of capitalism itself. The rhetorical figures that confer on things some properties of persons are thus* apostrophe, prosopopeia, anthropomorphism, *and* personification. *The parallel processes of turning persons into things does not offer itself in the form of a figure, but suggests that figures that increase humanness are by nature working against a decline of humanness and a thingification that go on all the time and have only accelerated with commodity capitalism. (22–23)*

In many ways, the scholarship of Johnson in the field of feminist deconstruction worked through literary and philosophical texts to see the manner in which figuration occurred—less to document thingification, as Aimé Césaire put it, or commodification, and more to assume that state and then to see how things moved toward or assumed the properties of personhood. In her attempt to understand the difference within, Johnson looked for the forms of monstrosity from which one attempts to emerge or from which selves occasionally emerge when self and identity already offer a foreclosed sense of being. The monstrosity of the emergent continuously addresses the doubtful presence or absence of being and the manner in which people come into view as personifications, barely visible faces that emerge, or signatures that are not yet visible. Figures appear as what she calls, in *A World of Difference*, the "originary vocative, which assures life even as it inaugurates alienation" (198). In a reading of Lacan in which she describes the verbal development of the infant that begins as a demand addressed to the mother, demand becomes a question about presence and absence, much as it has in her reading of Freud's notion of fetishism, in which the fetish is revealed to be less a substitute for the penis and more a substitute for the question of presence or absence.

The context of her discussion concerning the originary vocative is the essay "Apostrophe, Animation, and Abortion," in which she asks, "Can the very essence of a political issue—an issue, like say abortion—hinge on the structure of a figure? Is there any inherent connection between figurative language and questions of life and death, of who will yield and who will receive violence in a given human society?" (184). She chooses to address this issue through a discussion of the use of apostrophe in lyric poetry and brilliantly makes an argument elaborating the manner in which the ethical quandary of the political issue is that the attempt to find a language of demand is always articulated from the position of the child in rhetorical, psychoanalytic, and political structures concerning abortion. The political demand is therefore structured in the voice of the emergent human such that addressor and addressee of the demand somehow merge together, and the monstrous voice of the feminine and the child constitute a barely audible voice, much less a presence. In many ways, this speaks to the moment in feminist theory when there was an in-depth understanding of the way in which "any theory of the subject had always been appropriated by the masculine" (133–49), as Irigaray would put it, or as Johnson puts it: "[T]he monstrousness of selfhood is intimately embedded within the question of female autobiography. Yet how could it be otherwise, since the very notion of self, the very shape of human life stories, has always from Saint Augustine to Freud, been modeled on the man?" (*World* 154). But it also did something else. It gave to language the matter of politics and also gave to politics a need for understanding how difference functioned within language to refuse a subject position. And what occurs is the presence of the fetus and also, in her chapter, menstruation and the dead child, at the expense of the mother.

In considering figures of emergence in order to understand presence and absence, Johnson demonstrates how figures of speech conferring personhood of various sorts always also work to dissolve it, to demonstrate its lack of coherence and its lack of stability. A feminism built on that lack of stability is far from weak. At the moment in which deconstructive feminism became such a force, many doubted its ability to work politically, and it was unclear what it would mean to put deconstruction to work in the world. Johnson, and a handful of others, worked marvels in using a particular form of literary analysis to dwell on the sentence, the phrase, and the particular figure to demonstrate that its internal contradictions also spoke to the task of emerging from language that itself figures us. (Gayatri Spivak, Cathy Caruth, and Shoshana Felman, to name a few, worked in this vein.)

One of the challenges for Johnson and for readers of Johnson was the way in which deconstruction's political potential was doubted as a result of the revelations in the late 1980s concerning Paul de Man's writing for a Belgian newspaper that collaborated with the Nazis. An odd moment ensued in which Johnson seemed to feel responsible for addressing critical writing as historical writing that had to take into account such a moment as if de Man was already doing deconstruction at that time (obviously, he was not). The antipathy toward deconstruction and the speed with which people sought to bury it was one that took time for many to resist. Johnson wrote of the surprise of alterity at great length, the shock of an otherness that is in many ways endemic to the deconstructive form of reading. Writing, of course, can always pass into the hands of the unlikely reader. She also ties these questions to the notion of the allegorization of the figure of woman in politics and in journalism, focusing particularly on legal theorist Mary Joe Frug by considering what it means to proclaim someone or something as dead, how writing returns to you from death, and what it might mean to understand a body of work, like deconstruction, as dead or alive, personified in the moment of its much proclaimed demise (*Feminist*).

Johnson's work, whether on Barbie, Mallarmé, Freud and race, or Wordsworth, always looks to the question of the very tenuous structure of authority—in the law, in deliberately subversive texts, in considerations of sexuality, in poetic form. The difference within is always an address on the structure of authority and how one therefore can or cannot make demands within it. She wrote, in *The Feminist Difference*, "[L]iterature is important for feminism because literature can best be understood as the place where impasses can be kept and opened for examination, where questions can be guarded and not forced into a premature validation of the available paradigms. Literature, that is, is not to be understood as a predetermined set of works but as a mode of cultural works, the work of giving to-read those impossible contradictions that cannot yet be spoken" (13). If there is a wake to be had, it is as much for Johnson as it is for a mode of deconstructive thought that resists instrumentalist reason and quick conclusions. Looking archivally at the processes of ideation may instead allow for both a conceptualization of sexual difference and also a simultaneous undoing of that shaping as certainty.

Johnson's work, like Derrida's "Geschlecht," allows us to see again that sexual difference was rarely formulated in its narrowest rendition. Indeed, even for Freud himself, writing first in "On the Universal Tendency to Debasement in the Sphere of Love" (1912) and later in "The Dissolution of the Oedipus Complex" (1924), the phrase "anatomy is destiny" is first the Napoleonic phrase "geography is destiny," and it involves precisely the problem of ideation ("On the Universal" 189; "Dissolution" 178). Neglected in the civilizing mission of sexual education in the early essay are pleasure, anality, and indeed geography. In the later essay, the inadequacy of a form of feminism demanding equal rights without understanding the domain of the psychic in relation to the body is at stake. The narrowing and naming of sexual difference in terms of beauty, love, heterosexuality, and reproduction, in other words, must be framed within its own textual background if we are to see how the terms of sexual difference have been both demarcated by other differences and limited by them. The apparatus (or *dispositif*) of memory-making and naming has created boundaries out of ideological and conceptual necessity, ignoring the animal paw prints that make up the sexual, but have then failed to understand the import of that when formulating a more expansive notion of sexual difference.

Derrida, in "Freud and the Scene of Writing" (1967) and then later in "Archive Fever" (1995), explores the *dispositif* or apparatus of memory-making in terms of ideation and then of the necessary creation of an archive in a foreign land in the context of threat (referring to Freud's archivization in London where he had fled from Nazi Vienna). Reading Freud's *The Interpretation of Dreams* (1900) alongside "A Note upon the 'Mystic Writing-Pad'" (1925), Derrida further develops his notion of metaphysics and "the epoch of presence" begun in *Of Grammatology*. Derrida shows how Freud almost unwittingly reveals his own understanding of memory through the apparatus of the mystic writing pad that "there is no domain of the psychic without text" ("Freud" 198). Freud's minor text on the mystic writing pad reveals something for Derrida about the early, more significant text, *The Interpretation of Dreams*. Freud, he reminds us, employs filmic and photographic apparatus analogies in order to understand dreams (something that would become significant for theories of the apparatus from Jean-Louis Baudry and Roland Barthes to Thierry Kuntzel and Christian Metz).

In recent art criticism and curation, there has been much work on the question of the archive, ideation, sexual difference, and indeed the question of creating an archive in a foreign land and a foreign language. Hal Foster called this the "archival impulse in contemporary art," citing mostly international examples. Okwui Enwezor, in his catalog for the 2008 exhibition *Archive Fever* at the International Center of Photography in New York, cites the 1935 Marcel Duchamp piece *La Boîte-en-valise*, a miniaturized collection of all Duchamp's found object works placed in a briefcase as an early example of the archive form in modern art. Citing Benjamin, Derrida, and W. J. T. Mitchell, Enwezor considers how photography brought in a "change of artistic and pictorial parameters [and] became a specific phenomenon of modernity. The advent of mechanical reproduction initiated an archival formation that would overtake all relations to the photographic record" (10). He adds, "[T]his relationship between past event and its document, an action and its archival photographic trace, is not simply the act of citing a preexisting object or event [. . .], not merely a record of it." In the works he chooses, there is a sense that what is being analyzed is as much the *phainesthai*, the manner in which it is the technology that manages presence, as that which appears present.

In the context of the technologies of the visual in coloniality, one can think of numerous feminist and queer artists since the 1970s who have worked with colonial archives—and not only to denounce them but also to show that the desires and ideations we live with are products of the technologies of coloniality such that a simple oppositional relation is not possible. These constitute what I have elsewhere referred to as technologies of unbelonging, referring to such artists as Isaac Julien who engages Marc Allégret's camera work from when he made films of Africa as he traveled with his lover André Gide. Zineb Sedira looks at the ideation of belonging through her archival play on Algerian lighthouses to understand the technologies of borders and writing, and Mona Hatoum uses the epistolary in video art to show the letter that may not arrive. Walid Raad creates (artificial) archives of the names of those who died or disappeared in the war in Lebanon.

Assia Djebar's second film, *La Zerda, ou les chants de l'oubli*, falls into this category of works of and about the archive. It places sexual difference at its core and yet with the sense that this is not about naming

retrieved, previously forgotten figures or verifying or countering authenticity. Djebar called her films *images-sons* and understood them as part of a
feminist endeavor (*Ces voix*). When asked why she chose to transition originally from literature to film (although this turned out not to be a permanent
transition), she said she wished to work with colloquial Arabic, to work in
television so she could reach large audiences of Algerian women who may
not have access to literature, and to explore a medium that had always been
of interest to her in her writing. While the first two reasons seemed to suggest
a greater transparency in communication with women, it became clear that
her approach to feminism was ultimately more invested in the exploration
of different media and their forms of ideation. Djebar's *images-sons* (and,
indeed, her literature) consistently deals with the medium of representation, whether in her work on the painters Delacroix and Baya Mahieddine,
in urban architecture, on music, ritual, performance, the archival image,
or on the plural pure and impure languages that make up Algeria. In her
collection of essays, *Ces voix qui m'assiègent*, she writes of the different
media that permeate her works: oral transmission alongside text, her plays
bleeding into her novels, films infiltrated by still images, poems that are to
be sung and read but that also constitute critical essays, and films that are
in many ways contemplations on the signifier—images, sound, metonymy,
montage—and that resist narration.

    La Zerda, ou les chants de l'oubli is made up of archival images,
muffled sound, and apparently incongruous text. It is a film about the
archive, about memory, and about *genre*. But to say it is about something is
something of a stretch. The only consistency in the film is its lack of what
Michel Chion called "synchresis." There is rarely a relation between image
and sound. The disjunctive, the contrapuntal, is its dominant mode. Clarisse
Zimra has analyzed it in terms of Deleuzian notions of opsigns and sonsigns,
such that the disjunctive nature of filing creates a contemplation of time and
its technology rather than collapsing into a realist rendition that provides
a cut of the archive.

    Djebar made the film with Malek Alloula. They had been
informed that Pathé-Gaumont was going to throw away much of its colonial
archive material. This information provided the occasion for two projects
on the Franco-Algerian period: Alloula's well-known homage to Algeria and
Roland Barthes, *Le Harem Colonial* [*The Colonial Harem*], and *La Zerda,
ou les chants de l'oubli* [*Zerda, or The Songs of Forgetting*]. If *The Colonial
Harem* is haunted by a contemplation of photography as spirit-medium that

we see also in Barthes's *Camera Lucida* and *A Lover's Discourse*, with an epistolary response from nowhere, in *La Zerda*, we begin with a contemplation, too, of the technology of the screen. On the screen of the moving image, we are presented first with photography. Photography and film work with different versions of ideality, the former with a prolonged gaze, the latter with the cut. Both forms differently raise the question of whether photography and film record or constitute an entity. Benjamin, through Edgar Allan Poe, understands photography as providing the traces left by man rather than evidence as such ("Short").

Text enters Djebar's film not only for translation, titles, or clarity. In fact, rather than clarify, language serves to mystify. In words that bear no relation to the image on the screen, we see "La Mémoire est corps de femme" ("memory is the body of woman"). The phrase appears as suggestive of feminine difference, on the one hand, and overinscription on the other. It could refer to memories projected onto women's bodies, to woman as a screen—the metallic material that, as Irigaray puts it, reflects man; woman as the material that is the condition of possibility for the imaginary; woman as constituted through memory—woman as arche-trace, as origin.

Memory has been introduced thus between archive and screen through writing, as if to remind us that there is no simple transparency or opacity to a screen but that it is always a site of mediation. When we look to the screen for content over technique, we are bound once again to the epoch of presence in which transparency is presented as the solution to opacity.

The next words the screen receives, as if to emphasize this point, are "voile, voile, voile" ("veil," if the word were masculine, or "sail" if it were feminine, but gender is not designated) with the repetition beating the screen. Whether this is the sail of the boats across the Mediterranean or the veils of the women encountered there or the Republican illusion of a lifting of a veil as transparency or freedom, it brings together screen, memory, and the body of woman as mediators of the archive. Psychic life has been introduced into the arena of understanding the relationship between memory and archive as arche-trace, in which we understand that the archive is never simply a collection of the real or of origin, but, like screen-memories, is always a reciprocal product of technology and ideation.

It is also suggestive of the tedium of the presence of the veil in the archive and the idea of looking back. In the novel and autobiographical essay *Vaste est la prison* (1995), Djebar writes of the triangle spared of the veil on the face (one can think of the Arabian *niqab* or Turkish *yachmak*), whereby vision is channeled. The triangle at the eyes of the women becomes, for Djebar, a reference to the cinematic apparatus: the camera, the lens, the world view of the veiled women whom—or, perhaps, given their thingification, more appropriately, that—tourists love to photograph (195). The apparatus of the archive, with its lenses appropriately mediated by a third gaze of power, thus provides the occasion (following Kaja Silverman's reading of Lacan) for the filmmaker to map subjectivity in the traces and stains of difference on the screen.

The Zerda, the traditional festival presented in the archival footage, seems less than celebratory with the disjunctive music that disruptively accompanies the footage and the poems in voice-over that draw attention to the staged nature of all these ethnographic film clips and photographic images. The historically trained Djebar may indeed have wanted to preserve the archive in some way, but certainly not with the idea that something approximating North African authenticity was about to be lost. Nor is she appropriating the material, as it were, simply to return a gaze (even though the European onlookers of the Zerda are certainly rendered ridiculous as they appear to fail to understand ritual and fantasia as performance).

In the context of Djebar's work in which we see a change from a more romantic vision of a feminine oral culture in the earlier work, *La Zerda* marks a moment in which the technologies of colonialism—like photography and film—reveal the manner in which an apparatus comes to constitute a notion of the authentic, the documentable, and the originary as part of the nationalist project of colonial endeavor. Rather than counter this with another ideation of postcolonial nationalism or with the naming of authenticity, Djebar understands it, rather, as part of the failure (economic, material, and conceptual) of the economy of the same and the epoch of presence as a blindness to sexual difference.

Sexual difference becomes the name, then, not for an authenticity, or indeed for a future projection or ideation. Rather, it becomes the name for reading the technologies of ideation such that the trace of difference remains, and sexual difference is understood as that which is yet to be imagined.

RANJANA KHANNA is a professor of English, women's studies, and the literature program at Duke University. She works on Anglo- and Francophone postcolonial theory and literature and film, psychoanalysis, and feminist theory. She has published widely on transnational feminism, psychoanalysis, and postcolonial and feminist theory, literature, and film. She is the author of *Dark Continents: Psychoanalysis and Colonialism* (Duke University Press, 2003) and *Algeria Cuts: Women and Representation, 1830 to the Present* (Stanford University Press, 2008). She has published in such journals as *Art History, Diacritics, differences, Feminist Theory, positions, Public Culture, Screen, Signs, South Atlantic Quarterly,* and *Third Text.* She is currently completing two book manuscripts. The first is called "Asylum." The second is called "Un-belonging."

Works Cited

Agamben, Giorgio. *Profanations.* Boston: Zone, 2015.

Arendt, Hannah. *Love and Saint Augustine.* Chicago: U of Chicago P, 1998.

Barthes, Roland. "Upon Leaving the Movie Theatre." Cha 1–7.

Baudry, Jean-Louis. "The Apparatus." Cha 41–62.

——————. "Author and Analyzable Subject." Cha 67–83.

——————. "Ideological Effects of the Basic Cinematographic Apparatus." Cha 25–37.

Benjamin, Walter. "A Short History of Photography." *Screen* 13.1 (1972): 5–26.

Bersani, Leo. *Is the Rectum a Grave? And Other Essays.* Chicago: U of Chicago P, 2009.

Butler, Judith. *Gender Trouble: Feminism and the Subversion of Identity.* New York: Routledge, 1990.

——————. *The Psychic Life of Power: Theories in Subjection.* Stanford: Stanford UP, 1997.

Cha, Theresa Hak Kyung, ed. *Apparatus, Cinematographic Apparatus: Selected Writings.* New York: Tanam, 1980.

Chion, Michel. *Audio-Vision: Sound on Screen.* Trans. Claudia Gorbman. New York: Columbia UP, 1994.

Cixous, Hélène. *Dedans.* Paris: Grasset, 1969.

——————. *Vivre l'orange.* Paris: Des femmes, 1979.

Derrida, Jacques. "Archive Fever: A Freudian Impression." Trans. Eric Prenowitz. *Diacritics* 25.2 (1995): 9–63.

——————. "Freud and the Scene of Writing." *Writing and Difference.* Trans. Alan Bass. Chicago: U of Chicago P, 1978. 196–231.

——————. "Geschlecht: Sexual Difference, Ontological Difference." *Research in Phenomenology* 13.1 (1983): 65–83.

——————. *Of Grammatology.* Trans. Gayatri Chakravorty Spivak. Baltimore: Johns Hopkins UP, 1998.

Djebar, Assia. *Ces voix qui m'assiègent.* Paris: Albin Michel, 1999.

——————, dir. *La Zerda, ou les chants de l'oubli* [*Zerda, or The Songs of Forgetting*]. 1982. Radiodiffusion Télévision Algérienne.

——————. *Vaste est la prison.* Paris: Albin Michel, 1995.

Enwezor, Okwui. *Archive Fever: Uses of the Document in Contemporary Art*. Göttingen: Steidl, 2008.

Firestone, Shulamith. *The Dialectic of Sex*. New York: Bantam, 1970.

Foster, Hal. "An Archival Impulse." *October* 110 (2004): 3–22.

Freud, Sigmund. "The Dissolution of the Oedipus Complex." 1924. *The Standard Edition of the Complete Psychological Works of Sigmund Freud*. Trans. and ed. James Strachey. Vol. 19. London: Hogarth, 1923–25. 171–80. 24 vols. 1953–74.

——————. *The Interpretation of Dreams*. 1900. *The Standard Edition*. Vols. 4 and 5. 1953. ix–627.

——————. "A Note upon the 'Mystic Writing-Pad.'" 1925. *The Standard Edition*. Vol. 19. 1923–25. 227–35.

——————. "On the Universal Tendency to Debasement in the Sphere of Love (Contributions to the Psychology of Love 2)." 1912. *The Standard Edition*. Vol. 11. 1957. 177–90.

Hatoum, Mona, dir. *Measures of Distance*. 1988. Western Front.

Heidegger, Martin. *Being and Time*. New York: SUNY P, 2010.

Irigaray, Luce. *Speculum of the Other Woman*. Ithaca: Cornell UP, 1985. 133–49.

Johnson, Barbara. "Apostrophe, Animation, and Abortion." *Diacritics* 16.1 (1986): 28–47.

——————. *The Feminist Difference: Literature, Psychoanalysis, Race, and Gender*. Cambridge: Harvard UP, 1998.

——————. "My Monster/My Self." *Diacritics* 12.2 (1982): 2–10.

——————. *Persons and Things*. Cambridge: Harvard UP, 2008.

——————. *A World of Difference*. Baltimore: Johns Hopkins UP, 1987. 144–54.

Julien, Isaac, dir. *Fantôme Afrique*. 2005. DVD.

Kamuf, Peggy. "Derrida and Gender: The Other Sexual Difference." *Jacques Derrida and the Humanities: A Critical Reader*. Ed. Tom Cohen. Cambridge: Cambridge UP, 2002. 82–107.

Kofman, Sarah. *The Enigma of Woman: Woman in Freud's Writings*. Ithaca: Cornell UP, 1985.

Kuntzel, Thierry. "*Le Défilement*: A View in Close Up." Cha 232–47.

Mannoni, Octave. "Je sais bien, mais quand-même." *Clefs pour l'imaginaire ou l'autre scène*. Paris: Seuil, 1969. 9–33.

Marx, Karl. "On the Jewish Question." *The Marx-Engels Reader*. Ed. Robert Tucker. New York: Norton, 1978. 26–46.

Metz, Christian. "The Fiction Film and Its Spectator: A Metapsychological Study." Cha 373–409.

Perkins Gilman, Charlotte. *Herland*. Mineola: Dover, 1998.

Raad, Walid. *The Atlas Group (1989–2004)*. Reina Sofia. Madrid, Spain. June 2009.

Rubin, Gayle, and Judith Butler. "Sexual Traffic: Interview." *Feminism Meets Queer Theory.* Ed. Elizabeth Weed and Naomi Schor. Bloomington: Indiana UP, 1997. 68–108.

Scott, Joan Wallach. "Gender: A Useful Category of Historical Analysis." *American Historical Review* 91.5 (1986): 1053–75.

Sedira, Zineb, *Lighthouse in the Sea of Time.* 2011. Folkestone Triennial.

Silverman, Kaja. "Fassbinder and Lacan: A Reconsideration of Gaze, Look, and Image." *Visual Culture: Images and Interpretations.* Ed. Norman Bryson, Michael Ann Holly, and Keith Moxey. Hanover: Wesleyan UP, 1994. 272–301.

Varda, Agnès. *The Gleaners and I.* 2000. Ciné Tamaris.

Zimra, Clarisse. "Visual/Virtual Memory Sites: The Case of Assia Djebar." *Films with Legs.* Ed. Rosemary A. Peters and Véronique Maisier. Newcastle: Cambridge Scholars, 2011. 2–16.

Is Gender Studies Singular? Stories of Queer/Feminist Difference and Displacement

*I*n response to the "Mariage pour tous" movement for state recognition of lesbian and gay couples in France throughout 2013 and 2014, there was a profound religious and heterosexual backlash that sat somewhat at odds with the international fantasy of French tolerance for freedom of sexual expression.[1] At this point in time, those of us living in Europe or the u.s. are becoming increasingly used to seeing homosexual rights held up as a marker of democratic difference to police immigration and to demonize Islam as profoundly homophobic and patriarchal.[2] Yet in an interesting twist, homosexual rights were being marked out in this French context not as a marker of democratic freedom and progress, but as profoundly *un-French* and a specifically "American" import signaling the ills of globalization in contrast to national pride (Fassin, "La démocratie" and *Le sexe*). Indeed, this placing of homosexuality outside "Frenchness" was a move shared not only by members of the far right Front Nationale and Christian and Muslim religious groups but also by members of a more liberal coalition (Vinocur). The catalyst, the argument went, was the importing of "gender theory"—*la-théorie-du-genre* (singular)—which suggests that gender roles

Volume 27, Number 2 DOI 10.1215/10407391-3621721

are constructed rather than natural complements that make up the body politic, a view ostensibly leading to the inevitable *homosexualization* of the state and to a challenge to national pride and identity (Fassin, "National" 518; and Scott, *Only Paradoxes* ix–xi). Gender theory, this perverse coalition argued, was being taught not just in universities but also in primary schools, where innocent French children were having their natural difference upset by boys being forced to play with dolls and girls with trains, thus signaling the end of democratic Frenchness. Stories of the pernicious character of *la-théorie-du-genre* flooded the papers in the United Kingdom as well as in France as detractors insisted that "theorizing" gender would result in anarchy and called on concerned parents to take their children out of school on a national day of action (Bamat; Penketh; and Samuel). In contrast, the French people were called on to celebrate the natural and complementary gender difference seen to lie at the heart of the democratic French state.[3]

One might point to the irony of this staging by conservative forces of the links between gender, sexuality, and nation, while the Left and feminism have been trying for eons to make these same links visible with considerably less public success. This right-wing cultural and liberal cultural and political coalition knows indeed that when we challenge the biological base of gender, we erode the potency of the symbolic heterosexual couple that lies at the heart of the French democratic refusal of "difference," as Joan Scott has elucidated in *The Politics of the Veil*. Although that difference is framed primarily in racial terms (with its refusal being state mandated to the extent that racial statistics are not kept in France), its ambivalent recognition and repression relies on sexual difference as fully naturalized.[4] "Becoming French" as part of necessary assimilation necessitates not only relinquishing cultural, religious, and racial otherness but also recognizing the gendered complementarity that underwrites (heterosexual) *parité* (Scott, *Parité!*). To challenge that "nondifference," to make it visible, is thus to raise other spectres of difference in French politics and identity as never entirely eradicated and, indeed, Frenchness as never really achievable for those who cannot be assimilated into the emblematic white, secular Christian couple. In framing "gender as a social construction" as intolerable for the French nation, the reliance of French sexual exceptionalism and its veneer of tolerance are revealed as wholly conditional on the privileging of the male, heterosexual gaze. And in further framing this "incursion" into peaceful French sexual difference as an *immigration problem*, such disruption is positioned as a problem of globalization and homogenization. That this border transgression is from the United States rather than North

Africa, the more usual bête noire for French fantasies of the pure nation, is of course ideal: it marks the resistance to *la-théorie-du-genre* as articulated from the position of the underdog rather than that of the racist or xenophobe. In this sense, we might say that the figures of the "veiled woman," the "married gay or lesbian," or the "non-gender-legible child" constitute parallel interruptions to the unstated white, heteronormative order of French civil society and public space.

The response to this extraordinary set of representations and events from feminists and those on the Left has been to point out that there is no single theory of gender and to orient us toward multiplicity and away from singularity (Butler, Fassin, and Scott). Critics such as Éric Fassin have argued in a similar vein that these fantasies of a single theory of gender (one that demolishes French democracy and culture) strengthen the position of heterosexual women in particular as guardians of national identity, providing a useful alliance between antiglobalization and antifeminist sentiments without having to draw too explicitly on an increasingly controversial racialized anti-immigrant discourse (*Le sexe*). This call to multiplicity in the face of resurgent singularity makes complete sense for both political and theoretical reasons. Further, it is a way of pointing to the actually very long tradition of theorizing gender, sex, and sexuality in France, one that is so strong that the very anglophone scholars who are constructed as the "queer threat to French exceptionalism" might themselves be understood to have first borrowed from a diverse French feminist history in order to underpin their own epistemic and political challenges to sexed and gendered nationalism.[5]

This pluralizing response to conservative invocations of singular, fixed gender and sexuality as part of nationalist projects historically and contemporarily is a move not only in France, of course, but one shared across national and international sites of institutionalization. At the London School of Economics and Political Science (LSE), my own institution, our core course has been named "Gender Theories in the Modern World" for similar reasons: to pluralize terms that might otherwise conflate sex and gender within a colonial or nationalist history.[6] This simple "s" at once suggests that there are multiple theories and histories to the field of gender studies (also plural) and marks quite clearly the difference from a singular assumption of "gender" that will always default to a naturalized, complementary model. It gives me great pleasure, of course, to know that I might be able to resist the European spread of the Right with this same "s" and that I might be able to continue teaching this foundational course sure in the knowledge that I am resisting the reproduction of heterosexual and racist framings of gendered complementarity. Alternatively, that pluralization is demonstrated by multiplying the terms themselves rather than the theory, adding to a list of objects that makes plain the limits to singular thinking and orientations and the dangers of exclusion that attend the singularity of both object and politics. Thus we move from women's studies, historically, to gender studies and even to women's, gender, and sexuality studies (as at Yale). While some pluralization is implied already in the term *studies*, an issue of approach rather than object that I return to later in this essay, these displacements or additions primarily indicate a multiplication of sites and objects of study that resist the restriction of feminist and queer politics to singular objects. So in the case of a move from *women* to *gender*, what is often being marked is the opening up of the field to include men and masculinity, queer and transgender (as subjects and objects), an indication that we have learned from the determinist, or even essentialist, histories of our own modes of inquiry.[7] Such temporal and spatial pluralizations seek to make feminism less easy to coopt as a political and institutional project and mark it as always already running counter to the adoption of *gender equality* by neoliberal and neoconservative states and actors. Where "gender" belongs to "feminism" then, it must be plural in order not to be "singular" in precisely this French mode. The hope comes to reside in the object itself, then, and in its ability to carry both external plurality and the plurality of our own desires.

It does, of course, make sense to pluralize and multiply as a way of highlighting the problems of the singular (in the world and in our own institutional practices), but we also need to tune our ears to the alarm bells whose tones echo through the history of this politicized field. I want to suggest, in fact, that in moving too quickly to pluralization, we risk ceding the terrain of "gender," preferring to participate in a fantasy of escape that cleanses us of the amenability of this concept to the violence of nationalist projects rather than to explore the complex terrain of gender that we inhabit. In so doing, the mobilization of gender in ways we do not appreciate can be more easily framed as straightforward cooptation, though, of course, this raises the question of who the "we" is in such a fantasy of separation.[8] In wanting to be heroines of plural, multiple, international feminisms (not bad aims in themselves), the danger is that we accept the conservative framing of *singular* gender as precisely heterosexual, the property of certain women, essentialist and racist. In accepting that gender does not already signify multiplicity, I am concerned that alternative objects and perspectives are too readily positioned as doing *entirely different* work, as superseding (at best banal, at worst heteronormative, essentialist) gender with promises of freedom from conservatism. As Robyn Wiegman has pertinently noted in *Object Lessons*, this admirable desire to escape conservative alignments that coalesce in the object in the name of a false democracy with violence at its heart overinvests in optimistic progress narratives and in the capacity of some objects to resonate as more plural than others. For Wiegman, institutional feminism (in the academy) chases after the right object (whether "women," "gender," or "sexuality"), the one that will be plural and thus rescue feminism from its vexed relationship to the state or the nation.

In what follows, I explore the mobilization of queer theory (note we do not need to pluralize this, as its multiplicity is presumed) as that which displaces gender theory in a bid for ensured transgression. And I propose rethinking gender as a scene of multiplicity, a more accountable institutional and political mode.[9]

Histories

At a conference at Sussex University in 2013 titled (Im)possibly Queer International Feminisms, I found myself feeling increasingly boxed in by the presumptions attending the relationship between feminist and queer scholarship and politics. The conference was intended to be a forum for queer and feminist theorists to "update" and engage international relations theory. Despite the conference title, I increasingly noticed a move in which international relations as a discipline was being updated through its citation of and engagement with queer theory and practice over and above feminism, which was considered to be more aligned with mainstream international relations theory. This move was enabled by suturing feminism to its mobilization within an aggressive foreign policy in Europe and the United States through the familiar argument that "gender equality" is part of what is being exported in a range of violent interventions in the Middle East. Of course, and as I have been arguing so far in this essay, such uses are indeed part of the history of how gender has been taken up as a political alibi. But what was of particular interest to me at the conference was that this seemed to be the *primary* mode of citation of gender and feminism. Meanwhile, and hardly surprisingly, most of the conference attendees (particularly the younger ones) were keen, as a result, to align themselves with the queer critique over the feminist cooptation in order to mark their difference from the mainstream and from violence. Since queer theory was framed as displacing (critically and temporally) feminist approaches to politics, to align oneself firmly with queer theory over feminism also marked the people doing so as fully contemporary themselves, as part of the present and future rather than of a necessarily coopted feminist past. Predictably enough, I found myself following the pluralization route by raising the question of *multiple feminisms* past and present as a counter to this tendency but was also increasingly uncomfortable with the ways that this dynamic positioned me as a kind of "feminist mother" rather than the exciting and transgressive queer subject that I would, of course, prefer to be read as. In citing the multiplicity of feminism, I allowed myself the pleasure of the fantasy described above: that I could remain counterhegemonic and edgy if only feminism*s* were properly understood. But here the contest was not between those *feminisms* and the conservative forces that harness gender in ways I want to resist, but between a fully coopted feminism and a transgressive queer theory and politics. My response was to try for a third mode (plural feminisms) despite its confirmation of its object, gender, as indeed irrecoverable in singular mode.

This teleology, in which queer displaces feminism and is positioned as more theoretically and politically sophisticated and thus less amenable to cooptation, is of course hardly new. Indeed, one might say that the inaugural queer moment emerges precisely out of a consideration and ongoing tension in the relationship between gender and sexuality as objects of analysis and of queer and feminist projects as both different and interlinked. In her foundational piece "Thinking Sex," Gayle Rubin makes her case for separating out these key terms with the aim of rescuing a history of sexuality from a history of gender as structural oppression of women and allowing a distinct history of marginal sexualities freer rein. Rubin's concern here is less to demonize feminism, and gender as its object, than to try and open up a history of sexuality that challenges the moral panics that attend it. For Rubin, it is not possible to have a history of marginal and demonized sexuality if we subsume sexuality within gender, or lesbianism within feminism: the former cannot be entirely contained in the latter in each case.[10] But, in the process, we might say that feminist gender becomes overassociated with oppression. Eve Kosofsky Sedgwick similarly takes up Rubin's call as an institutional question of "proper objects" of queer and feminist studies, proposed as sexuality and gender, respectively, and in so doing she might be said to have performatively constructed these as different fields. While queer authors have always been generously critical of the pitting of the one against the other, Sedgwick and Rubin's understandable and important desire to inaugurate a field attentive to sexuality's *difference* from gender and to move away from a perceived feminist collapsing of the two has had a number of unfortunate effects.

Thus we might say that because of the history of emphasis, or even emphasis on history, the "separate" study of sexuality was always bound to attach to lesbian and gay (or bisexual) identities even as these were being deconstructed, because sexuality as an object was only becoming visible in the moment of its severance from gender. Sexuality, for Rubin and for Sedgwick, was proposed as *not gender*, *not only gender*, and *not gender in its heteronormative modes*; in the process, I want to argue, gender itself became fatally sutured to that heteronormativity. In this separation, then, feminism's (now) proper object, gender, was rather too easily reheterosexualized, first, as not providing enough of an account of that other sexual history (as Carole Vance suggested in her landmark book *Pleasure and Danger* in 1984) and, second, as denoting the most structurally reproductive and normative aspects of sexuality, precisely those that an emergent queer theory was keen to distance itself from. Thus, where sexuality rather than gender has remained attached to a *uniquely feminist* project, this has primarily been as a way of emphasizing its material miseries: sexual violence, trafficking, reproductive labor, and kinship. Where sexuality as an object is claimed as having a history other than that of the worst excesses of violence against women or male dominance, it is more easily sutured to queer theory, which has done its best to divest itself of these constraining modes. One institutional implication of this inaugural separation has been that courses on sexuality (particularly in the context of a gender and sexuality studies curriculum) are often actually LGBT or queer studies courses, since this is what the object has come to signify. It remains rare (though of course not unknown) for there to be sexuality courses that combine LGBT issues and queer theory and politics with sessions on abortion, romance, sexual freedom, or the sexualization of culture, reproductive technology, or tourism. A notable exception to this is often the inclusion of sessions on sex work/prostitution, but this is, of course, partly because the debate on this issue is itself split between one that focuses on structural and fundamental oppression and one that focuses on "choice" and alternative histories of labor and expression.[11] A further implication of such a supercessionist history is that lesbian feminism so easily becomes a curious relic, with lesbians forced to choose between allegiance to a "heterosexualized" feminism, with its structural modes of power, or a queer play that may not resonate particularly well with the experiences of being a lesbian in a male-focused LGBT or queer social world.[12]

In Anglo-American frames, this damning attachment of feminism to "its" proper object has been further reinforced through the characterization of the misnamed "French feminism" as having provided a whitewashed object—sexual difference—in contrast to a plural postcolonial subject aware of the multiple intersectional historical and contemporary forces that forge her. Gayatri Chakravorty Spivak's "French Feminism in an International Frame," in particular, secured a perception of sexual difference as irredeemably essentialist in sexual and racial terms, as hopelessly reductive and naturalizing, and importantly as "Eurocentric." Despite an earlier framing by u.s. theorist Toril Moi of sexual difference theory as *postmodern feminist* theory, such representations of sexual difference as accounts of the (unmarked) feminine resignification of phallocentrism persist. And despite Christine Delphy's deft intervention into the argument to challenge the characterization of "sexual difference" as specifically French and to highlight the variety of feminist theory written in France, the long history of French materialist feminism (which Delphy herself inaugurated) is consistently ignored.[13] Finally, Ranjana Khanna suggests in her essay for this special issue that "sexual difference" itself needs to be rethought and reclaimed from these renderings of it as essentialist or racist. Khanna argues that sexual difference theorists, and in particular Hélène Cixous, have in fact been consistently attentive to the character of French nationalism (particularly in relation to Algeria), challenging rather than reproducing the image of womanhood that underwrites the body politic as white and heterosexual. It is only in a transnational encounter with sexual difference that reads from an anglophone and particularly u.s. position, perhaps, that sexual difference can be marked as free of consideration of race and politics. For the purposes of my argument here, this erroneous critique of sexual difference as *racist*, in particular, and as heterosexist, in general (supporting oppositional gendered positions), has only shored up queer theory's attachment to sexuality as a potentially more fluid object than sex or gender. And indeed, the earlier postcolonial critique has meant that sexual difference remained a no-go area for anglophone scholars of a queer, postcolonial sensibility for some decades. Consider, even now, that where there are materialist "returns" to the body among anglophone scholars, they tend to go via Gilles Deleuze, Elizabeth Grosz, or Bruno Latour, not via Luce Irigaray or Cixous, whose work remains steeped in institutional and political anxiety.[14]

At no point have these categorical oppositions been uncontested, of course. The now classic text *Feminism Meets Queer Theory* from 1997 (from the 1994 issue of *differences*) troubled our assumptions about these relationships even as queer theorists were making their institutional mark. Thus, Butler, in her essay "Against Proper Objects," famously critiques the idea of proper objects at all, trying to open up the relationship among terms as unstable rather than fixed,[15] while Biddy Martin anticipates the problematic positioning of queer as transgression in terms of its implications for a sense of "the ordinary life" so important to queer people as a mode of survival. And in her landmark piece on "Sexual Indifference and Lesbian Representation" from 1988, Teresa de Lauretis positions gender as a vibrant scene of animation and fantasy central to sexual desire, refusing to endorse gender as someone else's heteronormative object and claiming its centrality to a queer imagination in all its slippery glory (see also de Lauretis, *The Practice of Love*). De Lauretis has much to teach us still, I think—about the openness of gender as a site of investigation (filled with misrecognition, displacement, and possessive intent as well as pleasure and resignification) and, too, about ways of opening up race and class identifications and reroutings as part of these same desiring scenes. For de Lauretis, race cannot and should not be evacuated from scenes of desire, however uncomfortable its presence may make us—a point I return to below. Again, the history of citation practices shores up these political and intellectual histories: de Lauretis and Esther Newton have seen much less citation than Butler, Rubin, and Sedgwick in the queer canon on both sides of the Atlantic.

Fast forward twenty years and this debate about feminist/queer relationships, about their proper objects and subjects, is still ongoing in some similar and some different ways that reflect patterns of institutionalization, location, and politics over this period of time. In work such as Janet Halley's *Split Decisions*, for example, feminist criticism is positioned as caught in the gender and sexual oppositions it wants to contest, while queer theory emerges to take up a more imaginative and freeing mantle. And, as I began with, at conferences in the last few years, I have found myself querying the implicit or explicit positioning of queerness on the side of everything that is transformative or creative, while poor old feminism is consigned to the reproduction of dull—and already fully known—critique. In the sexual division of theoretical labor, queer theorists and not feminist theorists still appear to be having all the fun. One of the keys in the contemporary staging of this relationship remains the question of race and identity, but one very important difference to the staging of this relationship in the present is that *both* feminism and sexuality studies have now had their objects roundly critiqued.

As discussed above, we might see anxiety around gender from a queer perspective as taking two main forms. The first, following Rubin and Sedgwick, is the unease with gender's ties to naturalized sex and heteronormative or reproductive frames (Butler, *Gender*). The second, following theorists such as Lisa Duggan, is its cooptation by the nationalist, militarist, or global corporate interests of late capitalism. The desire to liberate on the basis of gender equality in particular has for so long been part of colonial and contemporary acts of aggression and so linked to the fantasy of the racialized nonfree other that to even mention this feels vaguely redundant. The association of "women" or "gender purity" with nation and national interests so central to suffrage campaigns historically and postcolonial nation-building the world over is echoed in gender's mobilization as an alibi for interventionist violence and in its profoundly bureaucratic modes of mainstreaming. There are several fundamental ironies that attend these moves: take, for example, the demand for Turkey to demonstrate appropriate gender equality measures in order to join the European Union, while the United Kingdom's gender equality index score has become steadily worse over the last decade (it has the highest percentage of women in full-time employment in Europe, but wages are the most deflated). Or consider the World Bank's focus on "empowering women" in India (Wilson) or Mexico (Molyneux) to take loans for small businesses because they are more likely to pay them back (gendered behavior being perversely linked to gender transformations), while the same organization insists on low wages in ways we know have a disproportionately negative effect on women and children. Such paradoxes are the very stuff of gender, of course, and the ability to continue to believe in "gender equality" despite its history of contrary use is perhaps another sign of its extraordinary power as an open scene of fantasy attachments (to return to de Lauretis). These continuities between colonial pasts and colonial presents are not left uncontested of course. They are roundly critiqued as forms of the worst kinds of cooptation, cynical alibis that deflect attention from the vigor of capitalism, in Duggan's framing, or as colonial feminisms that inaugurate precisely the need for a pluralization.

Duggan is important because it is she who links the ways gender equality and sexuality have been taken up in the field of nationalism and as part of international agendas. While sexuality scholars may have historically sought to disidentify from feminism's purported object, we might say that they are now confronted with sexual identity as reducible to its mainstreamed rights modes in a familiar vein. Thus, as many theorists of homonormativity and, later, homonationalism have pointed out (Bracke;

Haritaworn; and Puar, "Mapping"), gay and lesbian subjects who are white, happily coupled or monogamous, and happily consumerist or nationalist (Hennessy), have come to occupy the position of a "national treasure" that acts at home, at the border, and elsewhere to ensure that contemporary citizenship can be represented as tolerant and democratic. As Jasbir Puar has pertinently noted with respect to the post-9/11 u.s. political and cultural context, white secular homosexuality stands as a marker of difference within an imagined clash of civilizations in particular, where Islam is always homophobic (as well as uniquely patriarchal) and u.s. identity is always sexually tolerant and in favor of gender equality (*Terrorist*). In a European context, as is familiar at this point from Butler's analysis of the citizenship tests in the Netherlands (versions of which can also be found in Germany, the United Kingdom, and Norway), not only must a would-be citizen show clear signs of recognition of the legal status of same-sex couples and the rights of women to bear their breasts in public, they must also demonstrate appropriate affect to show that they find displays of same-sex affection and women's breasts lovely or, better still, neutral, but certainly not disgusting or sinful ("Sexual").[16] Homosexual equality is not used as the primary alibi for going to war—yet—though instances of extreme homophobic violence are cited as markers of profound difference (e.g., in Afghanistan, Iraq, or, most recently, Syria, as well as Uganda, most typically) from the tolerance of countries that continue to demonstrate unremarked-on ambivalence toward homosexuality.

In this framework, queer studies and queer scholars can only retain their marginal transgressive potential (as compared to feminism) to the extent that they embrace the transnational critique of neoliberal capitalist and militarist interests. They are required—as feminists long have been with respect to gender—to divorce themselves from "sexuality" and LGB standpoints in order to be visibly anti-authoritarian and antinationalist. Queer studies used to be able to do this by moving away from gender as an object (as coopted, as heterosexual, even as whitewashed, but also as importantly *feminist*) in ways I have been suggesting throughout this essay; it now has to do this in relation to its own bourgeois and coopted object, and it has done so with considerable fervency. Called upon to decide between gay rights agendas and Muslim rights to recognition (or nonincarceration and freedom from torture), queer theorists have sided against identity and for transnational solidarity in ways that mirror feminist theorists. But as Fatima El-Tayeb, Jin Haritaworn, and Éric Fassin ("National") have all argued, to be asked to choose between gay rights or Muslim rights is, in fact, no choice at all.[17] There are also consequences to this fervent certainty of the right side to be on that bear on the questions of proper objects, pluralization, and the ground of transgressive critique. A queer critique of homonationalism in particular will appear on occasion to forget that heteronormativity is quite alive and well in most contexts of citizenship, policing the border as it long has and privileging opposite-sex couples with impunity; but one could be forgiven for thinking that gay and lesbian subjects were dominant across Europe, unless queering their own national attachments.[18] Furthermore, the sprinting away from the proper object of sexuality as fast as one can—for dear, transgressive, and critical life—produces its own crisis since one can only displace sexuality as an object so far.[19]

Ironically enough, perhaps, it seems that sexuality has become the same kind of poisoned chalice for queer studies as gender has been for feminism. Despite Rubin and Sedgwick's best efforts to keep the two objects separate, they may have come to do similar work in the end. For queer theorists, the price of inhabiting a transgressive, anticapitalist position in the present is the disavowal of the object that brought the field into being. Sexuality has to be displaced as the bad object that *someone else* carries or is sutured to, causing a splitting at the heart of the queer project, just as it does at the heart of the feminist project. So, too, the circularity of political critique in this evacuation effort bears some further scrutiny, since neither feminists nor (renamed) gay and lesbian scholars necessarily accept the gift of the singular that has been assigned to them. First, we are given our object (even if we refuse it, gender is yours, sexuality yours). Then, the object turns out to *represent* rather than dismantle the power relations that contain and constrain that object, and the subjects and fields so associated become similarly tarnished: old fashioned, outmoded, or dangerous and even violent. And well they may be. We must leave them behind in a progressive move toward multiplicity and away from singularity, away from power and toward freedom, away from cooptation and toward transcendence. But something else happens here, too, even if we think it might be a good idea to move away from objects that are about to blow. And this is that there is an overassociation of power with the *objects themselves*—and the people who do not want to relinquish them—rather than with the discursive and material power relations that give those objects meaning. Strangely, we make of the object a peculiar fetish at precisely the moment we turn away from it.

Interventions

There are several ways that scholars have attempted to intervene into these dilemmas to challenge the overassociation of certain objects with normativity and others with transgression in and of themselves. One approach is a theoretical one that challenges the assumed linear flow from one object to another, or from singularity to multiplicity as an inexorable historical movement. Wiegman's work on this issue is particularly helpful, in my view, as she seeks to suture the terms *queer* and *feminist* precisely in order to resist the displacement of the latter by the former ("Times"). For Wiegman, if we insist on representing the terms *queer feminist* as overlapping and mutually constitutive, we can reimagine queer history as sharing space with feminist history or even being indistinguishable from it at points. This tactic also positions *queer* as qualifying *feminist* rather than coming after or moving on from it. Wiegman's main strategy here is to privilege queer feminist entanglement over displacement, and as part of that project, she reframes Sedgwick's affective interventions, in particular, not as "coming after" debates about gender and sexuality as proper objects but as running parallel to them in mutually constitutive ways.[20] In my own work, too, I have employed similar tactics to Wiegman's, positioning Butler as a queer inheritor of a feminist tradition that she nevertheless remains within (Hemmings, *Why Stories Matter*). If Butler is understood as embracing Monique Wittig's sexual materialism as much as she does Michel Foucault's critique of identity categories, for example, the critical tradition that only sees her in opposition to feminism is disrupted. To play with Wiegman here, we might say that Butler is the feminist inaugurator of an emerging queer studies field; *feminist* could thus also be repositioned as the qualifier of the new rather than the drag on its enthusiasm.

What I underestimated at the time of writing, however, was the significance of international citation patterns and geopolitical location as a fundamental part of how the supercessionist relationship between feminism and the more sophisticated theories that displace it is represented. As my earlier discussion of a postcolonial representation of sexual difference theory suggests, the ability to position this body of theory as irredeemably Eurocentric is partially dependent on writing location. Consigning sexual difference to an essentialist and racist past from which a more attentive postcolonial body of scholarship can escape also depends on the spatial separation of continents and the designation of that older theory as "French," as we have seen.

In this frame, queer studies can only be European in its male antecedents (Foucault rather than Wittig) since its female or feminist foremothers are too fleshy a reminder of the difficulty of separating sex from gender in the first place. Close attention to what Spivak elsewhere refers to as the "politics of translation" ("Politics") might enable a more located set of interventions into the progress and loss narratives that underpin the teleology of queer/feminist separation and force another look at their broader citation as part of the maintenance of geopolitical ordering. Such an approach also requires thinking carefully about how postcolonial scholarship is crucial both to challenging the cooptation of "gender" and "sexuality" by forces outside of feminist and queer studies *and* to their pitting one against the other in a teleological vein. And to return to the contemporary problem of "sexual equality" as part of how Western democracies imagine themselves at the forefront of history, a transnational approach is essential in pointing to this hubris and its pernicious racist effects; yet such an approach also recasts "sexuality" itself as a tarnished object that queer scholars are loath to attach to (despite the impossibility of fully disentangling themselves from it).

As I began this paper by pointing out, the question of *la-théorie-du-genre* relies in the French case on the fantasy of gender theory as a u.s. import. This is, of course, a politically motivated and strongly homophobic move, but it points to an interesting area of resistance that does not require a *defensive* pluralization in response. We might, for example, want to point to the various geopolitical locations and histories of gender as an object of study in the first place. One approach has been to highlight the emergence of much u.s. gender theory through the encounter with European theory, shifting the presumption of import to one of export, as we have seen. But so, too, *gender* has an international institutional life that points to competing understandings of the term that are political as well as geographical and linguistic. We encounter this complexity each year in the international context of the LSE, where students' different locations and languages mean that gender never means only one thing and indeed often means something incommensurable rather than additive. Indeed, in many linguistic traditions it signifies in ways that resonate not with the Anglo-American traditions that suture it to *sex*, but rather with approaches that link it to *nation* (through its roots in *genus*), as Donna Haraway has argued ("'Gender'").[21] It may indicate a policy bent in Scandinavia or for South Asian students used to gender mainstreaming; or a preference for gender can reference a conservative history of depoliticization and erasure of the feminist peace movement in Croatia. In Portugal the significance of gender studies cannot be understood outside of the state's desire for full European participation, and its funding ensures that the field remains resolutely temporary and funded from outside national borders (Pereira), while the same designation can signal an openness to queer and transgender inclusion in the United States or the United Kingdom. Such layering of what gender means, let alone whether and how one can study it, is perhaps a slightly different mode of pluralization, one that is focused on complicating the *space of gender* rather than trying to move away from it in a teleology of displacement. Students and faculty have thus to negotiate these differences of meaning and political histories each year and consistently fail (of course) to reconcile such opposed meanings effectively. These negotiations might be said to make visible the geopolitics of the terrain of gender instead of ceding it, as students and faculty struggle to make sense of these various located histories.[22]

This understanding of gender as a space of negotiation and competing meanings at the institutional level finds resonance with a more psychoanalytic understanding of gender as a scene of complexity and negotiation. To return to de Lauretis: gender is never for her a static position or a hermetically sealed category; it is instead a dense site of fantasy, pleasure, and horror that is always already plural. It is a site of memory and displacement, pleasure, and attachment, and our participation in "gender as a scene" produces us as sexualized and raced as well as gendered subjects within a confusing yet compelling erotic economy. I am particularly interested in de Lauretis here because of the ways in which in her discussion of the film *She Must Be Seeing Things* she also centers race as part of that desiring scene of gender ("Sexual"). In the film, the butch, racialized (Brazilian) subject and the white femme (u.s.) subject play with and occupy these differences as sources of related pleasure and difficulty. To think of race and difference as part of the erotic scene of gender is a risky move, of course: it is to engage a history of fetishization of the other and risk eroticizing racialized power in ways that reproduce rather than challenge racism. Indeed, one critique of de Lauretis might be that she seems to engage in a flattening parallelism that sees all power relations as somehow mimetic (rather than having specific, if overlaid) histories. And yet, I think de Lauretis's risk is an important one, since her incorporation of racialized difference in the erotic play between protagonists in *She Must Be Seeing Things* seeks to theorize gender and sexual "scenes" of desire and disidentification as always already racialized.[23] For Ian Barnard, in his influential article "Queer Race," de Lauretis is unique in her early invitation to consider race as part of the erotics of queer gender play, and he is cautiously enthusiastic about her attempts to theorize this as part of, rather than antithetical to, desire (200–201). De Lauretis's surfacing of the vexed tension between race and gender, her placing of this tension at the center of her scenes of troubled gendered play and queer desire as her protagonists argue and make up, raises the question of the extent of the racialized nature of erotic encounter (with all its history) and at the same time suggests ways of treating difference across different modes of power. Her gendered scenes, then, propose open and constrained play in which no question of difference signifies in only one way.[24]

Continuing to think of gender as a malleable site of negotiation in both institutional and psychoanalytic terms, one might also foreground ways in which feminist epistemology has always insisted that *researching gender* is a process that performatively brings to life both the subject and the object of the research process and perhaps the field itself. For Lorraine Code, the task of "taking subjectivity into account" is central to feminist epistemology both in terms of challenging the idea of objectivity in the research field and with respect to the position of the knower who always has an influence on what can be known (23–57). We might say that feminist epistemology has always foregrounded gender as a dynamic and shifting, but always located, object and subject, as Haraway also suggests in "Situated Knowledges." Berger's work on u.s. and French queer and feminist encounters extends this tradition as she reminds us that gender is always relational, that it is actively engaged and transformed through the encounter between subject and object in ways that exceed and even challenge understandings of gender in terms of a heteronormative complementarity (*Queer* 11–82). For Berger, the relational character of gender and the field of queer feminist studies locates the critic in terms of attachments to that object they are never quite separate or alien from but also never identical to ("Petite"). It is Berger, in my view, who is particularly helpful in bringing together the institutional, transnational, and psychic dimensions of gender as a site of complex negotiation, investment, and dynamism without which there would be no field of gender studies.

Might these different visions of gender as a scene we already participate in, as do others but never in quite the same way, allow us to repoliticize gender as a conflicted psychic and geopolitical space that always risks reproducing its fusion with sex or nation but that cannot be reduced to this risk? Such an understanding of gender as an unfinished, conflicted site of engagement is echoed by Judith Butler, Éric Fassin, and Joan Scott in their roundtable discussion for *Représentations*, in which they propose gender as a way of asking questions of relationships and the world rather than as a closed concept with a singular (or even multiple but final) meaning. Perhaps then, and in line with Berger's intervention in *The Queer Turn*, we might think of gender as a scene of call and response, a dense site of exchange of power and privilege and of pleasure and possibility, rather than purely as a marker of distinct and naturalizing oppositions that must be pluralized or abandoned. In a sense, one might ask why gender is particularly helpful as a concept that can carry the weight of this work. Indeed, as indicated earlier, Khanna, in "On the Name," makes a similar move to mine in her desire to reanimate sexual difference as a site of complex intersectionality that already has race and colonialism in mind. So perhaps this would be a better site for thinking the real and fantasmatic history of sex, race, and space in ways I have been proposing throughout this article? But in thinking through why it is that I prefer to stick with exploring the multiplicity of gender rather than sexual difference, I have concluded that this best reflects my interest here in repoliticizing the inaugural separation of sexuality and gender as proper objects of engagement for queer and feminist studies, respectively. In other words, although sexual difference is clearly key for the transnational encounter between u.s. and French feminisms and the momentum of the field, it is *gender* more than sexual difference that is positioned as the lost object of feminism in the ascendency of queer studies as a unique site of transgression, at least from where I write.

But perhaps I am too hasty in wanting to keep these sites separate. In closing, might we think again about the similarities of feminist modes of engaging the body, desire, and relationality promised by feminist theories of gender as structural oppression, sexual difference theory in its most expansive rewritings of "woman-as-nature," and the Marxist-lesbian provocation of Wittig's that "a lesbian is not a woman" that I have suggested interrupts a queer/feminist teleology? Here, my interest is in returning to the lesbian figure I mentioned earlier, the one who falls outside of the competition between queer and feminist perspectives. She is associated with feminism in her guise as "lesbian feminist" and thus also with the anachronism that must be moved away from; yet she is also associated with queer transgression in her need for a history other than one in which gender can only signify pain and not pleasure. It is Wittig's citation as primary antecedent to Butler that has enabled me to reimagine a history of queer studies as a feminist one. But it is perhaps more accurate to say that Wittig allows me to reimagine the history of a queer/feminist relationship from the position of the ambivalent lesbian character that haunts the narrative (Hesford). Taking Wittig seriously challenges our "proper objects" in another way, too.

On the one hand, Wittig clearly participates in (or perhaps inaugurates) the queer tradition of proposing sexuality as different from gender. She famously insisted that a lesbian is not a woman, pointing directly to both the problem of heteronormative gender roles and to the inability to contain lesbian subjectivity within its confines. Wittig would surely agree, then, that sexuality needs a different history and analysis that feminism has not been attentive to. On the other hand, Wittig attaches firmly to her object, retaining *lesbian* as a category to challenge *woman* and yet simultaneously relying on it. Wittig's "lesbian as not woman" keeps us entangled rather than split, one might say, in her refusal to abandon the paradox of complicity.

CLARE HEMMINGS is professor of feminist theory at the Gender Institute, London School of Economics. Her book *Why Stories Matter: The Political Grammar of Feminist Theory* was published in 2011 (Duke University Press), and her book on Emma Goldman's importance for the history of feminist theory and politics is forthcoming (Duke University Press, 2017).

Notes

1   Joan Wallach Scott describes this fantasy of French tolerance in her groundbreaking book *Only Paradoxes to Offer*. For Scott the fantasy relies on gender complementarity within a heterosexual democratic imaginary.

2   See Butler, "Sexual"; and Puar, "Mapping." Indeed, the UK government did just this in the recent push for military intervention in Syria following the terrorist attacks in Paris, citing the particular barbarity of ISIS throwing gay men off buildings as well as systematically raping women. I will return to this issue of Western governments claiming gender and sexual equality as uniquely theirs to export and protect, despite ongoing homosexual inequality and pitifully low rates of prosecution of men for rape in both the United Kingdom and the United States, for example. See Wintour.

3   In her book *The Politics of the Veil*, Scott is more direct still in her identification of the heteronormative underpinnings of the French national imaginary. For Scott, the challenge of "the veiled woman"

is not her religious attachment but her refusal to participate in the fantasy of French "democratic heterosexuality," in which women are available to the male gaze as part of what makes up civil society.

4   Christine Delphy's recent work is instructive in this respect. In the context of increased right-wing anti-immigration feeling in France, she writes persuasively of the importance for feminists of not separating out sexism and racism ("Antisexisme"). And in her 2008 book *Classer, Dominer: Qui Sont Les Autres*, Delphy insists on an integrated, materialist feminist position that mobilizes a particularly socialist intersectional approach (see *Separate*).

5   Consider, for example, Judith Butler's debt to Monique Wittig and Luce Irigaray as the ground from which she departs in *Gender Trouble*; or Toril Moi's engagement with Simone de Beauvoir and Hélène Cixous in *Sexual/Textual Politics*.

6   There is, of course, a rather profound irony in pluralizing "gender

theories" only to retain the "modern world" as both singular and knowable. My thanks to Alyosxa Tudor for their critical insights on this point.

7 Importantly, however, these supposedly pluralizing shifts have been contested, with the shift to gender from women being seen by many feminist commentators as a depoliticization in line with institutional expectations of "inclusion" rather than the politicization of knowledge (Stromquist; Threadgold). Renate Klein takes the strongest position on this last issue, renaming gender studies "hetero-relations studies" (81).

8 I developed an argument about the amenability of feminist narratives in preference to cooptation in my book *Why Stories Matter* and extend that here as a way of thinking about gender itself.

9 Robyn Wiegman and Elizabeth Wilson have recently coedited a special issue of *differences* on the problem of antinormativity in queer theory. The demand for "queer" always to signal or enact a challenge to or subversion of the dominant, or "hetero-norms," is both politically and theoretically restrictive in their view. The burden of transgression is indeed a hard one to bear for queer theory as it continues to mark the opposite of cooptation *avant la lettre*, a burden that becomes harder and harder to carry, as I outline in the next section.

10 Rubin's foundational work is an engagement with the work of feminist theorists such as Adrienne Rich, for whom feminism and lesbianism must be thought together and for whom structural gender oppression is inextricably intertwined with sexual oppression.

11 Interestingly, these "object" splits also become disciplinary splits, with queer theory belonging more firmly to the humanities and feminism to the social sciences. So firmly entrenched is the view of this history as fact that Heather Love was able to make a plea for queer scholars to develop a fuller engagement with empirical methods, as though sexuality itself had not been studied outside of a humanities approach.

12 See Elizabeth Freeman's evocative article on the "generational" presumptions of a queer "exit" from a lesbian feminist past, which resonates with my argument here.

13 In a recent special issue of *South Atlantic Quarterly* on 1970s feminisms, Lisa Disch seeks to rectify this omission in her essay "Christine Delphy's Constructivist Materialism." The issue also reprints a piece of Delphy's earlier work, reintroducing it to a U.S. audience.

14 Of course, Elizabeth Grosz is a notable exception herself, engaging with Irigaray in considerable depth though interestingly not with her European feminist contemporaries, such as Rosi Braidotti, who make similar arguments about the importance of "vitalism." See Braidotti, *Metamorphoses*.

15 As Anne Emmanuelle Berger importantly notes in *The Queer Turn in Feminism*, her brilliant new book on French-U.S. feminist and queer intellectual circuits, Esther Newton—with her understanding of gender as theatrical in its queer sites as that which moves us—is probably better understood as Butler's interlocutor than Rubin in many ways. For Berger, too, in her commentary on the celebration DVD marking forty years of feminist scholarship at Paris 8 University, notes that shifts in

how we name the "proper object" of the interdisciplinary field we call home should be thought of as complementary rather than as a sequence of displacements. See the online documentary *Les quarante vies du Contre d'études féminines et d'études de genre.*

16   There are, of course, countries of origin not on the list (such that their citizens do not need to demonstrate such recognition or affect, and these include Western countries without same-sex rights or traditions of topless sunbathing, such as the United States), and, of course, money buys exemption.

17   Both El-Tayeb and Haritaworn have explored in detail the presumed contradictions of being queer and Muslim in Europe in the context of homonationalist rightwing consolidation and the consequences of this for those seeking to live lives in which these are inseparable terms.

18   See Brown for a trenchant critique of this tendency.

19   It is not accidental, of course, that most queer theorists (though not all) do in fact identify as queer, nor that the vast majority of queer work is in fact concerned with same-sex practices or with debunking heteronormative logics. There have been valiant attempts (Floyd; Halley and Parker) to entirely detach queer critique from its attachments to sexuality as both subject and object. But the queer focus will always tend back to sexual practice and subjectivity and circle around desire and its perversions. Indeed, without this movement, it might be hard to see what is distinct about queer theory (as compared to deconstruction in general).

20   Sam McBean makes a similar move in her book on *Feminism's Queer Temporalities*, in which she thinks again about the limits of an approach that marks feminism as less expansive than queer theory and practice, preferring to consider the ways they are sutured and scrambled.

21   See Braidotti's work on the range of different meanings and uses of *sex* and *gender* within a European geopolitical landscape ("Uses"). The now defunct journal the *Making of European Women's Studies*—part of the Athena project on mapping the field in Europe—published a range of interventions in a similar vein (see, e.g., Bahovec; Jegerstedt).

22   My own article "The Life and Times of Academic Feminism" maps some of these institutional as well as geopolitical conflicts over the meanings of *gender* and *women*, although it pays scant attention to the question of sexuality and queer studies.

23   José Muñoz's work on the importance of disidentification for a history of queer of color survival and desire, a mode of attachment that refuses full absorption into the dominant, extends de Lauretis's work in interesting ways (though Muñoz only briefly cites her work).

24   As Wiegman also highlights in *Object Lessons*, the question of race as so intimately linked to and sometimes standing in for social justice more generally (within feminism) means that direct engagement with an erotics of racialized difference that forms part and parcel of how racism works is forever displaced and even disavowed. Wiegman's work here is important both for her critique of the problematics of "intersectional" forgetting of a black feminist standpoint and for her address of Sharon Holland's proposition that there is an erotic life to racism that needs to be told.

Works Cited   Bahovec, Eva. "A Short Note on the Use of 'Sex' and 'Gender' in Slavic Languages." *Making of European Women's Studies* 1 (2000): 44–45.

Bamat, Joseph. "French Parents Boycott Schools over 'Gender Theory' Scare." *France 24* 30 Jan. 2014. http://www.france24.com/en/20140129-france-sex-education-gender-discrimination-protest-school.

Barnard, Ian. "Queer Race." *Social Semiotics* 9.2 (1999): 199–212.

——————. *Queer Race: Cultural Interventions in the Racial Politics of Queer Theory.* New York: Peter Lang, 2004.

Berger, Anne Emmanuelle. "Petite histoire paradoxale des études dites de 'genre' en France." *Le Français Aujourd'hui* 163.4 (2008): 83–91.

——————. *The Queer Turn in Feminism: Identities, Sexualities, and the Theatre of Gender.* Oxford: Oxford UP, 2013.

Bracke, Sarah. "From 'Saving Women' to 'Saving Gays': Rescue Narratives and Their Dis/continuities." *European Journal of Women's Studies* 19.2 (2012): 237–52.

Braidotti, Rosi. *Metamorphoses: Towards a Materialist Theory of Becoming.* Cambridge: Polity, 2002.

——————. "The Uses and Abuses of the Sex/Gender Distinction in European Feminist Practices." *Thinking Differently: A Reader in European Women's Studies.* Ed. Gabriele Griffin and Rosi Braidotti. London: Zed, 2002. 285–307.

Brown, Gavin. "Homonormativity: A Metropolitan Concept That Denigrates 'Ordinary' Gay Lives." *Journal of Homosexuality* 59.7 (2012): 1065–72.

Butler, Judith. "Against Proper Objects." Weed and Schor 1–30.

——————. *Gender Trouble: Feminism and the Subversion of Identity.* New York: Routledge, 1990.

——————. "Sexual Politics, Torture, and Secular Time." *British Journal of Sociology* 59.1 (2008): 1–23.

Butler, Judith, Éric Fassin, and Joan Wallach Scott. "Pour ne pas en finir avec le 'genre' . . . Table ronde." *Sociétés et Représentations* 24.2 (2007): 285–306.

Code, Lorraine. *Rhetorical Spaces: Essays on Gendered Locations.* New York: Routledge, 1995.

de Lauretis, Teresa. *The Practice of Love: Lesbian Sexuality and Perverse Desire.* Bloomington: Minnesota UP, 1994.

——————. "Sexual Indifference and Lesbian Representation." *Theatre Journal* 40.2 (1988): 155–77.

Delphy, Christine. "Antisexisme *ou* antiracisme? Un faux dilemme." *Nouvelles Questions Féministes* 25.1 (2006): 59–83.

——————. *Separate and Dominate: Feminism and Racism after the War on Terror.* Trans. David Broder. London: Verso, 2015.

Disch, Lisa. "Christine Delphy's Constructivist Materialism: An Overlooked 'French Feminism.'" *South Atlantic Quarterly* 114.4 (2015): 827–49.

Duggan, Lisa. *The Twilight of Equality? Neoliberalism, Cultural Politics, and the Attack on Democracy.* Boston: Beacon, 2003.

El-Tayeb, Fatima. "'Gays Who Cannot Properly Be Gay': Queer Muslims in the Neoliberal European City." *European Journal of Women's Studies* 19.1 (2012): 79–95.

Fassin, Éric. "La démocratie sexuelle et le conflit des civilisations." *Multitudes* 26.3 (2006): 123–31.

——————. "National Identities and Transnational Intimacies: Sexual Democracy and the Politics of Immigration in Europe." *Public Culture* 22.3 (2010): 507–29.

——————. *Le sexe politique: Genre et sexualité au miroir transatlantique.* Paris: Éditions de l'Ecole des Hautes Études en Sciences Sociales, 2009.

Floyd, Kevin. *The Reification of Desire: Toward a Queer Marxism.* Minneapolis: U of Minnesota P, 2009.

Freeman, Elizabeth. "Packing History, Count(er)ing Generations." *New Literary History* 31.4 (2000): 727–44.

Halley, Janet. *Split Decisions: How and Why to Take a Break from Feminism.* Princeton: Princeton UP, 2006.

Halley, Janet, and Andrew Parker, eds. *After Sex? On Writing since Queer Theory.* Durham: Duke UP, 2011.

Haraway, Donna. "'Gender' for a Marxist Dictionary: The Sexual Politics of a Word." *Simians, Cyborgs and Women: The Reinvention of Nature.* London: Free Association Books, 1991. 127–48.

——————. "Situated Knowledges: The Science Question in Feminism and the Privilege of Partial Perspective." *Feminist Studies* 14.3 (1988): 575–99.

Haritaworn, Jin. "Women's Rights, Gay Rights, and Anti-Muslim Racism in Europe: Introduction." *European Journal of Women's Studies* 19.1 (2012): 73–78.

Hemmings, Clare. "The Life and Times of Academic Feminism: Checking the Vital Signs of Women's and Gender Studies." *The Handbook of Gender and Women's Studies.* Ed. Kathy Davis, Mary Evans, and Judith Lorber. London: Sage, 2006. 14–34.

——————. *Why Stories Matter: The Political Grammar of Feminist Theory.* Durham: Duke UP, 2011.

Hennessy, Rosemary. *Profit and Pleasure: Sexual Identities in Late Capitalism.* New York: Routledge, 2000.

Hesford, Victoria. "Feminism and Its Ghosts: The Spectre of the Feminist-as-Lesbian." *Feminist Theory* 6.3 (2005): 227–50.

Holland, Sharon. *The Erotic Life of Racism.* Durham: Duke UP, 2012.

Jegerstedt, Kari. "A Short Introduction to the Use of 'Sex' and 'Gender' in the Scandinavian Languages." *Making of European Women's Studies* 1 (2000): 39–41.

Khanna, Ranjana. "On the Name, Ideation, and Sexual Difference." *Transatlantic Gender Crossings.* Ed. Anne Emmanuelle Berger and Éric Fassin. Spec. issue of *differences* 27.2 (2016): 62–78.

Klein, Renate D. "Passion and Politics in Women's Studies in the 1990s." *Out of the Margins: Women's Studies in the Nineties.* Ed. Jane Aaron and Sylvia Walby. London: Falmer, 1991. 75–89.

Les quarante vies du Centre d'études féminines et d'études de genre. 29 June 2015. Télédebout DVD. http://www2.univ-paris8.fr/ef/spip.php?article270 for the uploaded documentary.

Love, Heather. "Close Reading and Thin Description." *Public Culture* 25.3 (2013): 401–34.

Martin, Biddy. "Extraordinary Homosexuals and the Fear of Being Ordinary." Weed and Schor 109–35.

McBean, Sam. *Feminism's Queer Temporalities.* London: Routledge, 2015.

Moi, Toril. *Sexual/Textual Politics: Feminist Literary Theory.* London: Routledge, 1985.

Molyneux, Maxine. "Mothers at the Service of the New Poverty Agenda: Progresa/Oportunidades, Mexico's Conditional Transfer Programme." *Social Policy and Administration* 40.4 (2006): 425–49.

Muñoz, José. *Disidentifications: Queers of Color and the Performance of Politics.* Minneapolis: U of Minnesota P, 1999.

Newton, Esther. *Cherry Grove, Fire Island: Sixty Years in America's First Gay and Lesbian Town.* Boston: Beacon, 1993.

Penketh, Anne. "Can Boys Wear Skirts? France Divided by Gender Stereotyping Experiment in Primary Schools." *Independent* 30 June 2014. http://www.independent.co.uk/news /world/europe/can-boys-wear-skirts-france-divided-by-gender-stereotyping-experiment-in -primary-schools-9574297.html.

Pereira, Maria do Mar. "The Importance of Being 'Modern' and Foreign: Feminist Scholarship and the Epistemic Status of Nations." *Signs* 39.3 (2014): 627–57.

Puar, Jasbir. "Mapping U.S. Homonormativities." *Gender, Place, and Culture* 13.1 (2006): 67–88.

─────────. *Terrorist Assemblages: Homonationalism in Queer Times.* Durham: Duke UP, 2007.

Rich, Adrienne. "Compulsory Heterosexuality and Lesbian Existence." *Signs* 5.4 (1980): 631–60.

Rubin, Gayle. "Thinking Sex: Notes for a Radical Theory of the Politics of Sexuality." *The Gay and Lesbian Studies Reader.* Ed. Henry Abelove, Michele Barale, and David Halperin. New York: Routledge, 1993. 3–44.

Samuel, Henry. "French Parents in Panic over Warning of Lessons That 'Boys Can Be Girls.'" *Telegraph* 28 Jan. 2014. http://www.telegraph.co.uk/news/worldnews/europe/france/10602928 /French-parents-in-panic-over-warning-of-lessons-that-boys-can-be-girls.html.

Scott, Joan Wallach. *Only Paradoxes to Offer: French Feminists and the Rights of Man.* Cambridge: Harvard UP, 1996.

─────────. *Parité! Sexual Equality and the Crisis of French Universalism.* Chicago: U of Chicago P, 2005.

─────────. *The Politics of the Veil.* Princeton: Princeton UP, 2009.

Sedgwick, Eve Kosofsky. "Axiomatic." Introduction. *The Epistemology of the Closet.* Berkeley: U of California P, 1990. 1–63.

Spivak, Gayatri Chakravorty. "French Feminism in an International Frame." *Yale French Studies* 62 (1981): 154–84.

——————. "The Politics of Translation." *Outside in the Teaching Machine.* New York: Routledge, 1993. 179–200.

Stromquist, Nelly. "Gender Studies: A Global Perspective of Their Evolution, Contribution, and Challenges to Comparative Higher Education." *Higher Education* 41.4 (2001): 373–87.

Threadgold, Terry. "Gender Studies and Women's Studies." *Australian Feminist Studies* 15.31 (2000): 39–48.

Vance, Carole. *Pleasure and Danger: Exploring Female Sexuality.* New York: Routledge, 1984.

Vinocur, Nicholas. "French Parliament Allows Gay Marriage Despite Protests." *Reuters* 23 Apr. 2013. http://www.reuters.com/article/us-france-gaymarriage-idUSBRE93K08B20130423.

Weed, Elizabeth, and Naomi Schor, eds. *Feminism Meets Queer Theory.* Bloomington: Indiana UP, 1997.

Wiegman, Robyn. *Object Lessons.* Durham: Duke UP, 2012.

——————. "The Times We're In: Queer Feminist Criticism and the Reparative 'Turn.'" *Feminist Theory* 15.1 (2014): 4–25.

Wiegman, Robyn, and Elizabeth A. Wilson. "Antinormativity's Queer Conventions." Introduction. *Queer Theory without Antinormativity.* Spec. issue of *differences* 26.1 (2015): 1–25.

Wilson, Kalpana. "'Race,' Gender, and Neoliberalism: Changing Visual Representations in Development." *Third World Quarterly* 32.2 (2011): 315–31.

Wintour, Patrick. "David Cameron Puts Case for Syrian Airstrikes to MPs." *Guardian* 26 Nov. 2015. http://www.theguardian.com/politics/2015/nov/26/david-cameron-publishes-case-for-syria-airstrikes.

Wittig, Monique. "The Straight Mind." *The Straight Mind and Other Essays.* Boston: Beacon, 1992. 21–32.

Feelings of Injustice: The Institutionalization of Gender Studies and the Pluralization of Feminism

This is what a wrong [*tort*] would be: a damage [*dommage*] accompanied by the loss of the means to prove the damage.
—Lyotard

I would like to call a *differend* [*différend*] the case where the plaintiff is divested of the means to argue and becomes for that reason a victim.
—Lyotard

The limits of the discursive analysis of gender presuppose and preempt the possibilities of imaginable and realizable gender configurations within culture. This is not to say that any and all gendered possibilities are open, but that the boundaries of analysis suggest the limits of a discursively conditioned experience. These limits are always set within the terms of a hegemonic cultural discourse predicated on binary structures that appear as the language of universal rationality. Constraint is thus built into what that language constitutes as the imaginable domain of gender.
—Butler

*A*s its starting point, this essay addresses two issues that Anne Emmanuelle Berger and Éric Fassin posed in their *argumentaire*,[1] written in May 2014 for the celebration of the fortieth year of the Centre d'études féminines et d'études de genre at the University of Paris 8, as topics of discussion. The first issue, posed as a question, is this: "If feminism is both a movement and an increasingly institutionalized academic discipline, does the institutionalization of Gender Studies de-politicize feminism?" In what follows, I will connect this question with the contingent and pluralized history of feminism in the academy, with Jean-François Lyotard's notion of the *différend*, and with the transdisciplinary character of gender studies so as to argue that the movement and the academic institution might not be as opposed as they seem.

Volume 27, Number 2   DOI 10.1215/10407391-3621733

I suggest that the opposition of scholarship and politics is mistaken on two fronts. First, it ignores the strongly and decisively university-based environment of second-wave feminism. The assumption is that the feminist movement exists primarily outside of academia when, in fact, from the beginning of the second wave, feminism, the movement, was crucially based within universities and perhaps even conditioned by this exceptional conjunction. Second, the opposition downplays the evidence of the strong interdependence of feminist scholarship and politics. Scholarship not only gives strength to feminist and gender-deviant politics but also, crucially, complicates its stakes and often actually builds up its content, providing the space where that politics is generated and, indeed, often actually *is* that politics.

The history of forty years of gender studies testifies to the power of academic-activist commingling as conceptually creative, particularly in finding ways to express "wrongs" in the sense meant by Lyotard's notion of the *différend*. I maintain that gender studies has developed into a trans-discipline that, rather than generating "knowledge production" on gender or sexuality, instead intervenes by finding expressions for wrongs that are hard to express in the dominant language. In this endeavor, the separation of the movement from the scholarship is difficult and, I think, ultimately undesirable.

The second issue taken up by Berger and Fassin in their *argumentaire* concerns the content of gender studies as an academic discipline. Berger and Fassin discuss a tension within the discipline between the issues of women and gender, on the one hand, and sexuality and sexual minorities, on the other. The problematic they raise touches upon the history of the past four decades of academic feminism, within which the separation of "gender" issues from "sexuality" issues has been reflected in changes in the name of the entity that focuses on scholarship involving feminist issues. In some universities, the name changed from "women's studies" to "gender studies," and then, with the rise of queer studies, some academic institutions renamed their programs "gender and sexuality studies."

I argue that the issues of women/gender and sexuality/queer, however much they appear to diverge, in fact belong together in the academy, both institutionally and in terms of scholarly tradition. To make my argument, I will first revisit the fact that sexuality and the wrongs lived by sexual and gender minorities have been both present and contested issues within the second-wave feminist movement since its beginning; they were not introduced as separate issues later. During the earliest days, these issues were a wrong that was difficult, almost impossible, to express in words. More important, I will argue that the two issues—that of gender inequality and hierarchies between women and men, on the one hand, and that of cultural violence around sexual and gender minorities (LGBTQI), around gendering and, indeed, around the mere cultural existence of gender, on the other hand—are strongly implicated with each other: gender inequality and gender hierarchy are ultimately achieved through asserting and enforcing the necessity of gender and through what I will, with reference to Lyotard, call "the terror" of gendering, in which the threat to life replaces the legitimated violence of the various norms of gender.

Before proceeding with this argument, it is important to note a historically understood difference between two kinds of gender politics that have informed and been entangled with one another within academic feminism over the last forty years. First, there is the feminism that expresses the wrong done to women by being culturally dominated by men. That is about solidarity among women, and it could be called *sisterhood feminism*. Second, there is the politics that expresses the wrong of compulsory (binary) gender. This could be called *queer feminism*. While acknowledging this difference, I argue that the pluralization of feminist politics, which comprises both of these and more, is at the core of academic feminism as a transdisciplinary discipline. This is because the discipline ultimately distinguishes itself within the academy through being there *in order* to express injustices. The feeling of injustice persists and informs the field, its institutions, and activism after these forty years of pluralization.

The Movement and Academic Institutions

The issues of institutions versus politics and that of scholarship versus activism have been debated since the beginning of academic feminism, and it has perhaps even become a tradition to discuss these supposed tensions within the field. There are some misconstruals in this discussion, and through exploring them I would like to argue that the best way to think about academic feminism is not to oppose the movement and the institutions, but rather to see how they might, in fact, not be two different things at all.

That second-wave feminism actually developed within academic institutions from the beginning is evident particularly when compared to the first wave of feminism. Although it is true that the first wave was inspired by well-known writers and scholars, such as Olympe de Gouges (1748–93) and Mary Wollstonecraft (1759–97), women who used their brains and their pens, neither these women nor many of the suffragists of the first wave were active within scholarly institutions. Academic institutions were to a high degree marked by restricted gender access in the eighteenth and nineteenth centuries and for most of the early twentieth century, as scholarly institutions had been for ages within all three monotheistic traditions that condition the history of the universities. For centuries, women were not in these institutions at all, and only a few were admitted at the time of the first wave of feminism.

By the time the second wave started in the 1960s, gender segregation in education had crucially changed, which was to a large degree the result of the first feminist wave. Almost all of the women who were present and active in the making of the second-wave revolution were university students or had some academic studies in their background. Even those who were mostly known as journalists, such as Betty Friedan and Gloria Steinem,[2] and hard-core activists, like Valerie Solanas, had studied in the universities, and the core of the movement itself was largely part of the student movement. Academia and academic institutions were never very far from this activism, and academia may even have been one of the preconditions of the movement, which makes it hard to imagine them as separate. The issue was no longer women's access to these institutions, but the content and authority of the knowledge that universities produced.

Consider the campus of Columbia University in New York in 1971: Group 1, the first feminist consciousness-raising group, with its student and postgraduate membership, was active there. One of the strongest figures of this group, and one who stands out in public memory, is Kate Millett. Her *Sexual Politics* (1969), which later became a classic and core reading for gender studies courses in the history of feminist thought, was her doctoral dissertation. Millett wrote a thesis that challenged existing knowledge and intervened in scholarship in broad and multidisciplinary ways. Shulamith Firestone, who started as an art student in Chicago, did not write a doctoral thesis, yet her *Dialectic of Sex* (1970) also seriously discusses scholarly literature. Monique Wittig was a Sorbonne student when she took up activism and wrote *Les Guérillères* (1969). Although this was a literary work, the author was from that time onward deeply involved with academic institutions. All these books and many others that we now read as classics of early second-wave feminist thought were written by young university students who intervened within the institution, not outside of it, and with no fear.

Feminist work of the 1960s and 1970s, although initially marginal, nevertheless often originated with strong scholarly ambitions. Just consider, in addition to the work of Millett, Firestone, and Wittig, Juliet Mitchell's *Woman's Estate* (1971), Luce Irigaray's *Speculum de l'autre femme* (1974), Hélène Cixous's "Le rire de la Méduse" (1975), and Gayle Rubin's "The Traffic in Women: Notes on the 'Political Economy' of Sex" (1975). All these works published in or before 1975 were clearly academic in their ambitions but also fearlessly *un*disciplined, intervening within established frameworks within the academic setting.

Admittedly, some of this work took its inspiration from socialist and Marxist activist movements and writing, which were not initially based within academic institutions. Socialist and feminist thought were already close to one another during the first wave of feminism, but this was always within the revolutionary labor movement, from which academic circles remained socially distant. Nevertheless, Marxist heritage is also a scholarly tradition, and Marx's and Engels's work has strong roots in academic disputes among Hegelians and political economists. The liaison between Marxism and academia became intensive quite suddenly during the beginning of the second wave of feminism. This time, the socialist scholarly disputes moved within academic institutions proper as Marxist thought gained popularity and became hegemonic both in many areas of scholarship and within student movements. Socialist feminism also flourished within the academic institutions of feminism, and there were other traditions of thinking, learning, and writing as well that originated outside the academy but that at around this time merged with feminism within institutions of learning. These traditions included psychoanalysis as well as various traditions of fiction writing that were mobilized in feminist developments. Crucially, all this often came together within universities, within the nascent academic feminism of women's studies.

What followed was the rapid spread of a completely new academic discourse within the university: it first provoked feminist political intervention within multiple academic fields, producing challenges for the established content of teaching; it then compiled this multidisciplinary activity into separate courses with a focus on feminist intervention. Books, journals, and programs of study were followed by professorships and degrees: a whole academic discipline of its own, based on this new literature, came into being. Whether in the United States, in Britain, or in continental Europe—at Paris 8 University in France, in Berlin, Amsterdam, Helsinki, Copenhagen, Oslo, and Stockholm—teaching gender studies courses in the universities was at the time the sign of a feminist movement being brought into existence. It did not feel as if the nascent feminist institutions were outside of a more original movement that was constrained by institutionalization; instead, feminist intervention happened strongly within institutions and as an institutionalization of feminist thought.

The fusion of the movement and the academy was also how queer studies developed. "Queer" as a conceptual node started to circulate in a kind of movement-academia conglomerate from the late 1980s on. Again, the U.S. activist groups, such as ACT UP and Queer Nation, were never very far from the academy, and the new vocabulary of "the queer" circulated in between the academy and the street so quickly that it is hard to keep the two separate. Yet, the standard strong narratives paint a picture in which there was first a movement, which was only later followed by the development of academic thought.

It seems that academic disciplinary institutions provide nurture, time, and a protected and inspirational space for conceptual storms that feminist thought needs: seminars, symposia, talks, discussions, and events, which merge within the feminist and queer movement elsewhere, never maintaining complete separation. Together, they challenge the concepts, words, current teaching, academic content, regimes of truth, and the norms of right and wrong, contesting them with the means of expression that are created with instant connection to public discussion, to media, and to politics. Considering the intimate relation of second-wave feminism to the university, it is not surprising that the institutionalization of gender studies connected to feminism in the academy has also been centrally implicated within changes in feminism, feminist politics, and feminist thought. These discussion sites within universities have not only continuously complicated the content of politics but have also guaranteed continuous diversification of the movement and have been the sites for elaboration of the stakes involved.

I am thus skeptical about any assumed strong division between the movement and the institutions and sometimes wonder whether the assumption of a division is not only exaggerated but has become a kind of heritage story. It is important to celebrate the creativity and empowerment provided by public discussions, journals, leaflets, bookstores, demonstrations, clubs, events, art, and the numerous sites of political collectivity in campaigns. At the same time, while the movement was obviously much more than what happened in the academy, academic institutions as a site of struggle about concepts and conceptual creativity have been significantly implicated in all of it since the beginning of the second wave of feminism.

Contingent History

The feminist movement was stronger in some places than in others during the 1960s and 1970s. Another misperception concerning the institutionalization of gender studies is that while one could imagine that where the movement was strong the academic institutions of gender studies would also have grown strong, this does not necessarily seem to be the case: the role of the movement in the histories of institutionalization is in no way straightforward. In some places, institutions of gender studies with authority to grant degrees have been built successfully whereas they have not at all come into existence in some other places. It seems that the strength of the movement is not directly related to this uneven history; there is no direct correlation between a strong movement and strong academic institutions, nor between a strong movement and weak academic institutions. The history is much more contingent.

Within the anglophone world (the u.s., the uk, Canada, and Australia), activist movements have been strong and many universities in these countries have established academic institutions, which have a long and varied institutional history of ups and downs. In some countries, the feminist movement was strong, but institutionalization in the universities has not been successful thus far. Germany is one of these countries: in comparison to the u.s. and the uk, or the Nordic countries, there are few disciplinary institutions in German universities. The German feminist movement was strong and intellectually challenging in the 1960s and 1970s: feminist bookstores, magazines, parties, events, and discussions there were numerous. Moreover, the gay and lesbian movement has always been strong and intellectually active in Germany; yet, currently, there are very few active scholarly feminist institutions, and those that exist, such as the Queer Institute in Berlin, are often based outside the universities. One hears young scholars complain that it is next to impossible to build a career in the German-speaking academy on expertise in gender and queer.

Italy is similar. The Italian feminist movement in the 1960s and 1970s was particularly strong and has produced plenty of intellectual feminist work that has also spread abroad, such as that of Luisa Muraro and Adriana Cavarero. Yet there are no gender studies departments in Italian universities. In contrast, in the Netherlands, where the movement was equally active, one of the strongest disciplinary centers of gender studies was established at the University of Utrecht, for a long time led by Rosi Braidotti. The French movement was one of the leading ones, yet the French universities offer fairly few opportunities for study and teaching in gender studies, with the notable exception of the strong gender studies degree programs at the Centre d'études féminines et d'études de genre at Paris 8 University. Nordic countries all had fairly strong movements, yet Denmark, which was probably the strongest of them, has not developed gender studies degree programs, while Sweden, Finland, and Norway have developed very strong academic disciplinary institutions. Most research universities have well-developed degree programs in gender studies in these countries.

State and international interventions, rather than feminist activism directly, have also had a crucial role to play in the institutional successes and failures of some programs. In Finland, Norway, and Sweden, we can be grateful to state interventions for our academic gender studies institutions, although, of course, the state would never have pushed the universities to add gender studies had there not been strong feminist activist pressure that was channeled through the political parties into state action. The Academy of Finland has also been a positive agent in promoting gender studies. In Sweden, there have even been critical voices from within the scholarly community claiming gender studies as a nationalistic project (Liinason 75–81). Australia resembles Nordic countries in the positive role of the state in promoting gender issues. Quite often, though, the idea of "state feminism" is exaggerated since even in the so-called state feminism countries, feminist initiatives remain in the margins and gender studies institutions struggle to maintain their existence and resources.

New managerial university regimes, which work through competition and auditing, have been neither self-evidently positive nor negative in the institutionalization of gender studies; rather, their effect is contingent. At the moment in the United Kingdom, auditing politics seem to work against gender studies, but elsewhere, competition has sometimes enhanced the chances of gender studies in the face of conservative university structures. For example, competitively won external funding at some point brought EU money to gender studies in Europe, which helped to establish the Athena Network, later AtGender (through efforts of the Utrecht Centre); a new National Center for Scientific Research (CNRS) program has recently been established in Paris (led by Anne Emmanuelle Berger); the Nordic doctoral school of gender studies has been funded for a long time through competitive funding (through Nina Lykke's efforts); and gender studies has been very successful over the years in competitive research funding from the Academy of Finland.

In some places in Asia and Africa, development programs have had a role in promoting gender studies. After the fall of socialism in Eastern Europe, the Soros Foundation played a large role in building the gender studies program at the Central European University in Budapest, which is today a strong institution in the field. At that time, the European University at Saint Petersburg also had a period of strong teaching in gender studies. At times and in some places, even gender-segregated academic structures have helped to build institutions for gender studies.

For multiple reasons, this contingent history has resulted in many countries now having quite strong academic institutions for gender studies. An independent Internet site that compiles women's studies academic institutions currently lists nine hundred institutions worldwide (Korenman), many of which award master's and doctoral degrees in gender studies. Gender studies has evolved into an academic practice with its own right to judge quality and its own hierarchy of reference. These institutions grant degrees, they require students to read particular literature, and they provide teaching on the history of feminist thought and the movement as well as on various concepts of gender and sexuality, provoking new thinking on these questions.

Is this worrying? Does institutionalization mean depoliticization? In my view, although I can certainly understand the fear of such depoliticization, I see no evidence of it. On the contrary, it seems that where gender studies has had institutional success in the academy, there is also more politicized gender activity, more provocation, and more change. In the United States, academic gender studies has undoubtedly had a productive role in cultural changes around gender and sexuality, changes that are, if not entirely satisfying, then still clearly visible when compared with the situation of the early 1960s. The same is true in Europe. If one looks at the differences in the development of academic gender studies in Europe, it even appears that the existence of academic institutions of gender studies correlates with the division of labor in families and with the numbers of women participating in conventional politics. Nordic countries and the Netherlands have active gender studies programs and are also high in female political representation in comparison to other European countries (EIGE 1). Much more important, though, where gender studies thrives, local politics and media attract its graduates, and these holders of MAS and PhDs are particularly capable of opening up new areas of gendered conflict. It seems that in studying gender, what these people have learned is precisely to politicize issues. Why is that?

Transdisciplinarity and the Différend

What gender studies has institutionalized, as an autonomous practice, is something I would call "transdisciplinary disciplinarity." I have recently written about this elsewhere, arguing that the reason for calling gender studies a transdisciplinary discipline is not only because gender studies works across other disciplines, but more important, because it does not primarily aim at "knowledge production," which is the favorite phrase of research politics today (Pulkkinen). The academic study of gender is never done in order to produce knowledge of what gender is or what sexuality is; there are other disciplines that set these as goals, ranging from biology and medicine to sociology and sexology. Instead, gender studies stages interventions in existing notions and practices of gender and sexuality. With its roots deeply in the feminist movement, gender studies displays a transdisciplinarity that is connected to its habit of intervening, and this sets it apart in the academy. Gender studies by its very tradition contests and politicizes rather than establishes any truths and knowledges.

Here, I link the idea of intervention and transdisciplinarity to Jean-François Lyotard's *The Differend* and his *Just Gaming*, two books that date from 1983 and 1979, respectively, in their original French versions, and that continue to be relevant. In both of these works, Lyotard writes on judging, justice, and morals in a context of a multiplicity of criteria, and most interestingly, he writes about "feelings of injustice." His notion of the *différend* develops the idea that moral judgments are sometimes linked to feelings of injustice that are impossible to express in the dominant language when the available language is in the hands of those who commit the wrong. He believes there is an imperative to find expressions for such feelings, and it is here that I find a connection with what gender studies tries to achieve.

Lyotard is concerned with cases that are hard to bring to a court of justice because the language of the court is that of the perpetrator of the damage. This he calls a "wrong," instead of just a damage: "This is what a wrong [*tort*] would be: a damage [*dommage*] accompanied by the loss of the means to prove the damage" (*Differend* 5).

In these cases of wrong, not only is the victim silenced, but even more profoundly, it is impossible for the victim to even tell that a damage has been done:

> *In all of these cases, to the privation constituted by the damage*
> *there is added the impossibility of bringing it to the knowledge of*

others, and in particular to the knowledge of a tribunal. Should the victim seek to bypass this impossibility and testify anyway to the wrong done to him or to her, he or she comes up against the following argumentation: either the damages you complain about never took place, and your testimony is false; or else they took place, and since you are able to testify to them, it is not a wrong that has been done to you, but merely a damage, and your testimony is still false. (5)

Différends are situations where you know that something is terribly wrong but lack the means of bringing it to the knowledge of others. It is ultimately about lacking language: "The differend is the unstable state and instant of language wherein something which must be able to be put into phrases cannot yet be. [. . .] This state is signaled by what one ordinarily calls a feeling: 'One cannot find the words,' etc. [. . .] In the differend, something 'asks' to be put into phrases, and suffers from the wrong of not being able to be put into phrases right away" (13).

The notion of the *différend* accurately captures the dilemma of feminism in the academy in the early years. There was a strong feeling that something was wrong, that women did not have a chance, let alone justice, but that it was almost impossible to express what, exactly, was the problem. If women did find a way to complain about the feeling of being excluded and silenced, they were told that nothing was wrong because they obviously were there and could express themselves. There was just something that did not work and that could not easily be put into words. In Lyotard's view, "What is at stake in a literature, in a philosophy, in a politics perhaps, is to bear witness to differends by finding idioms for them" (13).

I suggest that this is what academic feminism has proceeded to do and that this is the main goal of gender studies: to find expressions, to be there in the first place in order to be able to make the case, to argue, to find the words for gender wrongs. In the past half century, the language to express the wrongs done to women has grown immensely: "gender inequality," "gender discrimination," "sexism," "sexual harassment," "glass ceiling," "gender gap," "empowerment," "intersectionality," and much more. The concept of *gender* itself was a conceptual innovation that the field of gender studies effectively spread (so much so that very powerful institutions, such as the Vatican, fight against the word), and after it, numerous other powerful conceptual tools, such as "heteronormativity," "queer," "transgender," and "cis" have appeared, while more are being developed all the time.

Universities have changed, at least to a degree. Starting from a position of complete segregation, with no women within these institutions, at present the "scissors diagram" of gender inequality rules in many universities (European Commission 17). In most disciplines, there is a distinct pattern: there are more women than men among undergraduate students and PhD level and early career academics, but then gender lines cross, and the higher up in academic hierarchies one looks, the fewer women there are. Only 20 percent of professorial and higher research leadership positions are occupied by women. And this wrong persists.

In the area of the natural sciences, in particular, difficulties in expressing the gendered wrong seem to be quite common. On the basis of studies of women's careers in science, Liisa Husu has observed something that sounds very similar to Lyotard's *différend*, which she calls "non-events."

> *In researching women in science and academia, I have found that it is not only the things that happen to women—such as recruitment discrimination or belittling remarks—that affect them in pursuing a career in science or that slow their career development. It is also the things that do not happen: what I call "non-events" [. . .]. Non-events are about not being seen, heard, supported, encouraged, taken into account, validated, invited, included, welcomed, greeted or simply asked along. They are a powerful way to subtly discourage, sideline or exclude women from science. A single non-event—for example, failing to cite a relevant report from a female colleague—might seem almost harmless. But the accumulation of such slights over time can have a deep impact. [. . .] Non-events are challenging to recognize and often difficult to respond to. Nothing happened, so why the fuss? Often, non-events are perceived only in hindsight or when comparing experiences with peers. Learning to recognize various non-events would help women scientists to respond to them, individually or collectively, with confidence and without embarrassment. (38)*

The non-events that Husu has identified are very close to the *différend*: there is something that is hard to put into words as being wrong when nothing happens. Gender studies researchers have continuously worked to find the words for things difficult to express, difficult to talk about, or that happened when nothing happened, things that used to have no name. Feminist thought, scholarship, and writing have produced and keep producing powerful tools, concepts, and phrases for expression and change.

During my professional lifetime, there has certainly been incredible change in the dominant standards of speaking of gender and sexuality and of feminism. I was recently reminded of this when my predecessor, Päivi Setälä, the first gender studies professor at the University of Helsinki, passed away in March 2014, and a group of us gathered to discuss organizing a memorial seminar. Päivi Setälä was among the leading forces in setting up institutions of gender studies in Finland. A very clever institutional agent during the 1980s, she engaged with the university, with politicians, and with the state, and she was instrumental in the establishment of the first feminist institution at the University of Helsinki in 1990 (the Christina Institute for Women's Studies) following the development of courses and study units in the late 1970s and 1980s. She was among those who pushed the state to sponsor nine professorships in gender studies in 1996, and she even managed to establish a national flag day for a Finnish female novelist, Minna Canth (1844–1897), who remains the only Finnish woman to be recognized with that honor. In the organizing committee for the memorial seminar, when we spoke of her achievements, I was reminded by Päivi's former students, who now hold various positions in public administration and academia, of the cunning advice she used to give to "her girls": "Remember," she used to say, "You can be a feminist, but you'd better not look like one!" I was suddenly sent thirty-five years back in time. I could not imagine this piece of advice being acceptable or welcome to young women more recently educated in the institutions Setälä helped to establish. The standards of what can be said about gendered appearances and how they matter are completely different now. And I realized that academic gender studies has, indeed, had a major part to play in this change.

The younger generations, now informed by academic institutions of gender studies, not only speak in a sophisticated manner about various gender performances; they also perform gender in different ways. If gender studies as an institution is famous for something, it is for promoting all possible looks, all possible gendered and nongendered bodily expressions. Departments usually strive to create the conditions in which people who study or teach gender studies do not have to comply with any given set of norms; in particular, deviant gender expressions are not policed. These institutions provide not only safe places, but more than that, they encourage gender nonconformity. There has been an enormous amount of work done to make explicit those norms that constitute the performance of gender, to point them out. That work has politicized norms governing gendered appearance, and instead of complying with them, gender studies institutions have widely contested them.

Gender versus Sexuality:
Different Issues or a Case of a Différend?

This brings me to the second of my topics from Berger and Fassin's *argumentaire*: the tension between gender, on the one hand, and sexuality and sexual and gender minorities, on the other. Päivi's "You can be a feminist, but you'd better not look like one" rings a loud bell in the history of the feminist movement and hides uncomfortable tensions. The issues around sexual minorities and gender identity, of femininity and masculinity within the feminist movement were already present in the nineteenth century: many feminist politicians and campaigners were ridiculed for wearing men's clothes, for apparently wanting to be men. Not respecting gender divisions was a major accusation against feminists, a frequent case made against them. Looking like a feminist quite often meant not looking feminine, and panic about lesbianism—or any other unnamed sexual or gender deviance—was only thinly concealed.

The beginning of the second wave of feminism includes painful memories of lesbians being policed by other women in feminist groups so that the groups could avoid the label of *lesbian*. As noted by Sidney Abbott and Barbara Love, who wrote in *Sappho Was a Right-On Woman* about the early women's liberation movement and its most influential group, the National Organization for Women (NOW), in the period between 1968 and 1971: "Lesbians were permitted to work behind the scenes and even found their way to top offices if they could pass for straight and if they kept silent" (109). When the consciousness-raising groups started, where women were open about their intimate lives in the spirit of the "personal is political," the fears of hidden lesbians in the groups spread both inside and outside of the movement. "Very active gay women who remained officially hidden had to work still harder to conceal their sexual preference as women began to discuss experiences with their male lovers and husbands." Some lesbians quietly left; some fought. "It was hard enough to have to hide from colleagues in the office, but to hide from other women in the movement was too much" (110).

A wrong also happened regarding a consciousness-raising group at Columbia University in 1971: Kate Millett was publicly humiliated as a lesbian in front of the whole nation on the cover of *Time* after disclosing her bisexuality in a feminist meeting, causing a public uproar that resulted in a major disruption in her personal life. Millett was not the only one to be "outed," as the constant fear of gendered and sexual deviance hovered around public presentations of feminism and demanded sacrifice.

I would argue that lesbians were, at the time, in a situation of *dif-férend* both outside and within the feminist movement, accused of something for which they did not have the idioms to communicate that they were victims. Given the abundance of the vocabulary available for gender and sexual deviancy now, it is hard to even imagine the weight of lacking expressions in 1971. The Stonewall riots of 1969 were only two years in the past, and even if the new word *gay* had made a huge difference as a term, it had only just started spreading the possibility of naming a personal and social identity around sexuality in a positive light (Weeks 85). In the feminist movement, "gay" women not only represented "the love that dare not speak its name," but they also lacked the means of expressing this love. The medically and criminologically burdened vocabulary of *homosexuality* and *lesbianism* was not an appealing way to self-identify.

Within the feminist movement, the forced closeting of lesbians and the homophobia of many fellow feminists could not yet be articulated as *closeting* or *homophobia* because the words were not available. There was very little one could say about the "uncomfortable feeling" that many straight feminists felt at the time, when such concepts as *heteronormativity* were not there to help the process of reflection. The people involved in the early feminist movement were in no way more homophobic than anyone else, but they were only beginning to develop the vocabulary for expressing the social power of normative sexuality, let alone to discover positive words of identifications for minorities. "Women loving women," "political lesbianism," "woman-identified-women," and numerous other expressions were signs of negotiating the social control around sexuality as well as sexual differences. Nevertheless, the issue of sexuality was actively present in the feminist movement at the time it was conceived as the women's movement, and those involved in developing women's studies were actively developing the means to express these issues from the very beginning.

With respect to Berger and Fassin's *argumentaire* and the history of academic gender studies, my main point here is that it is a misconception to think that first there were just women's issues in women's studies and the feminist movement, and then only later did sexuality issues join the agenda, as is often assumed. Sexuality and gender identity were present in feminist movements and feminist thought from the beginning, and they were increasingly identified as wrongs to be addressed. In Lyotard's terms, this was a case of a *différend*: sexual and gender minority issues were felt as a wrong within the feminist movement long before they were spoken aloud in actual terms and expressed with concepts that identified the wrongs through phrases such as *heteronormativity, sexual minorities, transgender,* or *cisgender.*

In current gender studies institutions, a plurality of gender expressions seems to have been purposefully promoted. "Looking like a feminist" can appear in very different ways; there are exaggerated performances of femininity as a celebration of womanhood and as a challenge to the traditions that regard femininity as being less valuable than masculinity; there are those who tone down any signs of gender as a challenge to the norm of having to actively perform gender; and there are those who actively repeat gendered norms in a different manner in order to create gender deviancy, such as Jack/Judith Halberstam, who is quoted as saying: "A lot of people call me he, some people call me she, and I let it be a weird mix of things" (qtd. in Sexsmith). There are also those for whom gender matters as a possibility of making the change from one to another, whatever the names and looks. There has always been a politicization of appearances connected with feminism and gender activism, and currently there is a clear proliferation of expressions of feminist appearance. This multiplying of feminist gendered performances and the abundance of genders also signal the pluralization of feminisms. The possibility of establishing one of these performances as "the" feminist one is very distant at the moment.

It is about this kind of state of affairs that Lyotard speaks of in *Just Gaming.* The book treats the issue of moral judgment in a context where there are multiple valid sets of rules, which Lyotard calls "games." While *Just Gaming* is marked by the Marxist university movements of the 1960s of which Lyotard had been a part, its analysis is more general: it reflects on the idea of one right judgment and on the relations of those who hold different truths and make different judgments, who play different games. For Lyotard, the end result of the conversation in the book is the notion of a multiplicity of justice games,[3] where the only universal rule is the prevention of any majority from becoming a majority in all or most of the games.

Lyotard's notion is much more nuanced as a plain argument for pluralism, as I will elaborate below. I find his discussion in *Just Gaming* particularly pertinent to the discussion on gender because there is such a strong undercurrent of threat that one particular majority, the one assuming just two genders and heterosexuality as the sole sexuality, is allowed to be conceived as the majority in all or most of the plurality of gender and sexuality games.

It is as important to acknowledge that there are different feminisms that make different judgments as it is that there is a multiplicity of gender and sexuality games with different norms. There are also different *différends*, and feminisms and gender studies work on different *différends* with various means. The pluralization of feminism in the continuum of feminist thought and politics means that there are genuinely different games that nevertheless have something in common: the goals of finding expressions for *différends* and of preventing any majority from becoming the majority in all games of gender and sexuality.

Different Feminisms:
Just Gaming *and Justice in the Games of Gender*

I was reminded of the plurality of serious feminisms in one of our own institutional settings of gender studies at the University of Helsinki, the Gender Studies Advanced Research Seminars (Christina Research Seminars) of 2013. Among others, we heard two talks of a more or less autobiographical kind, reflecting on the history of feminism in Sweden. The first was Ebba Witt-Brattström's "Sisterhood Is Powerful" and the second was Tiina Rosenberg's "Feminist Art and Political Hope." What struck me most strongly about these talks was that although both spoke of feminist struggle, they discussed two completely different projects. Witt-Brattström's paper concerned memories of 1970s militancy and promoted feminine solidarity on the basis of cherishing undervalued femaleness in order to gain more gender equality. The other, Rosenberg's reflection, was on queer struggles that started in the 1990s and promoted a challenge to the two-gender order.

There has been a tendency in Sweden, as elsewhere, to narrate this particular difference in feminisms sequentially, in a story of separated generations. It is as if there were the women's movement and women's studies first, then gender studies and queer studies, with a huge generational gap in between them. Witt-Brattström's account involves "the end of feminism," when sisterhood fades away with the questioning of the identity of "woman," while in another story, told by Mia Liinason, the questioning of identities, both sexual and national, is told as a positive breaking point. As Claudia Lindén notices, both Witt-Brattström and Liinason repeat in the story line of generational breaking points that Clare Hemmings has identified in many accounts of feminist scholarship in her *Why Stories Matter*. Lindén also notes that here, too, the story of feminism is told in generations, either as a defeat or a celebration, with poststructuralism as the breaking point and the unity of the category of *woman* as being left behind. For Witt-Brattström this is bad; for Liinason it is good. Nevertheless, for both, the story has the same structure (Lindén 305–10). Along with Hemmings, Lindén, and many others, I consider it easy to see how this story line has been reinforced through repetition and regard it as worth the effort to challenge the story with other possible accounts. In my view, different feminisms exist simultaneously, with multiple women's and gender issues constantly being fought. Solidarity did not cease to exist, and many other issues have surfaced that are meaningful for feminist struggles. Instead of periodizing, it is good to give recognition to the differences and *différends*, as well as to points of continuation.

Interestingly, while some of the fiercest struggles between different feminisms were portrayed publicly in Sweden during the building of a unique Swedish development, the feminist political party (Feministiskt initiativ [FI] established in 2005), the party manages to combine various feminist agendas in quite a concrete way. The party—which won a seat in the EU parliamentary elections while not making it over the threshold in the Swedish parliamentary elections in 2014—is clearly based on female solidarity while promoting equality issues between women and men such as equal pay and the legislation of equal parental leave, legislation for gender quotas on the boards of companies, and various other issues. Yet simultaneously, FI has also encouraged the use of the new gender-neutral pronoun *hen* in the Swedish language and has in numerous other ways promoted thought and education beyond the two existing options of masculine and feminine genders. Both sisterhood feminism and queer feminism seem to be combined here at the level of concrete politics, which is simultaneously influenced by and in dialogue with much of the work and thought done in academic gender studies.

The question can be asked in an even more profound way: why is feminism, which pursues gender equality between women and men through promoting female solidarity and pride in womanhood, so closely affiliated with the struggle for abolishing or disturbing the power of gendering altogether, that is, the queer struggle? Might there be a common source and agenda for both? I would suggest that an underestimation of femaleness and gender inequality is usually achieved by means of the same universalized notions of gender and sexuality that are the problem for queer thinkers. In Lyotard's terms, the wrong is perpetrated by enforcing one game as a valid rule in all games in the actual presence of a multiplicity of games.

Lyotard's ideas in *Just Gaming* on the games of justice, on rules, and on terror (a term he uses in a different sense from the meaning we encounter more frequently in the media today) are illuminating here.

They help us to see the difference between the legitimate violence of norms involved in the games of "being a woman," "femininity," and "heterosexuality," "homosexuality," "queer," or "transgender," on the one hand, and the "terror" of gender, on the other. Lyotard concludes his discussion on judging in conditions of multiplicity:

> *Yes, there is first a multiplicity of justices, each of them defined in relation to the rules specific to each game. [. . .] And then the justice of multiplicity: it is assured, paradoxically enough, by a prescriptive of universal value. [. . .] It prohibits terror, that is, the blackmail of death towards one's partners, the blackmail that a prescriptive system does not fail to make use of in order to become a majority in most games and over most of their pragmatic positions. (100)*

In these terms, the rule that establishes a universal order of two genders is a rule of terror, which poses the threat: be of one of the two genders, or do not be at all. Kate Millett's case in 1971 gives strong evidence of this terror and its connection to all kinds of feminist struggle. The key term in Millett's theoretical work was *patriarchy*, and her topic was the domination of one sex over the other. Millett was for sisterhood feminism, yet her claim was put down by the terror of gendering. She was violently pursued because, as an individual, she broke publicly against the order of the two sexes, two sexualities, two genders by appearing to be, as it were, beyond the rule of two, and therefore, in the logic of terror, not worth a life. The brutal workings of public shaming and generating mental stress that worked against Millett testify to the power of gendering. To me, this appears as the same power that made it necessary for Päivi Setälä to masquerade as a not-feminist by advising her students to adopt conventional appearances of femininity rather than challenge the gender division in an attempt to open up space for feminist action in politics.

In the justice of multiplicity that Lyotard envisions, the only universal rule is the rule against the possibility that any majority makes life unlivable for those not playing the same game. Terror, which is the threat of death in order to try to gain majority in all games, is not allowed. It is interesting to note that in this view, the norms themselves, that is, the rules of the games, are not the trouble. Norms are enabling as much as restricting; they make games possible in the first place. It is the terror, the threat of violence through universalizing, which is different from the legitimate norms of gender, that causes the problem.

Heterosexual difference is important in the heterosexual game; yet all feminists interested and involved in the games of heterosexuality know that observing the rules of these games does not require acceptance of a hierarchy between genders. Even more important, taking part in the seduction games of heterosexuality, however enthusiastically, does not imply the view that everybody else has to comply with the rules of the femininity/masculinity game in order to live a human life. Confusing the two is to confuse the legitimate violence of norms of a game with the universalizing terror of gender.

I would argue that the terror of gender is as troublesome to sisterhood feminists as it is to queer feminists, since it seriously limits the scope of any action through posing a life threat. Any feminist action is dependent on the exposing of the hegemonic claim of the terror of gendering in order not to be undermined as breaking a universal gender rule. It is also through this conjunction that I wish to make the point that sexuality has not actually replaced gender as an issue in more recent work on gender and sexuality. The two issues belong together, they have always belonged together, and they belong together in politics as well as in the academic transdisciplinary institutions of gender studies.

More precisely, it is because of the terror of gendering that issues of gender and queer belong together. The impossibility of expressing injustice is caused precisely by universalized regimes, and it is because of this that gender studies' task is to continue finding expression for feelings of injustice. This is because the discipline ultimately distinguishes itself within the academy through its purpose of expressing injustices and, in particular, injustices related to the terror of gendering. It is the common point of all feminisms within the academic discipline that the discipline politicizes these issues rather than merely study them.

There is clearly ample room for specialized journals in the field according to different *différends*: queer studies have been followed by trans studies, together with multiplying and critical theorizing, such as crip theory, critical animal studies, postcolonial studies, race studies, the intersection of class, gender, and race. All of them emphasize the idea that the most important legacy that the feminist movement has left in gender studies is the feminist movement's aspiration to find expressions for feelings of injustice, the *différends* that are hard to express but that are looking for expression.

Feelings of injustice persist and inform the field. There is something wrong; there is something we need not only to research but also to find words and expressions to describe for the sake of justice, something that motivates the academic field of gender studies. As a field of conceptual study, gender studies is alive and expanding. The work of current students and researchers in these institutions is sophisticated and courageous, and it continues to address, and to express, the wrongs of gender.

I presented the first version of this essay as a paper in May 2015 at the fortieth-year anniversary celebration of the Centre d'études féminines et d'études de genre at University of Paris 8.

TUIJA PULKKINEN is chair of gender studies at the University of Helsinki, Finland, and co-editor-in-chief of the journal *Redescriptions: Political Theory, Conceptual History and Feminist Theory*. Her publications include (with Antu Sorainen) *Siveellisyydestä seksuaalisuuteen: Poliittisen käsitteen historia (From Sittlichkeit to Sexuality: The History of a Political Concept)* (Suomalaisen Kirjallisuuden Seura, 2011) and the co-edited volume (with Kimberly Hutchings) *Hegel's Philosophy and Feminist Thought: Beyond Antigone?* (Palgrave Macmillan, 2010). She is currently working on a project on politics of philosophy in contemporary feminist theory.

Notes

1   The French *argumentaire* can be translated as a "*pitch*," as in the "pitch of an idea."

2   Betty Friedan (1921–2006) studied at Smith College, which was women only, from 1938 until 1942. She took up graduate studies at UC Berkeley but abandoned her academic career for journalism and activism. Gloria Steinem (b. 1934) also graduated from Smith College. Robin Morgan (b. 1941), subsequently a *Ms.* magazine editor, studied at Columbia University in the 1960s, and Susan Brownmiller (b. 1935) studied at Cornell in the 1950s.

3   *Just Gaming* is set as seven days of dialogues, a conversation between Jean-François Lyotard and Jean-Loup Thébaud.

Works Cited

Abbott, Sidney, and Barbara Love. *Sappho Was a Right-On Woman: A Liberated View of Lesbianism*. New York: Stein and Day, 1972.

Berger, Anne Emmanuelle, and Éric Fassin. *Argumentaire. Les paradoxes de l'institutionalisation*. Acte 5. 26–27 May 2014. Le printemps international du genre: Enjeux politiques et savants de l'institutionalisation et de l'internationalisation d'un champ d'études. Programme-livret. Les quarante vies du Centre d'études féminines et d'études du genre de Paris 8. Université Paris 8, Vincennes–Saint-Denis, 2014. 43–45.

Butler, Judith. *Gender Trouble: Feminism and the Subversion of Identity*. New York: Routledge, 1990.

EIGE. "Gender Equality Index." *European Institute for Gender Equality*. http://eige.europa.eu /gender-statistics/gender-equality-index/2012/domain/power/1 (accessed 5 Mar. 2016).

European Commission. "Mapping the Maze: Getting More Women to the Top in Research." *European Commission: European Research Area*. http://ec.europa.eu/research/science -society/document_library/pdf_06/mapping-the-maze-getting-more-women-to-the-top-in -research_en.pdf (accessed 11 Jan. 2016).

Hemmings, Clare. *Why Stories Matter: The Political Grammar of Feminist Theory*. Durham: Duke UP, 2011.

Husu, Liisa, et al. "Laboratory Life: Scientists of the World Speak up for Equality." *Nature* 495.7439 (2013): 35–38.

Korenman, Joan. *Women's Studies Programs, Departments, and Research Centers.* http://userpages.umbc.edu/~korenman/wmst/programs.html (accessed 11 Jan. 2016).

Liinason, Mia. "Feminism and the Academy: *Exploring the Politics of Institutionalisation in Gender Studies in Sweden.*" PhD diss. University of Lund, Centre for Gender Studies, 2011. http://lup.lub.lu.se/luur/download?func=downloadFile&recordOId=1761928&fileOId=1776392 (accessed 11 Jan. 2016).

Lindén, Claudia. "Temporality and Metaphoricity in Contemporary Swedish Feminist Historiography." *Rethinking Time: Essays on History, Memory, and Representation.* Ed. Hans Ruin and Andrus Ers. Huddinge: Södertörns högskola, 2011. 301–12.

Lyotard, Jean-François. *The Differend: Phrases in Dispute.* Trans. Georges Van Den Abbeele. Minneapolis: U of Minnesota P, 1988.

Lyotard, Jean-François, and Jean-Loup Thébaud. *Just Gaming.* Trans. Wlad Godzich. Minneapolis: U of Minnesota P, 1985.

Pulkkinen, Tuija. "Identity and Intervention: Disciplinarity as Transdisciplinarity in Gender Studies." *Theory, Culture, and Society* 32.5–6 (2015): 183–205.

Rosenberg, Tiina. "Feminist Art and Political Hope" [Feministinen taide ja poliittinen toivo]. Lecture. Christina Research Seminar. University of Helsinki. 9 April 2013.

Sexsmith, Sinclair. "Jack Halberstam: Queers Create Better Models of Success." *Lambda Literary* 1 Feb. 2012. http://www.lambdaliterary.org/interviews/02/01/jack-halberstam-queers-create-better-models-of-success/.

Weeks, Jeffrey. *Sexuality.* London: Routledge, 2010.

Witt-Brattström, Ebba. "Sisterhood Is Powerful: The Impact of Second Wave Feminism of the 1970s on (Swedish) Literature." Lecture. Christina Research Seminar. University of Helsinki. 12 March 2013.

"Territory Trouble": Feminist Studies and (the Question of) Hospitality

*A*s an echo of the paper I gave at the 2013 International Spring-time of Gender conference in Paris, this essay is an attempt to visit the field of feminism through the issue of hospitality. I first recognized the relevance of this approach while organizing in Geneva, along with Cynthia Kraus, meetings with and around the work of Judith Butler.[1] We were her hosts, and she was our guest. Like the International Springtime of Gender, the Geneva event raised questions of hosting and translating. Translation, exchange, appropriation, interpretation, and acculturation are all elements that commonly characterize scholarly meetings; however, something else was at play that involved feminist thought in a novel fashion. What if hospitality were essential to the idea of feminism? How could this potentiality be put to work and made productive as a resource?

I will focus, first, on what feminist thought and action have done and are doing to the social and political orders. The metaphor of *hospitality* is a way to question the inextricably linked domestic, public, and territorial issues at play. The figures of the outsider and of disorder raise questions of welcoming and rejecting; they question the nature of "our" feminist

Volume 27, Number 2   DOI 10.1215/10407391-3621745

engagement and "our" Westernness. Following Jacques Derrida, the idea is to progress from rejecting to welcoming, from the language of law to speaking up and, with Donna Haraway, from the idea of sudden emergence, of speaking as an individual, to the question of figuration and coalition. Hospitality raises questions of language and territory, of the intimate and the enemy, and is thus a good concept for universalizing feminist proposals and revealing what they disrupt in the domestic and national order of the political sphere.

After highlighting some of the promises and universalities of feminist thought, I will, in the more local context of French contemporary society, examine the inhospitable situation in which "women" subjects, homosexual subjects, and colonial or migrant subjects have been and are still positioned. The idea is not so much to address these questions in detail (they are too vast to comprehend) as to insist on their inextricably linked social, political, and epistemic dimensions. This will provide an opportunity for three narratives from *within* France, where knowledge and politics intermingle: 1) the history of the French historical tradition and its inhospitality toward gender studies and feminist issues—a question that, following other authors, I have recently addressed (Gardey, "L'histoire"); 2) the history of the situation of immigrants in a French (post-)colonial context and how the Republic, the nation, and alterity are revealed in that light—referring in particular to the work of Nacira Guénif-Souilamas; and 3) the renewed material and gendered history of parliamentarianism since the French Revolution and of the domestic nature of the political in a context of Western democracy—based here on my own recent historical work (Gardey, *Le linge*). The idea is thus to bring together the inhospitality of historical reason and knowledge, the definition of national and political territory, the production of the outsider and of otherness, and cultural features of democratic institutions in the French republican context.

In the third part of the essay, I question the facts and fictions of various feminisms as extraterritoriality. Is feminism a hospitable space? If so, for whom and on what conditions? If the history of feminism allows us to define it as a space for encounters and hospitality, what are the limits to this definition? Is what brought us together during the days of the International Springtime of Gender conference, and that continues in the editorial space provided here by *differences*, an unindexed space, an "international" or "transnational" space? Is it a Babel of sorts or a site that replays power relations and some unconsidered issues, in particular due to the domination of the English language and of a certain tendency to speak without considering the locality that is constitutive of the North American era of production as a specific territory and culture?

Finally, "non-national" and "trans-Atlantic" became a resource, or even a survival condition, for feminist studies (for example, in the French-speaking world since the end of the 1980s), but the issue of finding ways to articulate these territories remains, whether they be disciplinary, national, and non-national, or epistemic and political. What may the virtues of the feminist field be in a context of strong cultural standardization and institutional transformations of the scientific and academic field? How can we conceive of our undertakings in the age of the h-index, of the ranking of individuals and institutions, of all-out competition, of the propagation of neoliberalism and managerialism in academia and research? What is the future of feminist thought, and can it be imagined independently from the "humanities" and the way they will go? Finally, as the framing of issues and the style of explanations are more and more of an extrasocial—and most often infrapolitical—nature (cognitive psychology, genetics, neurosciences, evolution theory, etc.), what forms of writing and types of resistance can we craft?[2] In the face of operators whose scope of action appears to be boundaryless, can feminist territories still exist as a land of asylum?

Feminist Promises

Raising the Issue of Hospitality, Troubling the Order of the "Home"

As Judith Butler recalled in her second introduction to *Gender Trouble*, "to make life possible," which is one of her theoretical and political claims, could be seen as a means to invite persons who were "unauthorized" until then to move into a new life space, a new political and theoretical space, which could be defined as common ground (Gardey, "Définir").[3] It could be seen as defining a "home" in which to live and think, a "my place" that could also be "our place," in a definition "at large," as Donna Haraway would say ("Cyborgs"). It seems to me that this gesture, which Butler makes beautifully explicit, has been operating for forty years under the influence of the feminist movement and feminist thought. Increasing the number of subjects, expanding the range of possibilities, and redefining "homes" in terms of politics and science are among the mechanisms and motives of acting and thinking in most feminisms (Gardey, "Définir" 120).

In that sense, the social and political order is involved, as are science, philosophy, and academia. Admitting strange objects and subjects as guests (and not as enemies) through the doors of law, society, philosophy, scientific knowledge, and the university means transforming "the home order," subverting its codes and norms. In the end, it is about redefining what *home* is or could be. Here, the idea of hospitality refers to the diversity of objects, subjects, and issues raised by feminist thought and theory.

Let us now focus on what is opened in the sense of "transforming the home order" by Butler's work. Beyond feminism or queer thinking, in *Precarious Life: The Powers of Mourning and Violence*, Butler brings up hospitality in a wider social and political sense. *Precarious Life* is about the state, war, and the law. It deals with nomad subjects, foreigners, and those who are "in exile." It talks about those who find themselves excluded from protective territoriality (including that of the state, where legitimate violence is also perpetrated). It deals with tolerance and liberality, with the ways of preserving and accepting difference(s); it is about fundamental rights, of "precarious lives" or "bare life" in Giorgio Agamben's terms; it deals with protection and asylum.

From a historical perspective, the fact that this thinking originates from gender and sexual differences and the "right to live" of those who have long been described as "minorities" is significant. It is an unprecedented movement of hospitality and an overturning of what counts as the stigmata or the norm, the particular or the universal. The theoretical and political potential of these promises still remains to be explored (Haraway, "Promises").

While hospitality defines a space and a situation, it also defines a certain type of relationship in which peoples, cultures, languages, and ideas are mutually obliged. It is the very definition of what occurs that is engaged and made more complex and uncertain. As Jacques Derrida writes: "The host who welcomes, the one who welcomes the invited guest, the welcoming host who believes himself the owner of the house is in reality a guest welcomed in his own home. He receives the hospitality that he offers in his own home, he receives hospitality from his own home—which ultimately does not belong to him. The host, as host, is a guest" (*Adieu* 41). Thinking of oneself as the ephemeral guest of one's own house, conceiving a conditional presence that is conditioned by the relationship with others, would that not be a way to reformulate the order of knowledge and politics? What could be the promise of a territory thus made "other," this territory under tension whose quality or value would depend on the quality and value of the relationship with others? A "self" and a "home" whose interiority and privacy would be not abolished but rather fulfilled by this foundational "opening"? An "identity" that would thus be founded and redistributed by showing welcome? It is certainly interesting to think about the history of feminism, of what it has done and what it does to thinking and the world from that problematic angle, and about what is at play in terms of paradoxical relations. It would then be possible to explore its creative and universalizing potential.

Speaking Up, Showing a Figure, and Taking Position

Derrida's words are neither ironic nor out of step with reality. Hospitality is about actual and abstract situations, possible and impossible experiences, and happy and unhappy situations. Derrida does not leave out violence. He gives it a central position since it is centrally unperceived. Here, language becomes essential. It is the language that one speaks that others speak. It is the language of law and rules that are written. Language can be primary violence. "The foreigner is first of all foreign to the *legal language* in which the duty of hospitality is formulated, the right to asylum, its limits, norms, policing, etc. He has to ask for hospitality in a language which by definition is not his own." This is where the question of hospitality begins for Derrida: "Must we ask the foreigner to understand us, to speak our language, in all the senses of this term, before being able and so as to be able to welcome him into our country?" (*Of Hospitality* 15).

What language must one speak to be welcomed? What languages should be developed and maintained in order to exclude? Today's legal language is cast in the language of economics. Like the Argentinians before them, the Greek people are well aware of that. But let us come back to the issue of language and what it implies in terms of hosting, empowerment, and agency. For the "woman subject," for the "lesbian" or "queer subject," for the "subaltern subject" (immigrant, aspiring migrant, minority with migrant or colonial ancestry), isn't the question first and foremost that of the language he or she is asked to speak?

Women and other *others* have been and are "foreigners" in more than one respect. This is what makes Haraway's use of Sojourner Truth's soliloquy, of her amazing sermon, so strong. "Ecce Homo" is about the language that a black female slave can speak. It is about the act of speaking up itself. It is about the radical strangeness of a language that originates from physicality as a strength and as a *difference.* It is about what emerges and cannot be kept quiet because of the crushing experience of slavery and beyond that experience, in spite of the *precariousness* of bodies and an almost *bare* life. It is about the conditions of enunciation. Engaging in language, making language take shape, making it emerge and happen in its absolute locality: is that a basic condition? Must that language, that voice, be made to confront the language of law, that of the (white) fathers and brothers? Must it be made, by its existence, its strange sound, and its disruptive syntax, to leave its mark and stigmatize the language of the home, to reveal the locality of the language of law, to highlight the fragility of "neutrality" as a *force for law* and universality, and to underscore the contingency of the domestic space as political space (Gardey, "Définir")?

As Haraway suggests, a shift, a radical *opening*, is possible. Returning to Sojourner Truth, she asks: "Why does her question [Ain't I a Woman?] have more power for feminist theory 150 years later than any number of affirmative and declarative sentences?" ("Ecce" 92). "For me, one answer to that question lies in Sojourner Truth's power to figure a collective humanity without constructing the cosmic closure of the unmarked category. Quite the opposite, her body, names, and speech—their forms, contents, and articulation—may be read to hold promise for a never settled universal" (92).

The option is not posthumanist but humanist: "How can humanity have a figure outside the narratives of humanism?" asks Haraway. Her plea is in favor of new and feminist humanism *hic et nunc.* It is a utopian quest for a new and possible figuration: "How do we figure 'feminist humanity'?" she adds (93). Working on the "eccentric and mobile" figures of new "imagined humanity," to use de Lauretis's words from "Queer Theory," Haraway rejects the idea of a consistent subject as origin but seeks a "common language" for what Butler calls new "connections" or new "coalitions" ("Sexual"). The figure of Christ as a figure of dislocation and suffering serves as a point of entry in "Ecce Homo." Haraway speaks of blasphemy and expectation (Gardey, "Reading" 88). She also speaks of *critique.* But how to proceed with critique and blasphemy without falling into intolerance? "Is critique secular?", ask Talal Asad, Wendy Brown, Judith Butler, and Saba Mahmood. How can we give life to a public space where free speech and hospitality coexist? Isabelle Stengers's intuition in her comment on Haraway is that critique as blasphemy does not relinquish a certain form of expectation.[4] It is in that sense that it produces utopia, that is, an imaginary and real territory.

As we can see, defining this *common space*, this *topos* (this "home"?), means agreeing on the languages that are spoken within it and on what forms an individual (or collective) subject. The questions of subject, law, identity, and name are connected by the question of the question, or the "address." What is this about? It is, in fact, about interrogation, the paranoia that now bears the name of "security." It is the obsession with names that sets out and sets apart and, at the same time, puts forward and includes. Derrida asks, "Does hospitality consist in interrogating the new arrival? [. . .] Or else does hospitality begin with the unquestioning welcome, in a double erasure: that of the question *and* the name?" He continues, "Does one give hospitality to a subject? to an identifiable subject? to a subject identifiable by name? to a legal subject?" (*Of Hospitality* 29).[5]

Or should we not give up the obsession with the question and instead engage in the social and political experience of opening, of welcoming *precarious lives*, to use Butler's words? As we can see, the questions of territory and borders are essential.

The Past and Present of Inhospitality

Producing Knowledge in Inhospitable Territory: The Case of History in France

The question of the hospitality and inhospitality of national, social, and political territories, of the legal and actual treatment of individual and collective subjects, is of course linked to the way knowledge defines the boundaries of its own territory and the subjects that are relevant and legitimate within them. Playing a role in knowledge, becoming a producer of science, is a historical issue on which many feminist (and nonfeminist) women researchers have provided long narratives, filled with obstacles, within the different theoretical and practical fields of knowledge.[6] Bringing "outside" knowledge into science is another story, often related to the first; such is the extent to which the social and cultural conditions of knowledge production determine its conditions of exercise and happiness. The social history of science has highlighted the highly historical, nonlinear, and equivocal nature of what is considered relevant to the order of the home or the laboratory,[7] leisurely and amateur practice or scientific activity, and the world of the court and of monstration or demonstration.[8] In this respect, it should be noted that some epochs are more hospitable than others in terms of scientific poaching. The very territory of what is and what makes science appears historically contingent and thus potentially open . . . or closed.

Awareness of the historicity of knowledge, of the influence of context on methods of inquiry and research objects, is sometimes lacking in the experience that academic disciplines have of themselves. Indeed, self-definition and the limits placed on certain approaches are common. They participate in the work that scientific fields continue to undertake in order to exist. In the case of history in France, rejection of feminism was as much about flesh and blood individuals as ideas and thought. The "home" of social and human sciences, the "home" of the Republic, of science, and of universality have thus kept the ship on course for a long time. There is a dual exclusion (in practice and in thought) that is inextricably epistemic *and* political. In the following paragraphs, I will focus on a few symptomatic examples of inhospitality in the territories of historians.

The first example is Jacques Poloni-Simard's article published in *CLIO* in 2002. *CLIO* is the young and only French journal of women and gender history, and Poloni-Simard is the editor of *Annales. Histoire, Sciences Sociales*, the major history journal in France. Invited to report on the contribution of women and gender history to the historical field, he focuses on the (modest) *Annales* editorial policy regarding women and gender history, which he nevertheless judges positively. More interestingly, he clarifies what is "welcome" (and thus, conversely, what is less welcome) in the field by affirming several times what seems essential to him, which is "the definition or defense of a particular idea of social history." His words display an understanding of harmony and completeness: the history of women and gender cannot form a separate continent; it has a place as a component of social history on condition that it does not disrupt its "unity." The tone of the article is one of reserve and retreat, and it is tempting to wonder if the history of women and gender may be allowed to contribute only on condition of not being ambitious (in what it *is* and what it *does* to history). The idea (which is not new) seems to be that women's and gender history is useful if it is integrated (in reality, when it *integrates itself*)[9] rather than if it opposes, and when it "adds complexity" rather than when it becomes an "exclusive criterion" (108). The history of women and gender may keep its seat at the grown-ups' table if it conforms to the rules that apply to the sharing of the cake: respecting the founding principles imposed by those (*male*) peers who are its hosts. Indeed, in the same article, others ("Blacks, Indians, outsiders, and therefore also women or, more recently, subalterns and homosexuals") are asked not to impose a history "based on ethnic, social or sexual criteria" (108).

Through this inventory, all types of studies (cultural, postcolonial, queer) beyond gender studies are suspected of disrupting "unity" by "slicing" historical matter. Here, history sees itself, like that which is social (society? knowledge?), as a whole under threat of "fragmentation." Paraphrasing Alain Badiou's *De quoi Sarkozy est-il le nom?*, we are entitled to ask: What does *Unity* name? And what unity, and for what purpose? Why should social history remain united? United for whom, with whom, to conduct which types of projects and to exclude which others? The dramatic nature of what would happen if, by some mischance, such "unity" were disrupted is impressive, like a simple action that might be committed with consequences all the more disastrous for being unknown, eventually sweeping all away: History, its Unity, and Society—unless it were, in fact, Knowledge, the Republic, and eventually Mankind?

The second example is the journal *Genèses* and its cofounder, Gérard Noiriel, who published a book titled *Sur la "crise" de l'histoire* [*The Crisis of History*] at the end of the 1990s, which speaks of the same fear of "atomization," "fragmentation," and, eventually, the depreciation of history (113). Most of his argument consists of redefining history as a disciplined and methodical scientific community, at a distance from superfluous and sterile theorization. In the only section of his book dedicated to feminist history, Noiriel offers as an example of "sterile" the discussion between Joan W. Scott and Laura Lee Downs about social groups as "actual entities," or entities resulting from the "discursive aspects of experience."[10] Here, too much discussion between feminists is said to harm the method, unity, and communicability of history (144–48).[11]

In her review of Noiriel's book, Scott points out certain contradictions in the author's approach. To repeat and extend some of her comments: How can it be that Noiriel, who made a decisive contribution (I would be tempted to say as a result of his experience as an activist) in rewriting part of French national working-class history by working on the important but denied contribution of immigrants, became a scrupulous guard of the borders of what historical territory should and could be? As Scott writes, "Why does the historian feel authorized to criticize the Nation (using history against politics to produce change) and not the foundations of his own practices?" ("Border" 388). Later on, highlighting how Noiriel's defense of the discipline is a plea against philosophy (or any form of excessive theorization), she questions this "border patrol" work and shows surprise at the fact that a historian of immigration can be in favor of the expulsion of philosophy in the name of the community of historians. Scott concludes by wondering whether it is desirable for those who work at the frontiers of knowledge to be asked to "assimilate or migrate" ("Border" 388).[12]

Producing the Common in (Post)colonial Territory:
Immigrants from within France

Assimilate or disappear is one of the injunctions made to the populations that Guénif-Souilamas studies. For many years, she has focused on the figure of "the emigrant" and on the experience of migration in the French postcolonial context. In her recent work, she questions the reality of colonialism's posterity by showing what persists of colonial relations in French society ("Altérités"). Her work offers a rich vision of France as nation-state and focuses in particular on the management of mass emotions, the production of a hegemonic discourse on emigrants, and how both constrain the policies that are implemented and those that are possible. This work takes various forms.

First, Guénif-Souilamas sheds light on the obliteration of the voices and actual life experiences of the French people who are continuously reassigned to their "foreign" origins: as Arabs, Muslims, Africans, former colonial subjects—subjects who are spoken about but whose own ability to speak is taken into account very little, if at all. The question of the subject of enunciation (and that of knowledge) is, in addition, brought up on a personal level by the author as a French-Algerian woman and as a sociologist (who loves literature and, above all, writing). She therefore questions the standards of sociological and academic literature, and the calls to order that are made to her on a scientific as well as a political level. Can the (Muslim) sociologist (of Algerian descent) speak? Should she let herself be trapped in the identity and role of the integrated migrant promoted through scholarly achievement? Should she still, as always, obey the orders to be impartial that constitute the foundation and form, the appropriate scientific ethos, of the sociologist? Can she be assimilated, professionally and socially, or does she disrupt the codes of the profession and the public space of what can be expressed?[13] The biographical disruption is central in her more recent texts and continues in the vein of Harawayan fictions in the form of acting on and in the world.

In that respect, Guénif-Souilamas continues the work of undermining the good conscience of the Left undertaken with Éric Macé in *Les féministes et le garçon arabe* [*Feminists and the Arab Boy*]. In this seminal book, they highlight an essential social and political phenomenon that disturbs the feminist conscience in the form of the disqualification of Arab boys in the French suburbs or the attributing to young men of Arab origins a caricatured figure that is constantly reified. The book sheds light on the mechanisms through which Arab boys have become the enemy from within. It uncovers this characteristic societal phenomenon even in the writings of some feminists: shouldn't young Arab girls (the *beurettes*, as they are commonly called)[14] be saved from the "Arab boy"? Young men whose parents or grandparents were born in the Maghreb countries of Algeria, Morocco, or Tunisia, former French colonies, still suffer from permanent racialization and acute racism. These identity-based assignations and disqualifications are reworded today in the context of the anti-Muslim racism that developed in the West after September 11th. Kabyles and/or Christians, Arabs and/or Muslims, *beurs*, many of whom are French citizens, are kept in a subordinate condition, socially and politically experiencing subaltern citizenship on a daily basis. They are also reminded of their otherness, a difference that, it is said, cannot be assimilated, which is now expressed in the figure of the "Muslim."

In her work "L'altérité de l'intérieur" ("The Otherness from Within"), Guénif-Souilamas gives a more general outline of the contemporary characteristics of the (post)colonial French Republic. This essay deals with what it means to be constituted through constraint, acculturation, and norms imposed on those who can, have, and eventually "deserve" to be "French." It is about foundational unconscious and repeated structures and hidden or omitted skeletons. Guénif-Souilamas empties the closets of the nation. She shows how metaphors, ideas, concepts, theoretical resources, and/or ideological markers operate as reified elements that can be kept to hand and sorted out. She identifies the origin of a language that was established in the wake of the modification of the French nationality code in 1988, when a national doctrine of "integration" emerged. In a text titled in English translation "Liquidating Integration," she reviles the word and the concept: "Integration is not a tool of government or a measure of good government; it is one of the 'attributes' of the reigning president. It is not out of the picture for which it would provide an understanding; it is in the picture, and has become a quasi-fetishized object of figuration, to be considered as an indigenous category." She continues: "It is by weighing the political, normative, and yet human damage caused by this notion, which has become a watchword under the appearance of a European directive, that I have taken the measure of the damage caused by Europe's recolonization process that is hidden by this unassuming dirty word in the mouths of those who use and abuse it" ("Altérités" 191, my translation).[15] Butler highlights the normative and real consequences of this model: "[I]n other terms, the model of social integration depends on what is 'unintegrated,' or should be 'disintegrated' in order to maintain its hegemony. In that sense, social integration acts *against* substantial norms of equality and universality" (Report).

Finally, the work deals with this quality of (shared) territories and what produces and defines them *here and now*. With different biographical and linguistic crossroads (French and Arabic; French and English; writing and speaking), the territories covered by Guénif-Souilamas are defined from one coast to another, from the Mediterranean to the Atlantic. They include the relationship between center and periphery, between the lights of the capital and the working-class territories of Paris's northern suburbs in Seine-Saint-Denis. They take us from the metropolitan Paris area to the port of Marseilles by way of the streets and squares of Algiers. We thus find ourselves exploring physical, social, and psychological territories that are situated in between languages, between the settler and the colonizer, the dominant and the dominated, the universal and the particular, the black and the white, the Christian and the Muslim, the secular and the religious, the self and the other, and also history and the present. Guénif-Souilamas is interested in these territories for the very reason that the relationship between self and other is essential and inextricable. She thus helps to outline a surprising geography of contemporary worlds and to account for the way French society is, for example, interlocked in/with Algeria. Thus emerges modernity: territories that are always more complex and differently "other" than they seem at first, territories forever linked to this "other," the "outsider" who is yet an intimate part, territories that tend to delimit, contain, or deny, territories whose present substance is made of differentiated temporalities, inscribed or absent memories, and histories that have never been told yet are intensely vital.

Producing the Universal in Male Territory: Of Parliamentary Inhospitality

Working with the concepts of the *domestic* (nation, home) and the *other* (foreigner, Arab, Muslim), Guénif-Souilamas opens up in a particularly enlightening manner a series of unthought issues, "black boxes," paradigms, and "ready-made thinking" that structure the French contemporary political landscape. While apparently distant from this subject, my recent research on the history of the Assemblée Nationale, the French lower chamber of parliament, surprisingly echoes this undertaking. A fortuitous link can be seen in the vocabulary used by the first legislators (those who came together to form the Constituent Assembly under the French Revolution). In an attempt to delimit the perimeter of what forms the basis of the territory of their sovereignty, from the very first Assembly meetings, they regulated the access of outsiders (Poudra and Pierre). "Outsiders" must be understood here to be those who are not legislators (the king, the people, representatives of other authorities). As legal fictions and representative "bodies," legislative assemblies had thus to perform normative and material work to delimit the territory wherein they deliberated, thus expressing the historically unprecedented form of their sovereignty (Gardey, *Le linge* 29). Producing a space for deliberation and representation thus inevitably meant regulating and producing a physical territory. This original self-designation (the "representatives") and designation of the others (the "outsiders") brings us back to the inextricable link between the history of Western democracies and the territorial and political expression of the nation.

More generally, my work addresses how unprecedented ideas and principles (popular sovereignty, the universal character of the emancipatory promise of the Revolution in its principles of liberty, equality, and fraternity) were written and inscribed on walls, in formal and material arrangements, in social and gendered plans. The inquiry into the administrative or "private" archives of the French Parliament allows a revisiting of the history of Western democratic institutions as historically contingent and situated spaces and an exploration of the mechanisms by which they produced universal elements in producing difference and otherness. This anthropological study offers a new perspective on the long history, now well documented, of the exclusion of women from democracy in the French context. As masculine institutions in many respects, parliamentary assemblies substituted the body of the king with the "empty" and neutralized body of masculine representatives representing universality (Lefort 28). Democratic achievement was thus based on the actual repression of the "feminine," of emotions (in the sense of mass emotions) under the dual form of the crowd (the people) and the aristocracy (women and children of royal houses and high-ranking families).[16] Removed from the deliberative and sovereign space and the centrality of the political scene, things feminine were confined to the role of witness. To the exclusion of women from citizenship, the Republican parliamentary scenography added a specific "gendered architecture."[17] The masculinity of the parliamentary territory was enhanced by the definition of masculine grouping spaces around the Chamber (bar, hall of arms, salons), while the ladies were invited to contemplate the parliamentary scene from the boxes and galleries. The parliamentary theater took the architectural and social form of the theater itself and operated on accepted gender asymmetries: looking and being seen; speaking up and listening; representing and witnessing; being active or passive (Gardey, *Le linge* 41). This rendering contingent of the feminine is one of the tricks that came with the simultaneous and paradoxical production of the body of representation as a "body-less" body, neutral and universal while at the same time a masculine and bourgeois *corporation*.

The use of the territory and the gendered economy that it encompassed, however, was established and produced effects beyond the Chamber itself. My work, in fact, sheds light on the long-term inhospitality of the territory of French parliamentary assemblies (and in particular in the Republican context) for any feminine presence. Thus, from the point of view of a "politics of presence" (Phillips), it is not only that women were not present because they were not represented (and could not exercise citizenship) in the French democratic and republican context until 1945 (and beyond), but the whole "domestic" territory of the National Assembly appeared hostile toward any feminine presence, whether as elected officials or public servants. Archival analysis reveals the first domestic and familial dimensions of the Assembly's administration throughout the nineteenth and twentieth centuries in spite of the production of a Weberian ideal type of bureaucracy. These elements of tradition (recruiting of loyal and indebted staff drawing on families of public servants over several generations) are characteristic of the ancien régime and are continued into the twentieth century, enabling the establishment and the stabilization of the parliamentary institution. Side effects such as the fixing of traditions and their reproduction in fundamental structures gave this major institution of the French Republic (and democracy) its lasting "aristocratic" and "domestic" features.

Just as they were not allowed to "represent" in the sense of parliamentarianism, women (except for a few wives and widows of public servants working as linen maids) could not serve the parliamentary institution. In this regard, the culture of the Assembly's administration seems to have lagged behind changes witnessed in public and state administrations, where feminization and the access of women to higher ranks started earlier, in the last third of the nineteenth century and the early twentieth century, respectively, with controversial yet real access to positions as copywriters in the Ministries. The first office workers were recruited in the Assembly only on a temporary basis at the beginning of the twentieth century. Until the 1960s, no women worked in the Plenary Hall. After the refusal to integrate as a public servant a young woman who had passed the very difficult competitive examination for stenographer of debates, a job that is performed at the heart of the parliamentary arena and consists of taking notes of interventions and discussions to provide the official account of legislative proceedings, a claim was filed in 1972 before the State Council against the National Assembly for discrimination and noncompliance with the act on gender equality in public service (Gardey, "Scriptes" 207). Over the long history of the Fourth and Fifth Republics, the "weaker sex" remained de facto banned from the lower chamber, whether as elected members of parliament or as public servants.[18] The history of the National Assembly is thus that of a long-term constitutional and regulatory exception with regard to the texts that established gender equality in the wake of World War II within an Assembly whose liberty and sovereignty had been reconquered at great cost.

In bringing up the strictly political order that determined the "domestic in the political" aspect of a major institution in the history of Western democracy, in showing that the political included a domesticity that was dependent on certain social and gendered relations, my purpose is to qualify the matter and content of democratic institutions. In relation to the ongoing issue of women's political rights, of the genuine universalization of voting rights and representation, my work narrates the singular (conceptual and material) history of the territory of parliamentary assemblies, durably empty of feminine presence. The narrative I offer questions what actually lies behind the gender order in the French National Assembly and asks if another, more equal ecology could prevail today, that is, if a more hospitable parliament could be produced in terms of gender as well as diversity in culture and origin.

Presence and the Possibility of an Alternative Territory

The Politics of Hospitality versus the Politics of Domination in Feminist Territories

The three narratives above account for a specific arrangement the effects of which were lasting. They shed light on the origin and permanence of some overlooked elements and how these limit the range of possibilities. The present undertaking, about a country in which I live and work, does not mean that other countries (for example, the United States) and other models of democratic development do not deserve their own critique. There is no model that prevails; there are only forms of social and political lives that happen and on which we can base our thinking about alternatives.

In an enduring inhospitable domestic (or national) context, a transnational space has served as a resource and refuge to keep alive feminist research and contributions. But the costs of transaction and recognition have persisted. Just as she does not become "integrated" by being "disciplined," the historian of women and gender cannot become integrated by being "undisciplined," in particular when she intends, by poaching in foreign territories, to achieve emancipation from the paternalist and corporatist yoke of discipline.

The cost of access to another territory is incurred by anyone who wants access to it. She must learn the language, the habits, and customs, be socialized into certain ways of thinking and writing, and submit to certain mandatory norms and references. We must bear in mind the obvious limits of this feminist "extraterritoriality" in terms of hospitality. Feminist studies are not as cosmopolitan as one might think. They do not necessarily value cultural and linguistic differences in themselves. The time and space of these encounters—the time of the International Springtime of Gender that is now extended, written about, and inscribed in *differences*—seem to be that of productive diversity. The "spring" of feminism wants to be a "spring" of language and writing. Resisting the power of a single language, resisting what writing in a language implies in terms of formal habits and thought, and resisting also specific experience seem essential today. To stay alive, thought must remain plural. It has to be written with the intimacy and abundance of a native language, through exchange and proximity with other languages and the experience of loss and transformation produced by the fact of writing in a language other than one's own. Plurivocality, plurilocality are the price to pay for balanced exchanges, the quality of what makes a relationship, relationality. To me, defining what is common seems to depend on such an ecosystem. A politics of languages, that is, of the space left or not for alternatives and differences, should be considered an objective and an ardent obligation of the feminist field.

Beyond language, there is the question of feminisms' social and cultural diversity and how these open up and are opened to third parties. The history of the feminist field is not free from power relations and internal struggles. The expansion of feminist voices and subjects raises the question of borders, of the center and the fringe, of the included and the allies. What about the tolerance of other contributions and approaches, other subjects and thoughts in exile, or disturbing proposals?

As we know, feminism is not isolated from the world or social relationships. It is a space of friction and conflict, which are for the most part productive. The history of feminism is Western in the sense that it may be defined as a historically and culturally situated narrative. The critique is constantly repeated and renewed that feminism has accompanied and served cultural and political agendas such as colonialism. Colonial and North/South relationships, the issue of the religious and the secular, and the ways and promises of emancipation are all friction points in theory and practice. There are several options behind what is done today "in the name of feminism."

This matters for more recent developments. The "cause" of women is a resource that can be used by its enemies. Think about the rejection of the right to abortion for u.s. women by those who simultaneously used the suffering of Afghan women to legitimate the u.s. use of military force in their country.[19] Who speaks in the name of feminism and for what purpose? What is geostrategically and militarily at stake in this mobilization of feminism? How could the war in Afghanistan be justified "in our name"?[20] What is our responsibility in this name that seems to be ours and is thus engaged? The issue here is that of a pure politics of domination. Can we allow a "women's rights" kit to be brought in soldiers' suitcases or in the luggage of the NGOs that follow them? In what future disasters will we have to answer for our joint responsibility?

A Constrained Territory?
"Feminist" Thought in a Neoliberal Context

This corruption illustrates the constraints that we are now facing in terms of both action and thought. It reminds us of the way our knowledge is produced, the arenas that make it possible, and the norms to which academic circles must conform. Obtaining independence for feminism as a field of knowledge was first the object of a power struggle within the feminist movement—before it became a (particularly long-lasting, if we consider the French context) battlefield in the academic and scientific institutions of individual countries. The admission of feminist critique in the institutionalized space of the university was considered in its time a sign of irremediable depoliticization. This debate, which divided activists and academics in the 1970s and 1980s, was accompanied by other transformations, such as the institutionalization of part of the feminist program. *Gender mainstreaming* transformed political content and agendas,[21] the nature of the questions raised (in terms of struggle and action), and the forms and instruments to achieve them. For forty years, national and international institutional practices in the varied fields of public, social, and environmental policies, along with the politics of knowledge, have undergone deep transformations or have deeply transformed the space of legitimate questions and the framing of what renders them interesting or useful.

In addition to this practical and institutionalized integration and dissemination of feminist thought (for better and sometimes for worse), standardization has been imposed by the constraints characteristic of the contemporary academic game. The operating conditions of academic markets tighten the noose, reduce the range of possibilities, and shape methods of inquiry; they legitimate objects and forms of knowledge and ways to "do science" on feminist grounds. Ongoing neomanagerial transformations in the academic world over several decades have had an influence on individuals and teams. Productivism, "assessmentitis," and utilitarianism are only a few of our contemporary diseases. The ways research is funded and the general organization of competition between institutions, teams, and individuals are behind the standardization of objects, methods, contents, and ways of writing and thinking. They result in mandatory references and citations within the field of feminist studies itself.

Bibliometric indicators that have proliferated for the past two decades are the best possible example of the penetration of rationales from benchmarking and knowledge management in the academic and scientific worlds.[22] It should be recalled that these indicators are constructions with multiple biases and limitations. One such limitation, for example, is the favoring of the English language. Journals and norms of academic production are first and foremost Anglo-Saxon and only marginally "international."[23] Cultural domination and the asymmetry of power relations, plus all out competition of all against all, and the standardization of activities and products are the dominant traits of the epoch. In many respects, academics become workers like any other and share their experience of violent exchange in the neoliberal context.

The question of *freedom*, then, becomes essential—freedom in the use of one's time, in the way of working and writing, but also in collaborating and being held accountable to others, one's epoch, and contemporaries. Where will the desire to be recognized as "worthy knowledge"—in the sense of being legitimately worthy of being recognized and exercised as knowledge—lead us? This is a shared question today. It concerns all humanities and social sciences. Vinciane Despret and Isabelle Stengers make the following ironic comment: "Knowledge worthy of the name must not fear assessment, we are told, and this assessment has to be objective: how many articles, published in which journals? How many contracts?

How many collaborations with other highly prestigious institutions, thus contributing to the 'positioning' of the university on the European and world market?" (11).

Escaping these mapped, indexed, objectified, and "commensurated" territories is undoubtedly a primary obligation as are recovering spaces of freedom and promoting free, marginal, and hybrid zones. In my opinion, we have an obligation to resist, in writing, in our objects, methods, ways of life, and in comparing experience and knowledge outside and within the academic space. In this respect, the uncertain, nebulous, disorderly, or undisciplined character of the feminist field, and in particular its emphasis on *other* experience and knowledge, is most valuable and should continue to be promoted. This space should keep open and in conflict (keep unresolved) the political and epistemic questions that inhabit it. Hospitality must be the rule. Spaces for encounter between approaches in different languages, about social and political situations that may be similar or distant, unique or common across geographic and cultural territories, are still insufficiently developed. We need to take advantage of the richness of these confrontations. We must keep on doing science "in a different manner," promoting unpredictable, meaningfully *strange* encounters.[24] It is our duty not to let ourselves be consumed by deathly accounting obligations. We have to clarify under what conditions we want to become real players in the game and to participate in setting its rules: as insiders, as outsiders, or by adopting a hybrid "third space," an other space in the way we define what science could or must be.

Deterritorialization, Agency, and New Political/Epistemic Worlds

The well-established questions of feminism, postfeminism, and posthumanism have been discussed at length within and beyond the feminist field, and the emphasis in my conclusion may not be, exactly, on what is at play in these discussions. We can recognize the promises of Rosi Braidotti's decisive move when she claims: "The central concern for my nomadic subject is that there is a noticeable gap between how we live—in emancipated or postfeminist, multiethnic globalized societies, with advanced technologies and high-speed telecommunication [. . .]—and how we represent to ourselves this lived existence in theoretical terms and discourses" (4). If, in her words, "globalization" is about "the mobilization of differences and the deterritorialization of social identity" and challenges the "hegemony of nation-states and their claim to exclusive citizenship" (5), the question of how to act *from* and *in* a certain location (or territory?) remains—as does the question of the territorial and political frame in which political agency might be enacted. Confronted by the strength of capitalism, described by Braidotti as a "nomadic force" able to control space time mobility in highly selective ways, could we oppose the sole force of the "nomadic subject"? Becoming nomadic doesn't enhance empowerment in a persistant nation-state territorial context. Becoming emancipated is not an easy move in a neoliberal context where the autonomy of individual people and that of crucial institutions (such as the law or the public sphere) is subsumed in solely economic rationalities (see Brown). The future of the individual and collective subject depends on the opportunity that we happen to have to speak in the name of and about what is social, to uphold the social issues that are ours. It depends also on our capacity to define and invent new sovereign territories *from* which and *in* which to act. The very nature of the "new" territories that compose our present world (and define our present relation to the world) should be interrogated. The quest is both epistemological and political, as Haraway prophesied.

My last observation is on the joint demonetization of humanistic knowledge and of collective action in the contemporary world. Humanistic knowledge is confronted by its own internal critics and its lesser capacity to be heard and to operate. The loss of agency of most institutions and political stakeholders (in the context of Western democracies) under the reign of economic reason and the deterritorialized deployment of its own agency is an unprecedented event in the history of capitalism. What can institutions (even if they are coordinated, like the European institutions) do against the powerful forces of markets if not simply accompany them? How can one not see that in spite of the continuous changes in initiatives and coalitions, the market presides over and deeply transforms our lives, independently of any democratically coordinated or socially organized effort? For its objective is also and precisely to dismantle the socially and politically instituted chosen forms of life (Brown).

If we were right to criticize the humanistic program, then the recognition of the historical limitation of its emancipatory content postulated on humanist principles and linked to the deployment of "universal" scientific practices has both political and epistemological implications. Like the political, the theoretical seems disarmed. Conversely, other "reasons" or *épistémès* are highly valued and concretely able to perform and transform the world. Economics, behavioral psychology, and neurosciences are some of them. That the world may be described as postmodern or not makes no substantive difference. On the other hand, the colonization of our humanist (social and natural) worlds calls for the redefinition and recolonization of what counts as a territory *from* which and *in* which to act.

Economism, with its old, seemingly endless alliances, is a recurring threat to the definitions of what makes knowledge and what makes society. A double struggle is thus certainly taking place in the territory of lived realities as well as in those of thought and thinkable realities. New forces must be deployed to analyze and thwart the colonizing expansion of extrasocial explanatory registers of the social, such as cognitivist psychology, evolution theory, all-out genetics, and neurosciences. In her essay, "Sex, Cash, and Neuromodels of Desire," Isabelle Dussauge talks about "the lost and found social of neuroscience" (445). She insists on the behaviorist origins of "reward"—an intrinsically economic metaphor—and on the role it plays in neuroscientific experimental productions. "What kind of story of human action is being told through the figure of the reward system of the brain? What happens to economy, sex, and pleasure when framed as rewards?" she asks ("Valuation" 250). Far away from psychoanalytical theories that work with the complex notions of desire and pleasure, disciplines such as neuroeconomics, the neurobiology of addiction, and the neuroscience of sex or evolutionary psychology propose very simplistic definitions of human action. The cultural construct of the brain implies a framing of the human as "an individual subject detached from the world it lives in" (Dussauge, "Sex" 446). Here, neuroscience (or biology) doesn't position itself against the social and the social sciences; it embraces the social and substitutes for humanistic reason. As Dussauge emphasizes: "[N]eurosciences produce neural theories of the social—at the same time disregarding the social, the cultural and critical theories of the same" ("Valuation" 262). Science actively contributes to the material but also ontological definitions of what society is.

If we want to remain potential players in the world we live in, we must continue to prefer "humanistic" forms of explanation (historical, philosophical, sociological, literary, etc.) and the humanities and social sciences' own protocols to account for the social, cultural, and political realities of our time. This will probably entail developing new ways of describing and defining the world, as Haraway and Braidotti point out. For Haraway, the sciences, and in particular the life sciences, are matters too serious to be left solely to the specialists; by not leaving biology to the biologists one can envisage "a livable biology." There would be a veritable danger in permitting a sole language to dominate all those possible. We must take hold of the sciences, work with them, as practices of knowledge, as cultural practices and practical cultures. Yet again, the injunction here is not only of an epistemological or political nature—or merely a theoretical one—but is rendered necessary by our biosocial condition in the technoscientific context.

The fact that human and nonhuman entities are entangled in a "natureculture," defined by Haraway as our common *topos*, doesn't mean that we should not find ways to design emancipatory perspectives for the biosocial subjects we have become in that entangled territory.[25]

In that sense, the epistemic and political territory of the basis of our capacity for individual and collective emancipation still seems, more than ever, to be a territory to be recaptured. The possibility for such sovereignty to prevail and live in the context of a new, open territoriality, where hospitality "at large" is the rule, remains a challenge to this day.

DELPHINE GARDEY is professor of contemporary history and head of the Gender Institute at the University of Geneva (Switzerland), where she also directs the master's and doctoral programs in gender. Trained in France as a historian and a sociologist, she is a former fellow at the Institute for Advanced Studies (Berlin) and was a Humboldt Fellow at the Max-Planck-Institut für Wissenschaftsgeschichte and the Zentrum für Frauen- und Geschlechterforschung at the Technische Universität Berlin.

Notes

1   The book that resulted from these meetings is Gardey and Kraus, *Politics of Coalition*.

2   It is *infrapolitical* in the sense that it affirms itself as not political but conveys politics. It could be defined, then, as an "infrapolitics" of domination, the opposite of the "'infrapolitics' of the subalterns" conceptualized by James C. Scott in *Domination and the Arts of Resistance*.

3   Butler writes: "The dogged effort to 'denaturalize' gender in this text [. . .] was done from a desire to live, to make life possible, and to rethink the possible as such" (*Gender* 15).

4   Blasphemy as a critique *produced from within* should not be linked to insult, which is meant to harm and hurt. Differences of context and culture are manifest. What *secularizing* means cannot be universalized and detached from contingent forms taken by the relations between religion and politics in the Christian Western world. See Anidjar; or in the Muslim world, Asad, Brown, Butler, and Mahmood xvi. Following Haraway, blasphemy should not be renounced as long as it is *from within* and as long as we remember that "secular critique, if it is to remain critical, must be concerned with the epistemic limits on the knowable imposed by secularism itself" (Asad, Brown, Butler, and Mahmood xvi).

5   Written several months before the massive arrival of Syrian and Iraqi refugees at the gates of Europe, these lines have a whole new valence in this context.

6   From women in the history of science to feminist science studies, see, for instance, Fox-Keller,

Reflections; Harding; Kohlstedt and Longino; and Rossiter, *Women Scientists in America: Before Affirmative Action* and *Women Scientists in America: Struggles and Strategies.*

7   See Findlen; and Harkness.

8   We could refer to Biagioli; and Shapin and Schaffer. On the historiographical turn, see Pestre, "Pour une histoire sociale" and *Introduction*, and for a new and broad social and cultural history of science and knowledge since the early modern period, see the three volumes of *Histoire des sciences et des savoirs* edited by Pestre.

9   For a critique of *integration* (the word and the practice) in the contemporary French (neo)colonial context, see Guénif-Souilamas, "L'altérité."

10   This discussion is one of the intrafeminist episodes of a larger discussion about what has been called the "linguistic turn." For more details in the historical field, see Downs. Within the French feminist context, antagonism was also overplayed between "materialist" feminists and their past enemies (the so-called essentialist feminists), who seemed to return to France from the United States wearing new dresses. As Christine Delphy has remarked, "'French Feminism' is not feminism in France" ("Invention"). The controversy took place within a broader misunderstanding—or *because of* very well defined theoretical, cultural, and political agendas on both sides. In that sense, transatlantic exchanges didn't really occur, as academic French elites rejected most of what came (back) "from America." See Akrich, Chabaud-Rychter, and Gardey; Berger; and Kraus.

11   Noiriel is, in fact, the author of the *Le creuset français*, an essential contribution to the analysis of the role played by migrants in the identity of the working class and the definition of the French nation.

12   The persistence of this exclusion and this reluctance to accept the theoretical contribution of feminism to history is a mystery in itself. See, for instance, Delacroix; and Riot-Sarcey.

13   This question was discussed and replayed during Guénif-Souilamas's defense of her "habilitation thesis," reflecting the national, colonial, political, and disciplinary stakes at play and the importance of controlling the disciplinary territory of sociology, as in the previously mentioned case of history.

14   My translation of the Larousse French dictionary's definition of *beur*: "Youth of North African origins born in France of immigrant parents." About the word and concept, and the assignment and reappropriation of ways of naming oneself and being named, see Guénif-Souilamas, "Beurette."

15   It should be noted here that the models of "assimilation" and "integration" dominating the French debate are also the result of the politics of the European Union; the discourse of each European country has contributed to the formation of a shared doxa.

16   See ch. 1, Gardey, *Le linge.*

17   This occurred, more particularly, when the Republic finally managed to settle into the Third Republic (1871–1940).

18   French women gained the right to vote and be elected on April 21, 1944. The first Assembly elected by actual universal suffrage included 5.6 percent women in October

1945 and 6.1 percent in 1997. This disconcerting stability in the nonrepresentation of women led to the movement for parity at the end of the 1990s and to the voting in of constitutional laws requiring equal representation of men and women in electoral mandates. On the origins and the impact of the law, see Achin; Bereni; and Lépinard. On the French Republican paradoxes, see Fraisse; and Joan Scott, *Only Paradoxes.*

19   As we know, "the Bush administration and Laura Bush used the suffering of women to declare war on Afghanistan" (Mahmood). See also Delphy, "Une guerre?"

20   Vinciane Despret and Isabelle Stengers expand on the power (and risk) of what is done "in my name" or "in our name" (as women, feminists, or women of science) and insist on what we should refuse be done "in our name" (25).

21   As Sylvia Walby writes, "Gender mainstreaming is an essentially contested concept and practice. It involves the re-invention, restructuring, and re-branding of a key part of feminism in the contemporary era" (321).

22   Based on management methods dedicated to the private sector, these types of indicators were first transferred to the public sector (in the 1980s) and then to the universities (in the 1990s). Aggregated data, used in bibliometric contexts, became a management tool of the careers of researchers in the 2000s (Gingras 23). For an exhaustive perspective on the European "research market," see Bruno, "Comment?" and "La recherche."

23   On the cultural and linguistic biases in favor of American and English journals and productions in databases such as SCOPUS and ERIH and on the gap between standard bibliometric tools and the diversity of actual French scholarly production in the humanities and social sciences, see Dassa, Kosmopoulos, and Pumain. For commentary on the effectiveness of the international character of a journal such as the *American Review of Sociology* in comparison with *Actes de la recherche en sciences sociales*, see Gingras (77).

24   On such feminist explorations on the alternative ways of doing science *and* society, see Fox-Keller, *A Feeling*; Haraway, *Primate*; and Strum and Fedigan.

25   For additional comments on Haraway's ontologies and political propositions for a humanist (and not posthumanist) landscape, see Gardey, "Reading."

Works Cited

Achin, Catherine. *Le mystère de la chambre basse: Comparaison des processus d'entrée des femmes au Parlement, France-Allemagne 1945–2000.* Paris: Dalloz, 2005.

Agamben, Giorgio. *Homo Sacer: Sovereign Power and Bare Life.* Stanford: Stanford UP, 1998.

Akrich, Madeleine, Danielle Chabaud-Rychter, and Delphine Gardey, eds. "Politiques de la représentation et de l'identité. Recherches en gender, cultural, queer studies." *Cahiers du Genre* 38 (2005): 5–14.

Anidjar, Gil. *Semites: Race, Religion, Literature.* Stanford: Stanford UP, 2007.

Asad, Talal, Wendy Brown, Judith Butler, and Saba Mahmood. *Is Critique Secular? Blasphemy, Injury, and Free Speech.* New York: Fordham UP, 2013.

Badiou, Alain. *De quoi Sarkozy est-il le nom? Circonstances, 4.* Paris: Editions Lignes, 2007.

Bereni, Laure. *La bataille de la parité. Mobilisations pour la féminisation du pouvoir.* Paris: Économica, 2015.

Berger, Anne-Emmanuelle. *Le grand théâtre du genre. Identités, sexualités et féminisme en "Amérique."* Paris: Belin, 2013.

Biagioli, Mario. *Galileo, Courtier: The Practice of Science in the Culture of Absolutism.* Chicago: Chicago UP, 1993.

Braidotti, Rosi. *Nomadic Subjects: Embodiment and Sexual Difference in Contemporary Feminist Theory.* New York: Columbia UP, 2011.

Brown, Wendy. "Neo-liberalism and the End of Liberal Democracy." *Theory and Event* 7.1 (2003): 1–19.

Bruno, Isabelle. "Comment gouverner un 'espace européen de la recherche' et des 'chercheurs-entrepreneurs'? Le recours au management comme technologie politique." *Innovations* 36 (2011): 65–82.

————. "La recherche scientifique au crible du benchmarking. Petite histoire d'une technologie de gouvernement." *Revue d'histoire moderne et contemporaine* 55.4 (2008): 28–45.

Butler, Judith. *Gender Trouble: Feminism and the Subversion of Identity.* New York: Routledge, 1999.

————. *Precarious Life: The Powers of Mourning and Violence.* New York: Verso, 2004.

————. Report on Guénif-Souilamas's Habilitation. Unpubl. ms. 2010.

————. "Sexual Politics, Torture, and Secular Time." *British Journal of Sociology* 59.1 (2008). http://onlinelibrary.wiley.com/doi/10.1111/j.1468-4446.2007.00176.x/full.

Dassa, Michèle, Christine Kosmopoulos, and Denise Pumain. "JournalBase—A Comparative International Study of Scientific Journal Databases in the Social Sciences and the Humanities (SSH)." *Cybergeo* 484 (2010). http://cybergeo.revues.org/22864.

Delacroix, Christian. "*Espaces Temps* et l'histoire des femmes." *CLIO, Histoire, Femmes et Sociétés* 16 (2002): 111–18.

de Lauretis, Teresa, ed. "Queer Theory: Lesbian and Gay Sexualities." *differences* 3.2 (1991): iii–xviii.

Delphy, Christine. "Une guerre pour les femmes afghanes?" *Nouvelles Questions Féministes* 21.1 (2002): 98–109.

————. "The Invention of French Feminism: An Essential Move." *50 Years of Yale French Studies, Part 2: 1980–1998.* Ed. Charles A. Porter and Alyson Waters. New Haven: Yale UP, 2000. 166–97.

Derrida, Jacques. *Adieu to Emmanuel Lévinas.* Stanford: Stanford UP, 1999.

————. *Of Hospitality. Anne Dufourmantelle Invites Jacques Derrida to Respond.* Stanford: Stanford UP, 2000.

Despret, Vinciane, and Isabelle Stengers. *Les faiseuses d'histoires. Que font les femmes à la pensée?* Paris: La Découverte, 2011.

Downs, Laura Lee. *Writing Gender History.* New York: Bloomsbury Academic, 2010.

Dussauge, Isabelle. "Sex, Cash, and Neuromodels of Desire." *BioSocieties* 10 (2015): 444–64.

——————————. "Valuation Machines: Economies of Desire/Pleasure in Contemporary Neuroscience." *Value Practices in the Life Sciences and Medicine.* Ed. Isabelle Dussauge, Claes-Fredrik Helgesson, and Francis Lee. Oxford: Oxford UP, 2015. 247–64.

Findlen, Paula. "Masculine Prerogatives: Gender, Space, and Knowledge in the Early Modern Museum." *The Architecture of Science.* Ed. Peter Galison and Emily Thompson. Cambridge: MIT P, 1999. 29–57.

Fox-Keller, Evelyn. *A Feeling for the Organism.* New York: Freeman and Company, 1983.

——————————. *Reflections on Gender and Science.* New Haven: Yale UP, 1985.

Fraisse, Geneviève. *Muse de la Raison. Démocratie et exclusion des femmes en France.* Aix-en-Provence: Alinéa, 1989.

Gardey, Delphine. "Définir les vies possibles, penser le monde commun." *Le féminisme change-t-il nos vies?* Ed. Delphine Gardey. Paris: Textuel, 2011. 116–24.

——————————. *Le linge du Palais-Bourbon. Corps, matérialité et genre du politique à l'ère démocratique.* Lormont: Le Bord de l'eau, 2015.

——————————. "L'histoire, les Feminist & others' studies." *À quoi pensent les historiens? Faire de l'histoire au XXIe siècle.* Ed. Christophe Granger. Paris: Autrement, 2013. 209–24.

——————————. "The Reading of an Oeuvre. Donna Haraway: The Poetics and Politics of Life." *Feministische Studien, Zeitschrift für interdisziplinäre Frauen- und Geschlechterforschung* 32.1 (2014): 86–100.

——————————. "Scriptes de la démocratie. Les sténographes et rédacteurs des Débats (1848–2005)." *Sociologie du Travail* 52.2 (2010): 195–211.

——————————. "Turning Public Discourse into an Authentic Artefact: Shorthand Transcription in the French National Assembly." *Making Things Public: Atmospheres of Democracy.* Ed. Bruno Latour and Peter Weibel. Cambridge, MA: MIT P, 2005. 836–43.

Gardey, Delphine, and Cynthia Kraus, eds. *Politics of Coalition: Thinking Collective Action with Judith Butler.* Geneva: Seismo, 2016.

Gingras, Yves. *Les dérives de l'évaluation de la recherche. Du bon usage de la bibliométrie.* Paris: Raisons d'Agir, 2014.

Guénif-Souilamas, Nacira. "L'altérité de l'intérieur." *La situation postcoloniale.* Ed. Marie-Claude Smouts. Paris: Sciences Po, 2007. 344–53.

——————————. "Altérités (de l') intérieur(es)." Unpubl. ms. for Habilitation à diriger les recherches, vol. 2. Institut d'Etudes Politiques de Paris, 2010.

——————————. "Beurette, beur, rebeu." *Dictionnaire de l'adolescence et de la jeunesse.* Ed. David Le Breton and Daniel Marcelli. Paris: PUF, 2010. 113–16.

Guénif-Souilamas, Nacira, and Éric Macé. *Les féministes et le garçon arabe.* Paris: L'Aube, 2004.

Haraway, Donna. "Cyborgs at Large." Interview with Constance Penley and Andrew Ross. *Technoculture.* Ed. Constance Penley and Andrew Ross. Minneapolis: U of Minnesota P, 1991. 1–20.

——————————. "Ecce Homo, Ain't (Ar'n't) I a Woman, and Inappropriate/d Others: The Human in a Post-Humanist Landscape." *Feminists Theorize the Political.* Ed. Judith Butler and Joan W. Scott. New York: Routledge, 1992. 86–100.

——————————. *Primate Visions: Gender, Race, Nature in the World of Modern Science.* New York: Routledge, 1990.

——————————. "The Promises of Monsters: A Regenerative Politics for Inappropriate/d Others." *Cultural Studies.* Ed. Lawrence Grossberg, Cary Nelson, and Paula Treichler. New York: Routledge, 1992. 295–337.

Harding, Sandra. *The Science Question in Feminism.* Ithaca: Cornell UP, 1986.

Harkness, Deborah E. "Managing an Experimental Household: The Dees of Mortlake and the Practice of Natural Philosophy." *Isis* 88.2 (1997): 247–62.

Kohlstedt, Sally Gregory, and Helen Longino. "The Women, Gender, and Science Question: What Do Research on Women in Science and Research on Gender Have to Do with Each Other?" *Osiris* 12 (1997): 3–15.

Kraus, Cynthia. "Anglo-American Feminism Made in France: Crise et critique de la représentation." *Cahiers du Genre* 38 (2005): 163–89.

Lefort, Claude. *L'invention démocratique.* Paris: Fayard, 1981.

Lépinard, Éléonore. *L'égalité introuvable.* Paris: Sciences Po, 2007.

Mahmood, Saba. "Do Muslim Women Want Rights?" Gender, Islam and the West Conference. Grace Cathedral, San Francisco. 10 Feb. 2009. ies.berkeley.edu/resources/curricula/ssrc/labulughodsmahmood.html.

Noiriel, Gérard. *Le creuset français: Histoire de l'immigration XIXe–XXe siècle.* Paris: Seuil, 1988.

——————————. *Sur la "crise" de l'histoire.* Paris: Belin, 1996.

Pestre, Dominique. *Introduction aux Sciences Studies.* Paris: La Découverte, 2006.

——————————. "Pour une histoire sociale et culturelle des sciences. Nouvelles définitions, nouveaux objets, nouvelles pratiques." *Annales. Histoire, Sciences Sociales* 50.3 (1995): 487–522.

Pestre, Dominique, ed. *Histoire des sciences et des savoirs.* 3 vols. Paris: Seuil, 2016.

Phillips, Anne. *The Politics of Presence.* Oxford: Oxford UP, 1998.

Poloni-Simard, Jacques. "*CLIO-Annales*: 'Histoire des femmes, histoire sociale.'" *CLIO, Histoire, Femmes et Sociétés* 16 (2002): 107–11.

Poudra, Jules, and Eugène Pierre. *Traité pratique de droit parlementaire.* Paris: Chambre des Députés, 1902.

Riot-Sarcey, Michèle. "L'historiographie française et le concept de 'genre.'" *Revue d'histoire moderne et contemporaine* 47.4 (2000): 805–14.

Rossiter, Margaret. *Women Scientists in America: Before Affirmative Action, 1940–1972.* Baltimore: Johns Hopkins UP, 1995.

——————. *Women Scientists in America: Struggles and Strategies to 1940.* Baltimore: Johns Hopkins UP, 1982.

Scott, James C. *Domination and the Arts of Resistance: Hidden Transcripts.* New Haven: Yale UP, 1990.

Scott, Joan W. "Border Patrol." *French Historical Studies* 21.3 (1998): 383–97.

——————. *Only Paradoxes to Offer: French Feminists and the Rights of Man.* Cambridge, MA: Harvard UP, 1997.

Shapin, Steven, and Simon Schaffer. *Leviathan and the Air-Pump: Hobbes, Boyle, and the Experimental Life.* Princeton: Princeton UP, 1985.

Stengers, Isabelle. "Fabriquer de l'espoir au bord du gouffre. A propos de l'oeuvre de Donna Haraway." *La Revue internationale des livres et des idées* 10 (2009): 24–29.

Strum, Shirley, and Linda Marie Fedigan. *Primate Encounters: Models of Science, Gender, and Society.* Chicago: Chicago UP, 2002.

Walby, Sylvia. "Gender Mainstreaming: Productive Tensions in Theory and Practice." *Social Politics* 12.3 (2005): 321–43.

Gender and the Lure of the Postcritical

Since at least the turn of the millennium, there has been a conviction among a number of scholars that critique—seen as the legacy of Marx, Nietzsche, and Freud—is exhausted. As Jeff Pruchnic comments in a review essay on the question, while the demise of theory has often been proclaimed, this may be the first time that its death is attributed to its own success. Witness Bruno Latour's "Why Has Critique Run out of Steam?" in which he vents his frustration at how skillfully the Right has appropriated elements of left critique: in its denials of climate change, its elaborate conspiracy theories, its masterful truth claims on contentious subjects.

Concerns about the demise of critique have led not to intellectual paralysis but rather to a rush of speculative work on the future of theoretical thinking in the fields of philosophy, political theory, science studies, literature, and art.[1] Here, I turn to two literary critical essays that have received a good deal of attention in the United States: Eve Sedgwick's 2003 "Paranoid Reading and Reparative Reading, or, You're So Paranoid, You Probably Think This Essay Is about You," and Stephen Best and Sharon Marcus's 2009 "Surface Reading: An Introduction." With these two essays

Volume 27, Number 2   DOI 10.1215/10407391-3621757

as a point of departure, I ask what the lure of the postcritical might be, how gender is implicated in it, and what the so-called postcritical bodes for the future of critical and political thinking.

The Suspicion

Eve Sedgwick begins her celebrated essay recollecting a conversation she had with Cindy Patton about the origins of HIV. At a time when many believed the epidemic to have been deliberately developed and spread by the U.S. military, Sedgwick was eager for Patton's opinion on the speculation. In fact, Patton confessed she had little interest in the question. Even if one were certain of all the elements of a conspiracy, she said—"that the lives of Africans and African Americans are worthless in the eyes of the United States; that gay men and drug users are held cheap where they aren't actively hated," and so forth; "[s]upposing we were ever so sure of all those things—what would we know that we don't already know?" (123). It is this long-ago response of Patton's that made Sedgwick ever more suspicious of suspicion. For her, Patton's comment "suggests the possibility of unpacking, of disentangling from their impacted and overdetermined historical relation to each other some of the separate elements of the intellectual baggage that many of us carry around under a label such as 'the hermeneutics of suspicion'" (124).

For Sedgwick, there are political stakes involved in the disentangling. How to know in the AIDS case, for example, whether or not to put energy into the exposure of a plot? The choice is not self-evident, she says. To be suspicious of suspicion is to shift from the question, "'Is a particular piece of knowledge true, and how can we know?' to the further questions, 'What does knowledge *do*—the pursuit of it, the having and exposing of it, the receiving-again of knowledge of what one already knows?'" (124). To cast knowledge as performative is not news, Sedgwick acknowledges. But those very critical practices themselves founded on the performative seem to have forgotten their own grounds, and this, she argues, is the "unintentionally stultifying side effect" of what Paul Ricoeur calls the "hermeneutics of suspicion." For Ricoeur, the practice of interpretation has two warring sides, the suspicious side represented by Marx, Nietzsche, and Freud, and the other—"interpretation as recollection of meaning"—which Ricoeur claims as his own (28). Following Ricoeur, Sedgwick argues that since the Marx-Nietszche-Freud trio has for some time clearly dominated U.S. literary critical practices, practices that have generalized suspicion to the occlusion of everything else, it is time for something different. Thus she proposes "reparative" reading as a counter practice, born of a marriage of insights gleaned from the theories of Silvan Tomkins and Melanie Klein. What fuels Sedgwick's argument is her view that much of cultural criticism had become formulaic and predictable, with reading after reading dedicated to the exposure of the obvious: "How television-starved would someone have to be to find it shocking that ideologies contradict themselves, that simulacra don't have originals, or that gender representations are artificial?" (141). Moreover, she warns that by continuing to teach the "infinitely doable and teachable protocols of unveiling," we risk not only closing off epistemological possibilities but may "unintentionally impoverish the gene pool of literary-critical perspectives and skills" (143–44).[2]

The seductive power of this 2003 essay is undeniable. How to resist Sedgwick's wit, her audacity, her rhetorical brilliance, let alone her resonant indictment of so much of the criticism of the time? And what to think of the political stakes the essay claims? Sedgwick warns that the danger of an impoverished literary-critical gene pool is its "diminished ability to respond to environmental (e.g., political) change" (144). For younger members of the literary-critical profession, the danger she signals has to have seemed at least as alarming professionally as politically. In any case, the essay was for many liberatory in its irreverence for critical protocols that had long held sway in the academy.

"Paranoid Reading and Reparative Reading" is not a manifesto. There are no blueprints for reparative reading, no prototypes offered. Rather, Sedgwick offers provocative speculations as to what might be gained by readerly attention to *weak theory*. "You probably think this essay is about you," Sedgwick quips, because in Silvan Tomkins's terms, paranoia is a strong affect and, as such, takes over, ordering more and more of experience so that nothing else seems able to survive. For Tomkins, the affect system—innate response patterns to internal and external stimuli modeled on cybernetic feedback—displaces Freudian drives. Affect theories can be weak or strong, he explains: "To the extent to which the theory can account only for 'near' phenomena, it is a weak theory, little better than a description of the phenomena which it purports to explain. As it orders more and more remote phenomena to a single formation, its power grows" (qtd. in Sedgwick 134). Furthermore, for Tomkins, strong theories are—like paranoia—often *negative* affects that seem immune to refutation.

These are the psychological theories that Sedgwick adapts by analogy to the practices of reading and interpretation. And for the reparative rescue of critical studies, she inflects Tomkins's theories with Melanie Klein's paranoid-schizoid and depressive positions. She argues that allowing weak textual elements to interact with the strong could produce a rich reading practice, and allowing the positive to interact with the negative could produce a different "ecology of knowing" that might undermine the epistemology of enmity (145). It is not a question, Sedgwick insists, of a glass half full and a glass half empty. It is not that a reading that looks to weak positive affect is any more or less realistic than one in line with a strong negative affect: "In a world full of loss, pain, and oppression," she writes, "both epistemologies are likely to be based on deep pessimism: the reparative mode of seeking pleasure, after all, arrives by Klein's account, only with the achievement of a depressive position" (138).

What is important for Sedgwick is that there be some *possibility* for reparative reading and that the critical experience not be tautologically known in advance. For Sedgwick, who had long fumed against everything needing to say the same thing, reparative reading precisely does not know how reparation will be made. Which is to say that those who read her essay as contributing to the burial of critique fail to notice that it is critique that Sedgwick aims to repair. By theorizing the strong suspicious reading as consolidating the already known—that is, by offering a vigorous critique of suspicion—Sedgwick positions the reparative reading as one that doesn't know in advance what it will find, the very claim of critique.[3]

If Sedgwick's essay turns on an open notion of the reparative that preserves the indetermination of critique, Stephen Best and Sharon Marcus's 2009 "Surface Reading: An Introduction" takes the more determinative form of a manifesto. Like Sedgwick, Best and Marcus are frustrated with current criticism: "Those of us who cut our intellectual teeth on deconstruction, ideology critique, and the hermeneutics of suspicion have often found those demystifying protocols superfluous in an era when images of torture at Abu Ghraib and elsewhere were immediately circulated on the internet; the real-time coverage of Hurricane Katrina showed in ways that required little explication the state's abandonment of its African American citizens; and many people instantly recognized as lies political statements such as 'mission accomplished'" (2).

But where Sedgwick frames her critique of demystifying protocols in terms of the occlusion of the unknown by the known, Best and Marcus frame their argument on the thematics of surface and depth. It is curious that they turn to that theme given how worn out it might be seen to be, but it clearly offers a convenient rhetorical device for the reversal of all that Best and Marcus find outmoded in the critical practices inherited from the 1970s. As the introductory essay for a special issue of *Representations* titled *The Way We Read Now*, "Surface Reading" signals a set of critical practices that the editors identify as the *now* that counters the protocols of *then*. Although the essay claims that surface reading is not antithetical to critique (18), that it broadens its scope, the reader never knows just what is meant by "critique." What the essay does want to emphasize is that the critical reading of the past saw as its mission the revelation of deeply hidden truths, a practice that now seems superfluous and futile. Where Sedgwick's call to seek the reparative operations of weak theory is forceful but vague, Best and Marcus, by contrast, tell us where to go.

The turn to the surface for Best and Marcus is a sharp turn away from what they call "symptomatic reading." Although it is Louis Althusser who first uses "symptomatic" (*symptomale*) to characterize Marx's reading of the classical political economists, Best and Marcus draw their understanding of the term from Fredric Jameson's *The Political Unconscious*, the book that in their view popularized symptomatic reading in the United States (3). And although Best and Marcus's use of the term is very different from Althusser's—a difference I'll return to—it fits seamlessly with the theme of surface and depth. For them, symptomatic reading is the very *other* of surface reading. Drawing on language from *The Political Unconscious*, they evoke symptomatic reading as interpretation that seeks "a latent meaning behind a manifest one," that "reveals truths that 'remain unrealized in the surface of the text'" and the interpreter as one who rewrites "the surface categories of a text in the stronger language of a more fundamental interpretive code" (Jameson qtd. in Marcus and Best 3).[4]

Best and Marcus's call for the reversal of depth and surface is driven in part by a concern for "political realism." Tracing the roots of symptomatic reading to Marx and Freud, those alleged hermeneuts of suspicion, they wonder if the critical projects of today might well aim to be less "heroic" in nature. Their speculations grow, they write, "out of a sense of political realism about the revolutionary capacities of both texts and critics, and doubts about whether we could ever attain the heightened perspicacity that would allow us to see fully beyond ideology." These doubts lead to even more dramatic ones: "We also detect in current criticism a skepticism about the very project of freedom, or about any kind of transcendent values we might use to justify intellectual work" (16). Best and Marcus hasten to add that the neutrality they recommend, the call to relinquish "the freedom dream that accompanies the work of demystification," signals not an indifference to the constraints on peoples' lives but rather a state of mind that might be "equally valuable, though less glamorous" (17): "Instead of turning to literature for models of how to overcome constraint, or for a right way to live under capital, or to register the difference between our critical freedom and the limits placed on others, we are interested in how to register the ways that constraints structure existence as much as breaking free of them does" (18).

Gender

However the essays by Sedgwick and by Best and Marcus differ, one can understand why the two exhortations to "reparative" reading and "surface" reading have come to be seen as representing similar messages of frustration. As the explosive theoretical developments of the 1960s through the 1980s were gradually institutionalized in academic departments, as their unsettling strangeness was assimilated over time to the familiar, it was inevitable that what was once transformative would be lost to the formulaic. It is not just *l'esprit de contradiction* that drives current displeasure with the long dominant critical protocols—though *l'esprit de contradiction* can be valuable—but rather a deep dissatisfaction with the limits of demystification. Sedgwick looks to open up criticism by turning from the strong to the weak and from the paranoid to the reparative. Best and Marcus wager that letting go of belief in the depths will allow us actually to see the surface. And both interventions find their force in the observation that *times have changed* and that the changing times have overtaken critique as we have known it.

While it is not hard to understand the calls for a criticism that knows times have changed, a number of questions arise about these particular calls. How did critique—the practice that endeavors to think what we can't know in advance—come to represent the opposite, the already known? Is there more to the question than the formulaic dulling that comes from institutionalization? How did the forms of critique of Marx, Nietszche, and Freud—which famously *break* with hermeneutics—come to be labeled by Ricoeur as the hermeneutics of suspicion, a characterization embraced by Sedgwick as well as by Best and Marcus? How did symptomatic reading come to be seen as the revelation of latent meaning hidden underneath the manifest? And how to think about the implications of reparative readings and surface readings for the political?

I will begin with the last question by posing another: if critique is ineffectual, how to think about a phenomenon such as misogyny, arguably feminism's fundamental problem? Perhaps there is no longer any way to think about it *theoretically.* Indeed, the issue of misogyny can be seen to support arguments that critique has failed. After decades of feminist critique and activism, there is little indication that the phenomenon has diminished or is less ubiquitous. Women may have made political and social advances in some parts of the world, but misogyny seems to have its own energy, one that may correlate positively or negatively with such advances but that cannot be fully explained by them. Some might put misogyny in the same category as Abu Ghraib or Katrina: a display of violence that speaks for itself. Seemingly timeless and ubiquitous, it appears to have the kind of self-evidence that renders critique superfluous.

What can be said, then, for the critical possibilities of reparative reading and surface reading with regard to misogyny? Here it is necessary once again to distinguish Sedgwick's argument from that of Best and Marcus. For as much as the two have been seen to be congruent,[5] Sedgwick's cannot be said to be "postcritical." Sedgwick's formulation of the reparative—her shift from strong theory to weak theory—is designed to enhance critique, not to dispense with it. Thus, it is not impossible to imagine a reparative reading of misogyny. A careful reading of a text dominated by a strong theory of misogyny might well yield weak theoretical routes, perhaps even reparative ones. And how such a reading might avoid a further elaboration of the already known is an open question, not a closed one.

The situation is quite different in Best and Marcus's "Surface Reading." Fundamental to their formulation of "surface" is the idea that critical meaning resides there and that it is accessible through *description.* Indeed, although "attention to surface as a practice of critical description" is offered as only one approach among several (11), the practice of description is in fact indispensable to all forms of surface reading. If criticism "is not the excavation of hidden truths" (13), then critical attentiveness necessarily consists of various modalities of description. As Best and Marcus write: "Description sees no need to translate the text into a theoretical or historical metalanguage in order to make the text meaningful. The purpose of criticism is thus a relatively modest one: to indicate what the text says about itself" (11).[6]

If we were to give a patient surface reading, then, to all the textual elements that structure the misogynistic text, would we have a finer understanding of the ways misogyny constrains existence? Perhaps. But what would we have gained with a phenomenon that is so familiar that descriptive expansion seems superfluous and useless? The answer seems to be the modest, pragmatic one that Best and Marcus offer: critical reading is not the answer to misogyny; it can do some things, but we need to recognize finally that certain problems are outside the critical domain.

So what, then, is to be done with the question of misogyny? Should one see it as simply an epiphenomenal problem, its manifestations assimilable to other political and social analyses? Perhaps one should be suspicious of the very idea of misogyny, too universalizing in its reach, too close to "woman," now considered disreputable as a critical category. There certainly is some validity in such reservations. Like *patriarchy*, *misogyny* can be used as a broad brush, covering over social, political, and cultural complexities with convenient swaths of coherence. At the same time, misogyny as the hatred and fear of women does exist, and unlike systems of ultimately legible power relations, misogyny can be elusive. Those who try to grasp the dangers that misogyny sees lurking in the feminine invariably come up against the veiled disavowal that characterizes symbolic registers—a veiling that points back, of course, to critique.

Let us use the problem of misogyny to look more closely at the knot of questions that arise with the notion of the postcritical, including the implications entailed for feminist criticism. Misogyny is particularly useful, not only because it seems, in its elusiveness, unthinkable outside of critique but because its history as a critical object sheds light on the ways times have changed. By looking at two critical essays on misogyny separated by almost thirty years, we gain a view of changes in critical practices, changes that revolve around the category of *gender*, which itself changes in significant ways. Both essays are concerned with an elusive misogyny, both practice critique—one employing *gender* and one not—and together they offer a perspective on critique's "demise." The first essay is Howard Bloch's "Medieval Misogyny," published originally in a special issue of *Representations* in 1987, then two years later in the volume *Misogyny, Misandry, and Misanthropy*, which Bloch edited with Frances Ferguson. The second is Nancy McLoughlin's *Jean Gerson and Gender: Rhetoric and Politics in Fifteenth-Century France*, published in 2015.

Bloch, whose field is medieval literature, quips that "medieval misogyny" might seem redundant given that Western women hating, which reaches back to the Old Testament and the Greeks, seems synonymous with "medieval" (1). He looks at the discourse of misogyny and the ways the discourse is bound up with practices of medieval hermeneutics as well as with epistemological associations that persist into the present. For Bloch, the practices of medieval hermeneutics are inscribed in misogynist discourse because there seems to be no way to escape the latter. Woman as riot or chaos is a topos in medieval literature and as such contaminates the very language that cannot contain her. With example after example, Bloch shows how "[t]he riotousness of woman is linked to that of speech and indeed seems to be a condition of poetry itself" (5). Moreover, woman's very coming into being—from the rib of Adam—is seen as a scandalous metaphor, a perversion of the literal: "Since the creation of woman is synonymous with the creation of metaphor," Bloch writes, "the relation between Adam and Eve is the relation of the proper to the figural, which implies always derivation, deflection, denaturing" (11).

Bloch attributes the almost monotonous ubiquity of medieval misogyny to the "citational mode" of the misogynist discourse, "whose rhetorical thrust is to displace its own source away from anything that might be construed as personal or confessional and toward the sacred authorities," whose source in turn is absent and possibly nonexistent. "This defining tautology," Bloch goes on, "emphasizes the elusiveness of misogyny as well as the pertinence of the question of reading" (6). And while Bloch recognizes the historical disenfranchisement of medieval women, he cautions that although these material underpinnings are real, "they are not the same as misogyny, and one has to be careful not to move too easily between the domain of institutions and the discourse of antifeminism" (9). Similarly, he points to the futility of looking for the source of misogyny in authors' personal attitudes: "If misogyny is a topos, a virtual element, found in almost any work (including those that are overwhelmingly profeminine like *Aucassin et Nicolette*), how ascribable is it to something on the order of individual authorial intention?" (7).

Moving between institutions and discourse is precisely what McLoughlin does in her study of Jean Gerson, an early fifteenth-century theologian and chancellor of the University of Paris, renowned both for promoting rational and just government and for developing concepts of European witchcraft. McLoughlin is more than aware of the risks against which Bloch cautions. Indeed, she explicitly distinguishes her study of Gerson from the work of the majority of historians who "attribute his well-known misogynist polemics to either his personal feelings about women or the general misogynist attitude of the medieval clergy in a manner that suggests that Gerson's use of gendered language is only relevant to our understanding of his personal psychology or the history of women" (1). For McLoughlin, such reductive assumptions confirm the impression among historians "that gendered hierarchies and discourses do not inform and are not reproduced within [Gerson's] writings on seemingly non-gendered topics, such as representative government and equitable justice" (2). In other words, while other historians keep the two sides of Jean Gerson apart, separating the intellectual, theological, and political Gerson from the misogynist creator of witches, McLoughlin takes on the whole figure in order to shed light on his "enigmatic legacy."

To do this, the historian McLoughlin relies strongly on the critical category of "gender," a term virtually absent from Bloch's literary critical essay, and she enthusiastically credits Joan W. Scott's theorization of the term: "Gerson provides a perfect case study for demonstrating the need for medievalists to adopt the most radical aspect of Joan Scott's treatment of gender as a critical lens for understanding history, namely to apply gender analysis to the study of the relationship[s] between male institutions" (2). By employing *gender*, McLoughlin aims in her study to find the working relationships between the two seemingly contradictory aspects of Gerson's thought, "his reputation as a defender of the oppressed and his infamous misogynist polemics" (3). Her aim is also to influence the practice of medieval history, and she is thus careful to be as clear as possible about her approach: "Since the exact meaning of the term gender remains the subject of much confusion and debate, I would like to emphasize that I am using this term exactly as Scott originally intended" (4). Scott's original intent refers, of course, to her formulations in the essay "Gender: A Useful Category of Historical Analysis," published in 1986 in the *American Historical Review* and then two years later in *Gender and the Politics of History*. McLoughlin goes on to clarify her own use of the term by citing from Scott's introduction to the second edition of *Gender and the Politics of History* (1999), where Scott reflects on her earlier use of the term *gender*:

> *Gender provided a way of investigating the specific forms taken by the social organization of sexual difference; it did not treat them as variations on an unchanging theme of patriarchal domination. Instead it required careful reading of concrete manifestations, attention to the different meanings the same words might have. "Gender" might always refer to the ways in which relationships between men and women were conceived, but neither the relationships nor the "men" and "women" were taken to be the same in all instances. The point was to interrogate all of the terms and so to historicize them. (Scott qtd. in McLoughlin 4)*

McLoughlin thus reaffirms in her 2015 book the efficacy of Scott's "original" formulation of gender, which is to say, the efficacy of critique. As a feminist medieval historian, she is interested more in unsettling her own conservative field and in studying the still pertinent question of medieval misogyny than in aligning herself with those in other fields who see critique as exhausted. Of course, the 1999 revised edition of *Gender and the Politics of History*, from which McLoughlin cites, is the very text in which Scott declares *gender to be the exhausted term*. Whereas a decade or so earlier, *gender* had had the ability to denaturalize and disturb received understandings of sexuality—as it still does for McLoughlin's work—by the end of the 1990s, in Scott's view, it had lost its legibility in many fields as an instrument of critique. As she says, the term had taken on various meanings in common usage, "routinely offered as a synonym for women, for the differences between the sexes [both ascribed and 'natural'], for sex" (xi). But however unsettled it was in common parlance, in critical usage it was, in too many cases, no longer *unsettling*.

We might keep Scott's 1999 reconsideration of gender in mind when thinking about "gender and the lure of the postcritical." Might we think of gender not as tangentially related to the postcritical, but centrally implicated? Perhaps it is the failure of gender-as-critique that signals if not the collapse of critique then at least a shift in the terrain in which critique does its work. Such a speculation would coincide with a major shift that occurred in the u.s. academy in the 1990s. For at least two decades, leading-edge criticism in the United States had been dominated by French poststructuralist theories. Consider the critical orientations of Joan Scott and Howard Bloch, for example, whose essays on gender and misogyny appeared within a year of each other in 1986 and 1987. Although Bloch does not use the critical term *gender*, and although as a literary critic his approach is different from Scott's, there are more similarities than differences between the two scholars: both are in fields of French, both are informed by deconstructive theories of language, and both are engaged in critique. And although Scott draws on Michel Foucault's work in her focus on historical questions, her Foucault is quite different from the Americanized version that soon came to absorb u.s. criticism. By the turn of the century, however, the kind of French theoretical work represented by Scott's and Bloch's essays of the mid-1980s was no longer dominant.

While I am rarely inclined (and certainly not qualified) to make historical generalizations, my guide in this case is the title of the journal *differences*. It was founding coeditor Naomi Schor who had the brilliantly prescient idea of the marked "s" of the title, the set-off "s" that would signal a particular theoretical and geographical split. A line from the journal's mission statement tells the story: "*differences: A Journal of Feminist Cultural*

Studies first appeared in 1989 at the moment of a critical encounter—a head-on collision, one might say—of theories of difference (primarily continental) and the politics of diversity (primarily American)" ("Journal").

For a time, the two approaches—that of difference and that of differences—coexisted and were mutually enriching. But by the time Scott declared the exhaustion of gender-as-critique in 1999, the discourse of diversity had made the theoretical space of difference relatively unintelligible.[7] Of course, one must not overstate the degree of unintelligibility. Poststructuralist theories of difference remain at work today in a number of quarters, including in the work of Judith Butler, which continues to theorize in powerful ways the explosive conjuncture of difference and differences.[8] Nevertheless, the slide to differences has brought about a major shift in the problematic or theoretical framework of much of u.s. feminist criticism. Whereas theories of difference look at the ways language—meaning—works through differential operations with no autonomous positive entities (every positivity produced differentially), the politics of differences engages with positivities in their appearance as *identities*, however multiple, contingent, and fluid these identities might be. The two problematics are very different and are not congruent—which does not mean that one cannot work with the productive friction between the two in theoretically and politically effective ways. Nonetheless, there is something like a consensus that the balance has finally shifted for good and that difference has finally given way to differences, that differential operations with no positivities have lost the ground to the multiplication of identities. And with this shift, the terrain of critique changes, and those who embrace the shift to differences come to view the work of critique as pointless. Who needs critique when the differences we embrace are there for all to see?

For critique, indeed, never stops at the surface. As Barbara Johnson writes, "[C]ritique reads backwards from what seems natural, obvious, self-evident, or universal in order to show that these things have their history, their reasons for being the way they are, their effects on what follows from them, and that the starting point is not a (natural) given but a (cultural) construct, usually blind to itself." Copernicus's critique of Ptolemy's conception of the universe, she writes, "is not an *improvement* of the idea that the sun goes around the earth. It is a shift in perspective which literally makes the ground move. It is a deconstruction of the commonsense perception of the obvious" (Translator's xv).

Having dismissed critique as pointless demystification, surface reading is thus free to pursue the commonsense perception of the obvious.

What renders this dismissal of critique particularly interesting is that it occurs at a time when gender, in its display of differences, has become ever more pervasive and plural now that it is powerfully inflected by categories such as *transgender* and *genderqueer*. In the context of this convergence, let me pose two additional questions: If, as the proponents of surface reading suggest, what you see is what you get, what is it that we see when we see gender? And if critique is seen to be exhausted in these times, how have the changing times contributed to this impression of exhaustion?

Suspicion of Suspicion

There is a way in which Best and Marcus's essay on surface reading is a frame-up. It is a frame-up aimed at exposing the vain effort of "symptomatic reading" seen as a practice of critique that looks to find a latent meaning in the manifest when all is actually there to be seen. Now, to say that critique is framed in Best and Marcus's essay is not to imply, with narrow suspicion, that there is a conspiracy to indict. This would be improbable given the critical acuity of the authors. But it does suggest that "Surface Reading" makes its argument against symptomatic reading within a frame that is at odds with the actual theoretical framework of critique. That is to say, critique is accused of doing something that it would not know how to do. *Why* the essay takes the form of a frame-up is a question I will defer until the end of this section. The question first is how the frame-up works.

Once again, I turn to the notion of the *problematic*, that particular framing concept developed by Louis Althusser. The problematic is not, as Althusser says, a worldview, but a theoretical or ideological framework in which any word or concept is thought. We do not think in isolation, he argues, but rather within a field of intelligibility and unintelligibility that changes historically. Drawing "on a fact peculiar to the very existence of science," a term he extends to all theorized knowledge, he writes: "[Science] can only pose problems on the terrain and within the horizon of a definite theoretical structure, its problematic, which constitutes its absolute and definite condition of possibility, and hence the absolute determination of the forms in which all problems must be posed, at any given moment in the science" (25).

Althusser derives the concept of the problematic from Marx, of course, for whom knowledge issues not from an idealist realm of thought but from materialist practice. For Marx, knowledge is *produced*, and it is produced differently in different historical conjunctures. "This thought,"

Althusser writes, "is the historically constituted system of an *apparatus of thought*, founded on and articulated to natural and social reality. It is defined by the system of real conditions which make it, if I dare use the phrase, a determinate *mode of production* of knowledges" (41). It is through such historically materialist analysis that Marx observes, for instance, that capitalist economics could not emerge until notions such as democracy, equivalence, and abstraction were produced and available.[9]

To see "Surface Reading" as a frame-up of critique, I draw thus on Althusser's reading of Marx and Freud as opposed to Ricoeur's. For Althusser, Marx and Freud are both materialist theorists who break with the fundamentally theological grounds of Enlightenment rationalism. This is not a break with which the philosopher Paul Ricoeur concurs. Nor is Ricoeur at all coy or evasive about the problematic that frames his philosophical formulations. He writes in his 1965 *Freud and Philosophy: An Essay on Interpretation* that his approach is based on "a confidence in language: a belief that language, which bears symbols, is not so much spoken by men as spoken to men, that men are born into language, into the light of the logos 'who enlightens anyone who comes into the world.'" This is the belief, Ricoeur says, that animates his work (29–30).

For Ricoeur, hermeneutics entails questions of symbolism and of interpretation, the *symbol* defined as having the structure of double or multiple meanings and *interpretation* as the work of deciphering symbols. What distinguishes modern hermeneutics, Ricoeur argues, is a crisis of language that causes the interpreter to oscillate between the restoration of meaning, on the one hand, and demystification, on the other (27). Those interpreters who focus on demystification belong to what he calls the "school of suspicion." What the practitioners of this school are suspicious of, Ricoeur says, is consciousness. And because for Marx, Nietszche, and Freud, "consciousness is not what it thinks it is," they as interpreters must establish "a new relation [. . .] between the patent and the latent," a new relation that corresponds "to the one that consciousness had instituted between appearances and the reality of things." According to Ricoeur, then, for Marx, Nietzsche, and Freud, the fundamental category of consciousness is the relation "hidden-shown" or "simulated-manifested," and the hypothesis they have in common is that of "false consciousness" (33–34).

It is within this problematic of Ricoeur's that Best and Marcus situate symptomatic reading, the practice that in their view endlessly and vainly seeks "a latent meaning behind a manifest one." The problem is that for Althusser, who coined the term, symptomatic reading framed in this way would be unrecognizable. As he formulates it, symptomatic reading is, rather, a practice that *breaks* with the very idea of a continuous or coherent relationship between manifest and latent. Such a continuous, coherent whole would be what Althusser calls an "expressive totality," a totality in which parts and whole express one another. Yet, it is precisely this totality that frames Ricoeur's notion of the ways the symbolic structure of multiple meanings operates. In the realm of religion, for example, Ricoeur writes that "it is a word [. . .] that *declares* the cosmic expressiveness, thanks to the double meaning of the words earth, heaven, water, life, etc. The world's expressiveness achieves language through symbol as double meaning." Similarly, in the realm of dreams, "the manifest meaning endlessly refers to hidden meaning; that is what makes every dreamer a poet" (14–15).

The contrast with Althusser could not be more striking. For Althusser, there is a theoretical and political imperative to relinquish the fantasy of the expressive totality:

> *Need I add that once we have broken with the religious complicity between Logos and Being; between the Great Book that was, in its very being, the World, and the discourse of the knowledge of the world; between the essence of things and its reading;—once we have broken those tacit pacts in which the men of a still fragile age secured themselves with magical alliances against the precariousness of history and the trembling of their own daring—need I add that, once we have broken these ties, a new conception of discourse at last becomes possible? (17)*[10]

Both terms in Althusser's formulation of symptomatic reading are telling. *Reading* ceases to be the revealing or decipherment of concealed or encrypted knowledge and becomes the work of engaging with the ways a given text might open up gaps and blind spots in its problematic. This, too, Althusser learns from Marx. That is, he looks at how Marx discovers the epistemological break that capital represents, by attending not to what the classical political economists say but to what they don't know they are saying.[11] As for *symptomatic*, far from being an *index* to the unknown as in the medical model, the symptom for Althusser refers to unconscious operations that are legible only in their effects. In this case, it is Lacan whom Althusser credits for having shown him how Freud reads the unconscious. In fact, one can go directly to Freud for the insight. Unlike Ricoeur, who sees the relationship between the conscious and the unconscious—between "the patent and the latent"—as just a reworking of the familiar relationship between "appearances and the reality of things," Freud sees structural dislocations at work between conscious reality and "the other scene." In his 1900 *The Interpretation of Dreams*, he looks at the way "dream-work" transforms the latent "dream-thoughts" into the manifest content of the dream. While analytic interpretation can ultimately elucidate the dream-thoughts, it is the dream-work, Freud insists, that is the essence of the dream. As he underlines in a later footnote in 1914: "It has long been the habit to regard dreams as identical with their manifest content; but now we must beware equally of the mistake of confusing dreams with latent dream-thoughts" (580n1). And in an even later footnote in 1925, he expresses his frustration with analysts who cling with "obstinacy" to the idea that the essence of the dream resides in its latent content, thus overlooking that "dreams are nothing other than a particular *form* of thinking" and that "[i]t is the *dream-work* which creates that form, and it alone is the essence of dreaming" (506–7n2).

Because of the dream-work, the relationship between the latent and manifest for Freud is not simply hidden, as Ricoeur asserts, but distorted. And the work that produces distortion is particularly evident in the case of *overdetermination*, in which chains of associations can have multiple meaningful sequences on multiple levels of interpretation—due to condensation, displacement, and so forth—without there being any coherent unity. Indeed, for Freud, the very relationship between the conscious and the unconscious is characterized by an irreducible break.[12]

Moreover, the break is not limited to the Freudian unconscious. To read Marx and Freud through the Althusserian problematic rather than that of Ricoeur is to see a break in *reality itself*. Ricoeur declares that the new relation between "the patent and the latent" will correspond to "the one that consciousness had instituted between appearances and the reality of things." Read through a different problematic, there is indeed a new relationship between "the patent and the latent," but not only does it not correspond to the familiar relationship between appearance and reality, but that familiar relationship itself has changed. With Freud and Marx, there is a dislocation in the real.

∎

Perhaps the best way to see the dislocation in the real is to consider Marx's formulation of the logic of capital, the logic that dominates the *now* to which Best and Marcus refer. Recall Marx's analysis of the commodity form, which he calls the cell form of capital. As he writes in the first chapter of *Capital*, the commodity appears to be "a very trivial thing, and easily understood," but upon analysis one discovers "that it is, in reality, a very queer thing" (76). To evoke its queerness, Marx uses the figure of the *fetish*, the name early mercantile traders gave to what they believed to be objects of worship among West African peoples.[13] For Marx, the capitalist commodity, like the fetish, takes on magical properties, not because of what it is, but because of what it does, how it produces its value.

You will remember the warm and wooly coat Marx uses to illustrate how fetishistic magic works. In the capitalist mode of production, he writes, the value of a coat comes not from its warm wooly nature but from how much labor-time goes into making it. Such labor-time is not that of the individual tailor, of course, but the abstraction of flesh and blood labor into an average amount of time required for industrial production. It is thus that the market value of the coat-as-commodity is dependent upon the labor-time required to make it, and that equivalence is expressed through the commodity form of money.

It is not, therefore, its wooly warmth that determines the coat's value, but another commodity. Here, however, is where the fetish magic comes in. The commodity coat presents itself, Marx says, just *as if* its value—its price—emanated from its warm wooly nature. There is a kind of double displacement at work. The relationship between the commodity coat and the commodity money is made possible by a social relationship among people based on the exploitation of the commodity labor power and the extraction of surplus value—an exploitative relationship that is hidden by the exchange of one commodity for another. But—and here is the second displacement—that relationship between things does not proclaim itself as such. On the market, it *seems* as if the coat's value, its cost, has to do with the use-value of its wooly warmth. But if, on the market, appearance and reality can seem to realign, commodities know the truth. "If commodities could speak," Marx writes, "they would say this: our use-value may interest men, but it does not belong to us as objects. [. . .] We relate to each other merely as exchange-values" (176–77).

■

There is something about the commodity fetish that might shed light on the mystery as to why "Surface Reading" frames critique the way it does, why it pins on critique the misleading story of surface and depth. Indeed, the frame-up is particularly baffling considering the contrast Best and Marcus establish between the *then* (when the authors "cut their intellectual teeth" on deconstruction, ideology critique, and symptomatic reading) and the *now*. In fact, it was the Marx and Freud of Althusser's reading that dominated then, certainly not Ricoeur's hermeneutics of suspicion.[14] Assuming Best and Marcus do not aim to reinscribe a pretheoretical, ontotheological problematic, one must look elsewhere to understand their frame.

I can only speculate (with a nod to Sedgwick) as to why the strong thematics of suspicion seem to eclipse all other theoretical considerations. The reason might well have to do with the authors' claims that times have changed. Examples they give of the change are events like Abu Ghraib and Katrina, events that seem to require no demystification. These are persuasive examples, and there are surely many reasons why critique seems so superfluous in such cases: the development of visual culture, the twenty-four-hour news cycle, the dominance of the political Right. At the same time, it is worth noting how charged the irritation with demystification is, a charge nowhere more striking than in Best and Marcus's calls for "political realism." Given their doubts as to ever attaining the "higher perspicacity" to see beyond ideology, it is time, they say, for a "less heroic" view of what criticism can achieve, time to abandon the "freedom dream that accompanies the work of demystification."

I would suggest that the reason demystification is such a charged concept in the Best and Marcus essay has something to do with the particular way the logic of capital works in these times. Consider the difference between 1867, the year *Capital* was published, and now. On the one hand, although finance and global capitalism are a good deal more complicated than the industrial economy of Marx's time, the fundamental logic of capital as expressed by the primitive commodity form remains the same. On the other hand, our relationship to it does not. In 1867, the capitalist form of value was a recent enough phenomenon that it could pass itself off as precapitalist, as if the commodity coat's value emanated from its warmth. And for decades, critics worked to warn us about such trickery and about the pitfalls of false consciousness. But that was then. Today we need to be reminded *not* that the commodity has a magical secret but *why* commodity fetishism was once considered magical. As consumers, we view the commodity fetish much as the sexual subject views his fetish: we know we are dealing with commodities and not wooly warmth and we don't care. We know that what we see is not simply what we see; but we also know that there is no true thing behind what we see, and we don't care. We are all practiced fetishists. Hence the irritation, perhaps, with seemingly anachronistic commitments to critique. Of what use can demystification be when the commodity has lost its magic and when the alluring surface offers so much more?

The Lure of Gender

Recent inflections of gender in the forms of transgender and genderqueer are not strangers to commodification. Beginning at least as early as January 2014 with the Barney's ad campaign that featured some twenty transgender models, the transgender brand has proved successful. And although many transgender activists are highly critical of the marketing of figures such as Caitlyn Jenner, such commodification can be seen to reassure a general public that what might seem unsettling is actually business as usual. What is of more interest here, however, is not the commodification of gender, but some structural similarities between gender as commonly understood, on the one hand, and the commodity fetish, on the other. Both claim as theirs a certain freedom from foundationalism.

Clearly, it is important to move carefully here. No progressive critic or activist of the last forty years would want to relinquish gender fluidity. No one who has struggled against misogynist and homophobic essentialism has any interest in restoring the foundation of the "natural body." The challenge is to know how to think about the historical conjuncture in which we work. As Catherine Malabou asks in the context of her work on neuroplasticity: "What should we do so that consciousness of the brain does not purely and simply coincide with the spirit of capitalism?" (12). Might we, in an analogous vein, ask about gender and the logic of capital?

Capital's logic is, indeed, most wily in its power. In this world of advanced global capitalism, we have fluidity: freedom from the limits of foundational essences; freedom purportedly to choose, to change, to perform what we want to be. At the same time, all of this freedom and flexibility is contained within a globe, that smooth figure of totalization. What triumphal figures, the fetish and the globe, the fetish offering unalloyed foundationless freedom within a global sphere that forecloses all alternatives and shuts out the horizon by the curve of its arc. Our legacy then: the fetish that tells us there is nothing worth knowing and the globe that guarantees there is nothing more to know.

Gender as commonly understood—the gender of the problematic of *differences*—is wily in its own right in that the register in which it works is that of the lure. A lure is something that attracts and entices, normally through imitation, as with a decoy. And as with the decoy, the enticement is to *identify*.[15] With gender, however, unlike with the hunter's decoy, gender identification can be said to be its own reward, the reward of being self-same even if multiple, fluctuating, or indeterminate—but *only* on the condition that identification is felt to be free of coercion, free of cultural demands that seem to be murderous of one's true being. The celebrants of gender fluidity see gender as finally freed from the realm of demand. Whereas yesterday it was coerced, today freedom is its to claim.[16]

There are critiques, of course, that put this celebratory freedom in question. Butler has repeatedly argued that the performativity of gender, as she theorizes it, is incommensurate with notions of "freedom of choice." Some psychoanalytic critics see the lure of gender freedom leading—like the hunter's lure—to a fantasmatic trap. The trap would consist of imagining that if anatomy doesn't determine gender, there are, in fact, no limits. But for the psychoanalytic critics, there is indeed a limit, one that Freud calls "castration," the break that introduces the human subject into the bounds of *finitude*, the break in being that permanently dislocates the real.

In a reading of Freud's essay "The 'Uncanny,'" Samuel Weber evokes the structure of castration, remarking that it is not "an event or mere fantasy," but "as a structure bears implications both for the articulation of the subject and for its access to reality" (1113). The problem is that the child's discovery is a "nondiscovery." "Not only," Weber writes, "do the eyes present the subject with the shocking 'evidence' of a negative perception—the absence of a maternal phallus—but they also have to bear the brunt of a new state of affairs," that the subject "will never again be able to believe its eyes, since what they have seen is neither simply visible nor wholly invisible. [. . .] What is involved here," he goes on, "is a restructuring of experience, including the relation of perception, in which the narcissistic categories of identity and presence are riven by a difference they can no longer subdue or command" (1113). Indeed, as Barbara Johnson has remarked, *castration* is an interpretation not of presence and absence but of irreducible difference ("Frame" 243).[17] It is thus, Weber says, that castration has no referent but itself, ushering in the undecidability of signification and the unknowability of sexual difference. And it is thus that the "phallus" comes to designate for psychoanalysis the irreducible break between signifier and signified. With no definitive answers forthcoming, with no repair in sight, there is nothing for the subject to do but to assume castration—or not.

For if, following the Freudian reading, there is no way to escape castration, there are certainly many fetishistic ways to refuse it—if we understand the fetishistic structure of disavowal not just in its restricted sense but as a more generalized response to castration.[18] Psychoanalysis cautions that the refusal of castration has its costs and that only by renouncing the fantasy of plenitude and of total satisfaction can one have access to some satisfaction. That is to say, a fantasy of unfettered freedom can be seen to undermine all freedom. But freedom can be a difficult challenge in the context of finitude. Psychoanalyst Ona Nierenberg reminds us that the whole purpose of the phallic function—the "paternal" no—is "[t]o signify the impossible as the prohibited." She elaborates: "The fact that signification itself makes it appear that the unattainable is forbidden keeps producing the illusion that we can remove or at least protect against the obstacle as such. [. . .] What the subject as well as theory must admit is that we cannot have access to the impossible by removing the prohibition: the operation is irreversible. [. . .] The only vector for our little piece of freedom is via the paradox of assuming castration in all its incompleteness, with all its limits and losses" (10–11).[19]

One must be careful, of course, not to collapse the clinical into the critical: there are limits to the ways the two registers overlap. At the same time, the elaboration of gender-without-castration—which is the dominant formulation within the problematic of gender-as-identity—risks mirroring not only the logic of capital but also the neoliberal rationalism that underpins it. How paradoxical that the fetishistic logic of capital should be underwritten by a triumphal rationality that has little use for magic. And if we forget the unconscious, if we allow reason to persuade us that what we see is what we see, as Best and Marcus suggest, what resources do we have to think about questions of sexual violence, of misogyny, of homophobia, of racialized hatred, and the like? How can we think even more fundamentally about the position of the human subject-of-finitude within the universalized circulation of capital without limits, a capital that never dies? None of these questions can be addressed by surface reading. Nor by the formulaic critical practices that Eve Sedgwick excoriates, those practices that know in advance what they triumphantly uncover. To practice critique in times dominated by the logic of capital means not only that one cannot know in advance what one will find but that *knowing* itself has its structural limits.

When it comes to gender, *castration* is the limit. The move in the 1990s on the part of queer theorists to separate sex from gender may have restricted gender's critical terrain, but it also served to free gender from castration.[20] That is, by moving away from Freud's formulation of sexuality to a more legible Foucaultian one, the new sex/gender divide put gender firmly within the problematic of identity and hence safe from the unknowability of sexual difference.[21]

At the end of his essay on Freud's uncanny, Weber cautions that "it would be precipitate to ontologize 'castration' before having clarified its relation to [. . .] historical factors." The historical factors he refers to are those of capital and the commodity: "[C]apital is also described by Marx in terms of the return of 'dead labor' of the past, which 'lives like a vampire sucking up living labor, and which thrives all the more, the more it devours'" (qtd. in 1133) For Weber, it is cheering to recognize that in the face of such vampiric force the uncanny "has lost little of its actuality." Surely one can say the same of sexuality.

ELIZABETH WEED is founding coeditor, with Naomi Schor, of *difference*s, which she currently edits with Ellen Rooney. She is emerita director of the Pembroke Center and emerita member of the Modern Culture and Media faculty at Brown University. Her work in progress is (still) "Reading for Consolation."

Notes

1   In the philosophical turn to speculative realism, for example, Quentin Meillassoux's *After Finitude* gleefully discards critique along with the constraints of the Kantian notion of transcendental knowledge.

2   Commenting that screwball conspiracy theories have come to resemble "a teachable version of social critique," Latour sees a danger in continuing to teach critical unveiling: "What if explanations resorting automatically to power, society, discourse had outlived their usefulness and deteriorated to the point of now feeding the most gullible sort of critique?" (229–30).

3   Critique, which asks the conditions of possibility of a given knowledge, cannot know in advance what those conditions are. It is worth noting that Sedgwick makes her argument for weak theoretical reading by means of a strong one, something she acknowledges (see 145). For more on this, see Love.

4   Absent in Best and Marcus's reliance on *The Political Unconscious* is any acknowledgment of Jameson's spirited engagement with Althusser's notion of structural causality.

5   Best and Marcus are among those who see congruence (10–11).

6   See Rooney on the question of description.

7   It was then that *woman* became illegible as a critical term, replaced (some would argue corrected) by *women* and later *intersectionality*. The new problematic that replaced "French theory" was gradually introduced into France. See Berger's analysis of this transatlantic (ex)change.

8   Nonetheless, Butler's readers can often miss the challenges to intelligibility that her work engages.

9   See, for example, *Capital* 163–77.

10   See also Lacan, who writes that Marx announces that "history is instating another dimension of discourse and opening up the possibility of completely subverting the function of discourse as such, and of philosophical discourse, strictly speaking, insofar as a world view is based on the latter" (*On Feminine* 30).

11   For Althusser's reading of the way Marx thus formulates the unposed

question of "labor power," see part 1 of *Reading Capital*.

12   In "Psychoanalysis as Anti-hermeneutics," Jean Laplanche argues that symbolic associations block access to the unconscious: "[A]ccording to Freud, *when symbolism speaks, associations are silent*" (8). It is the notion of overdetermination that enables Althusser to theorize the Marxist totality as a "structure in dominance" as against the (more legible) expressive totality of base and superstructure.

13   In the imagination of the Portuguese traders, the people taken to be primitive natives were seen as worshipping inert objects, hence the Portuguese name *feitico*, from the Latin *facticius*. See Pietz.

14   Ricoeur was indeed viewed by many poststructuralist theorists as an adversary.

15   See Lacan's discussion of the lure in *Seminar XI*, particularly the relationship between the lure and *méconnaissance*, a relationship that sheds light on the lure as *bait* as well as *decoy* (*Four*).

16   Of course, there is no one stance with regard to the fluidity of gender, but rather a spectrum ranging from the subject who expresses the need to correct the relationship

between gender and anatomy to the radical genderqueer subject.

17   Addressing the question of the referential status of the missing phallus, Johnson writes: "[E]ven on this referential level, is the object of observation really a lack? Is it not instead an interpretation—an interpretation ('castration') not of a lack but of a *difference*? If what is observed is irreducibly anatomical, what is anatomy here but the irreducibility of difference?" ("Frame" 243).

18   See Tracy McNulty's essay "Speculative Fetishism," which argues that current philosophical movements such as speculative realism and the new materialism can be read not just as classic instances of fetishistic disavowal of maternal castration but, in their embrace of the absolute, as radical refusals of the linguistic turn, contestations of the signifier itself.

19   Best and Marcus's interest in "the ways constraints structure existence" ironically parallels the psychoanalytic view.

20   See Weed and Schor.

21   The relationship between a cordoned-off gender and the question of misogyny has not, to my knowledge, received serious critical attention. This deceptively legible question would demand critique.

Works Cited

Althusser, Louis, and Étienne Balibar. *Reading Capital.* Trans. Ben Brewster. London: Verso, 1979.

Berger, Anne Emmanuelle. *The Queer Turn in Feminism: Identities, Sexualities, and the Theater of Gender.* Trans. Catherine Porter. New York: Fordham UP, 2014.

Best, Stephen, and Sharon Marcus. "Surface Reading: An Introduction." *The Way We Read Now.* Spec. issue of *Representations* 108.1 (2009): 1–21.

Bloch, R. Howard. "Medieval Misogyny." *Misogyny, Misandry, and Misanthropy.* Ed. R. Howard Bloch and Frances Ferguson. Berkeley: U of California P, 1989. 1–24.

Freud, Sigmund. *The Interpretation of Dreams (Second Part)*. 1900. *The Standard Edition of the Complete Psychological Works of Sigmund Freud*. Trans. and ed. James Strachey. Vol. 5. London: Hogarth, 1953. 339–686. 24 vols. 1953–74.

Jameson, Fredric. *The Political Unconscious: Narrative as Socially Symbolic Act*. Ithaca: Cornell UP, 1981.

Johnson, Barbara. "The Frame of Reference: Poe, Lacan, Derrida." *The Purloined Poe. Lacan, Derrida, and Psychoanalytic Reading*. Ed. John P. Muller and William J. Richardson. Baltimore: Johns Hopkins UP, 1988. 213–51.

————. Translator's Introduction. *Dissemination*. Jacques Derrida. Trans. Barbara Johnson. Chicago: U of Chicago P, 1981. vii–xxxiii.

"Journal." *Pembroke Center for Teaching and Research on Women*. https://www.brown.edu /research/pembroke-center/journal (accessed 25 March 2016).

Lacan, Jacques. *Encore: On Feminine Sexuality, the Limits of Love and Knowledge, 1972–1973: The Seminar of Jacques Lacan, Book XX*. Trans. Bruce Fink. Ed. Jacques-Alain Miller. New York: Norton, 1998.

————. *The Four Fundamental Concepts of Psychoanalysis: The Seminar of Jacques Lacan, Book XI*. Trans. Alan Sheridan. Ed. Jacques-Alain Miller. New York: Norton, 1998.

Laplanche, Jean. "Psychoanalysis as Anti-hermeneutics." Trans. Luke Thurston. *Radical Philosophy* 79 (1996): 7–12.

Latour, Bruno. "Why Has Critique Run out of Steam? From Matters of Fact to Matters of Concern." *Critical Inquiry* 30.2 (2004): 225–48.

Love, Heather. "Truth and Consequences: On Paranoid Reading and Reparative Reading." *Criticism* 52.2 (2010): 235–41.

Malabou, Catherine. *What Should We Do with Our Brain?* Trans. Sebastian Rand. New York: Fordham UP, 2008.

Marx, Karl. *Capital: A Critique of Political Economy*. Vol. 1. Trans. Ben Fowkes. New York: Vintage, 1977.

McLoughlin, Nancy. *Jean Gerson and Gender: Rhetoric and Politics in Fifteenth-Century France*. London: Palgrave Macmillan, 2015.

McNulty, Tracy. "Speculative Fetishism." *Konturen* 8 (2015): 99–132.

Meillassoux, Quentin. *After Finitude: An Essay on the Necessity of Contingency*. Trans. Ray Brassier. London: Bloomsbury, 2014.

Nierenberg. Ona. "On the Specificity of the Phallus: Some Considerations." Lecture. 6 July 2014. Affiliated Psychoanalytic Workshops Study Weekend. Seminar 4: Object Relations. International Colleges, Dublin.

Pietz, William. "The Problem of the Fetish, 1." *RES: Anthropology and Aesthetics* 9 (1985): 5–17.

Pruchnic, Jeff. "Postcritical Theory? Demanding the Possible." *Criticism* 54.4 (2012): 637–57.

Ricoeur, Paul. *Freud and Philosophy: An Essay on Interpretation*. Trans. Denis Savage. New Haven: Yale UP, 1970.

Rooney, Ellen. "Live Free or Describe: The Reading Effect and the Persistence of Form." *Reading Remains*. Spec. issue of *differences* 21.3 (2010): 112–39.

Scott, Joan Wallach. "Gender: A Useful Category of Historical Analysis." *Gender and the Politics of History*. Rev. ed. New York: Columbia UP, 1999.

Sedgwick, Eve Kosofsky. "Paranoid Reading and Reparative Reading, or, You're So Paranoid, You Probably Think This Essay Is about You." *Touching Feeling: Affect, Pedagogy, Performativity*. Durham: Duke UP, 2003. 123–51.

Tomkins, Silvan. *Affect Imagery Consciousness*. 4 vols. New York: Springer, 1962–92.

Weber, Samuel. "The Sideshow, or: Remarks on a Canny Moment." MLN 88.6 (1973): 1102–33.

Weed, Elizabeth, and Naomi Schor, eds. *More Gender Trouble: Feminism Meets Queer Theory*. Spec. issue of *differences* 2–3 (1994).

Gender is/in French

Against Theoretical Nationalism

*I*n 1987, when I first came from France to start teaching in the United States, a graduate student at Brandeis University asked me: "Do you like Theory?" Unfortunately, I could not hear the capital "T," nor understand her use of the term at the time; but, given my national origin, she assumed that I did. I must have disappointed this literature student from the United States by responding less as a Frenchman than as a social scientist: I naively invoked Émile Durkheim's epistemology (derived from that of Claude Bernard) to reject any opposition between empirical and theoretical work. I later realized the nature of our misunderstanding, however: she was obviously thinking of Jacques Derrida and other French authors then in vogue in u.s. academia, especially in some literature departments. As a French academic in the United States, with an interest in public controversies such as the one raised that very same year by Allan Bloom's *Closing of the American Mind*, I soon felt obligated to catch up with Theory, eventually becoming one of François Cusset's informants as he wrote an intellectual history of "French Theory." The title of his book may sound English, but its Frenchness becomes apparent when used in a sentence. While "Theory" is

Volume 27, Number 2   DOI 10.1215/10407391-3621771

an intellectual construction from the United States, it translates into French as "*la* French Theory."[1] Conversely, the phrase seems to have entered the English language only with the translation of Cusset's book by a u.s. press: "French Theory" turns out to be French—literally.

This transatlantic crossing was already explicit in Derrida's own writings. In 1984, at the University of California, Irvine, he provocatively proclaimed: "America *is* deconstruction," an italicized exclamation reinforced by the Gallicism in the French version: *l'Amérique, mais* c'est *la déconstruction*. The irony of this proposition became even more explicit during a conference organized around the French philosopher at New York University in 1993, published two years later in a book under the same title: *Deconstruction is/in America*. In his keynote address, as he quoted his own declaration from the previous decade, Derrida attempted a definition undermining identification through the deconstruction of the copula: "And perhaps deconstruction would consist, if at least it did consist, in precisely that: deconstructing, dislocating, displacing, disarticulating, disjoining, putting 'out of joint' the authority of the 'is.'" This was no anticipation of a famous legal defense by Bill Clinton ("it depends upon what the meaning of the word 'is' is"). Rather, it was the theoretical condition preventing any essentialization of "Frenchness" or "Americanness": "Deconstruction, as we know it, will have been first of all a translation or a transference between French and American (which is to say also, as Freud has reminded us about transference, a love story, which never excludes hatred, as we know)" (Derrida 25–27). I wish to borrow from Derrida's paradoxical exclamation, and from the ambiguous title of the 1993 conference, to dispute the alleged "Americanness" of gender.

My argument comes in response to the dominant definition in French public debates of sexual issues in terms of national identity. The conference I co-organized in May 2014 at the University of Paris 8 with my colleague Anne Emmanuelle Berger, leading to this special issue of *differences*, was titled Le printemps international du genre. This "international spring" ironically echoed an echo: in reference to the media phrase "Arab Spring," "Le printemps français" ("The French Spring") had taken over from "La manif pour tous" ("Demonstration for All"), a reactionary movement that mobilized against *Mariage pour tous* (*Marriage for All*), the bill opening marriage (and therefore adoption) to same-sex couples. A year after the passage of the law, the international (and not just French-u.s.) program of our conference was a response to the culturalism of enemies of both equal rights and gender studies. Indeed, one of their banners read: "Mariage pour tous = théorie du gender pour tous." This eloquent slogan signified that so-called gender theory and equal marriage partake of the same logic (as the Vatican had long argued). Moreover, despite the fact that the 2013 Taubira law preceded the 2015 U.S. Supreme Court decision *Obergefell v. Hodges* on marriage, writing the word *gender* in English suggested that this logic is American, and therefore un-French.

The connotation needed no explanation: in France, the resistance to gender studies has played on this nationalist theme for decades. Indeed, anti-Americanism and antifeminism have long been happily "married," as Judith Ezekiel, a U.S. academic based in France, wrote in 1995. The very same year, Mona Ozouf, a French historian until then better known for her work on the Revolution than on feminism, published an essay that confirmed this argument. With respect to femininity, she claimed and proclaimed the existence of a "French singularity" defined in opposition to an American countermodel: the cultural legacy of the Old Regime in France, based on the art of conversation enjoyed in the salons, mitigated "democratic passions" and allowed for a kinder, gentler version of feminism than in the United States; Ozouf thus contrasted the aristocratic "commerce of the sexes" with the "war of the sexes" allegedly defining "America." Feminist historian Joan Wallach Scott responded critically: why nationalize gender issues thus, if not to undermine feminism itself? My own analysis of this transatlantic controversy focused on two questions: "If what we are discussing is gender, why should national character play such a prominent role in the debate? And if we are discussing transatlantic matters, what's love gotta do with it?" (Fassin, "Purloined" 117).

This polemic resurfaced in 2011 at the time of the DSK (Dominique Strauss-Kahn) scandal, when the French head of the International Monetary Fund (IMF) was arrested in New York on charges of rape. When the *New York Times* asked U.S. academics for their reactions, while feminist historian Bonnie Smith insisted that "the Strauss-Kahn saga has nothing to do with Frenchness," her colleague Scott denounced the persistent rhetoric of Frenchness in French intellectual life—namely those, like Ozouf and her disciple Claude Habib, who had long rejected feminism as "a foreign import" that they perceived as a threat to a glorified "art of seduction" understood as "a trait of national character" (Scott, "Feminism?"). The counterattack launched in the French press by sociologist Irène Théry and later joined by Ozouf and Habib only validated this critique by reclaiming *le féminisme à la française*. The difference between the two perspectives was clear: while Théry needed no scare quotes as she identified with a supposedly French brand of feminism, Scott characterized it as a political trope disputed not only in the United States but also by numerous feminists in France. Indeed, in the French press, some of the latter disputed the nationalist argument developed by authors whose Frenchness was better established than their feminism. "French feminism has no existence," they claimed: "[I]n the 1970s the 'F' in MLF [the French Women's Liberation Movement] stood for 'Femmes,' not 'French'" (Fassin, "Au-delà" 51). In other words, there is still no good reason, except for conservative purposes, to nationalize feminism—and therefore gender.

Refuting both the essence of a French feminism and the fundamental Americanness of gender is necessary to respond adequately to another, more challenging critique that has been leveled not from a conservative but, on the contrary, from an anti-imperialist perspective. At the end of the 1990s, French sociologists Pierre Bourdieu and Loïc Wacquant warned against "the cunning of imperialist reason": not only does cultural imperialism apply to dominant categories, such as economic ones; according to them, it also extends to fields "perceived to be marginal or subversive" that are equally caught "in this huge international cultural import-export business." It is true that *gender* as such is not named in this piece, which is worth noting, considering that the article is contemporaneous with Bourdieu's *Masculine Domination*, a book that certainly cannot be accused of importing American gender studies into France. But while the primary target of their critique of critical discourses is "race" (along with "minorities"), the range of the attack is wide, including "Cultural Studies, Minority Studies, Gay Studies or Women's Studies" (50–51). Should one not worry that this anti-imperialist critique resonates, though for opposite political reasons, with that of conservative supporters of "La manif pour tous" who denounce gender studies as an American import alien to French culture? In order to respond both to conservatives and to anti-imperialists, one might argue that the international circulation of *gender* is about translating, rather than importing—the difference lying in contextualization.

Grammatical Gender

Thinking in terms of translation, and therefore of language, helps move beyond a merely negative contention that simply rejects the nationalization of theory. It will not suffice to deny the untranslatability of gender studies. On a positive note, I want to argue here, in a somewhat counterintuitive fashion, in favor of the "Frenchness" of gender. Obviously, the idea is not to make a plea for a French origin of gender studies, which would amount to reinstating the theoretical nationalism that I have just argued should be discarded. Of course, in response to antifeminist critics of "theory of gender for all," it might be tempting to establish Simone de Beauvoir as a founding mother of the field. "One is not born, but rather becomes, a woman": it is true that this famous axiom from *The Second Sex* in 1949 could very well be considered the theoretical principle underlying the feminist appropriation of the concept of gender by young u.s. anthropologists such as Gayle Rubin a quarter of a century later; but the more interesting point might be that these feminists made international circulation explicit in their own foundational moment as they invoked French references, starting with Beauvoir. From this point on, Frenchness should be understood not in broadly cultural but in specifically linguistic terms: moving beyond the nationalization of gender, the argument is about the inscription of gender in the French language.

This implies taking grammar seriously. Scott's landmark 1986 article defining gender for several generations opens with an epigraph borrowed from Fowler's venerable *Dictionary of Modern English Usage*: "Gender. n. a grammatical term only. To talk of persons or creatures of the masculine or feminine gender, meaning of the male or female sex, is either a jocularity (permissible or not according to context) or a blunder" (qtd. in Scott, "Gender" 28). The irony of this quotation suggests that feminist studies must look beyond grammar to make gender into a "useful category." Today, while continuing Scott's work, could we not turn things around and consider grammar itself from a gender perspective? This is what I suggested in a *disputatio* that took place in 2011 in the Cathedral of Rouen with a Catholic theologian, Véronique Margron, on what the publisher of the resulting book, *Hommes, femmes: quelle différence?*, in the context of emerging public polemics about biology textbooks, was to label the "theory of gender." "In French, the word *gender* is familiar to all. Starting with primary school, we hear about the gender of nouns—contrary to what happens with the English language. Masculine, feminine (to say nothing of neuter): early on, we understand that gender is but a convention. *La chaise* (chair) is no more female than *le fauteuil* (armchair) is male" (Fassin and Margron 25).

My argument went on. "The comparison between languages is also a reminder: for example, the different gender of moon and sun is reversed if one speaks in German instead of French. The arbitrary nature of the sign, according to Saussure, is equivalent to the arbitrary social conventions of gender. According to usage, women are expected to sit on restaurant benches (*banquettes*), men on chairs (*sièges*); but from this it would be absurd to conclude that the former are male, and the latter female" (Fassin and Margron 25). The fact that my translation of the original text leaves words in French is but a reminder that grammatical gender does not translate into English, at least as far as nouns are concerned. The experience of the language suggests that an understanding of the nongrammatical definition of gender is facilitated by the grammatical practice in French. This stands in sharp contrast to those who argue that because feminist theories of gender are rooted in an English-language intellectual tradition, the concept itself must remain unintelligible to French speakers. Relating grammatical gender and gender studies is not simply an analogy, nor is it a mere pun. The experience of gender in the language is much more than metaphorical.

While it is well known that the language is a key to French national identity, it is worth emphasizing that mastering the language is very much considered a matter of spelling: even today, twenty-five years after it was first decided, implementing a minor reform in education that affects relatively few words still raises a storm: for spelling is about schooling. Indeed, far from being a theory of the language, what is called *grammar* only developed as a practical tool for pedagogical purposes. Historian of education André Chervel has demonstrated that school grammar is but an *ex post* justification of the vagaries of spelling, developed for the sole purpose of educating masses of children, starting with the Revolution, and to a greater degree under the Third Republic. In fact, the central exercise in primary school (even more than the multiplication tables) has long been *dictée*, which to this day remains a nostalgic political site if not one of Pierre Nora's *lieux de mémoire*. Dictation has functioned as a litmus test, selecting candidates based on their results for the diplomas of *certificat d'études* and *brevet*, and consequently for access to employment (especially in government administration). This explains why such an austere school exercise has fascinated French society for ages, as attested by the twenty-year-long public success of the *Dictée de Bernard Pivot* (presented on television by the most famous literary journalist).

But these dictations are not mere spelling bees; syntax is crucial. This is where gender plays a crucial role. Much of syntax is about singular and plural, but also about masculine and feminine, namely both number and gender. Socialization in the French language is thus also a form of socialization in gender. The point is not just what linguist Marina Yaguello has amusingly called "the sex of words." More important, perhaps, gender is inscribed in grammatical agreement. Of course, this is true for every person that uses the language, especially with the intricacy of the rules of agreement of past participles following the auxiliary verb *avoir* when preceded by a direct object pronoun (not to mention the ultimate difficulty: those of pronominal verbs). But this is especially true for women. Speech in the first person is a gendered exercise in gender: to speak in the feminine, one needs to pay attention to spelling and pronunciation in almost every sentence. This is even more the case in writing (since the addition of a feminine "e" cannot always be heard in conversation). The point is not just that men and women speak a different language; in practice, whether writing or speaking, women can never forget their own gender as they try to conform to grammatical rules. Gender is inscribed in the language; but as a consequence, the French language inscribes gender in speakers, especially female ones.

This rather obvious point is often overlooked. But one should not imagine that it has gone unnoticed throughout French history. In fact, it sheds light on the political battles concerning gender in the French language. The most visible today probably concerns the feminization of titles and names of professions. The political nature of this issue surfaced in a recent public controversy: on October 7, 2014, a conservative *député* was fined for his insistence on calling the Socialist Sandrine Mazetier, who then presided over the National Assembly, *Madame le Président*, thus rejecting her repeated request for the feminine version: *la Présidente*. (In an earlier incident, on January 16 of the same year, she had ironically responded by feminizing his title: *Monsieur la Députée*.) This representative invoked the authority of the French Academy that refuses systematic feminization on account of the gender neutrality of functions; but on this occasion, the Immortals disagreed as they made it clear that the rule must "give way to the legitimate wishes of individuals" (Académie).

In a short historical essay on the gender politics of the French language, Old Regime specialist Éliane Viennot reverses the question, speaking of "masculinization" rather than "feminization." Her argument is that there has been a concerted misogynistic effort by grammarians and other specialists of the language, starting with the seventeenth century and up to the end of the nineteenth, to establish the masculine gender's grammatical preeminence, and thus its social authority. A case in point is precisely *autrice*—the feminine version of *auteur*: what is at stake, beyond the word itself, is the reality behind it, that is, the existence of female authors who question the monopoly these men want to maintain on language and literature. This masculinization led to the imposition of a rule of agreement that all schoolchildren learn to this day: "the masculine prevails over the feminine" (*le masculin l'emporte sur le féminin*). Until the sixteenth century, proximity agreement was the rule, as it was in Latin: the closest noun defined the gender and number of the adjective. In the next century, starting with Malherbe, this rule came under attack. The new grammatical logic that he and his successors imposed was explicitly modeled after social hierarchy. As Vaugelas (among the first members of the French academy) put it a generation later, "the masculine gender is nobler"; but as yet another grammarian, Beauzée, explained in the eighteenth century, that is "because of the superiority of the male over the female" (Viennot 65–75). In reaction, some feminists are fighting today to restore proximity agreement (including the publisher of Viennot's book). Indeed, the gender politics of the French language clearly reflect gender politics in France.

The Theater of Words

Grammar is a political battleground, or perhaps the stage on which the battle scene of gender is performed. A play first presented in July 2015 during the Avignon theater festival illustrates this most . . . dramatically. The French-Swiss author Valère Novarina is one of the most recognized living playwrights in France. His new opus is called *Le Vivier des noms* [*The Pool of Nouns*]. Novarina's theatrical work is about language itself, as this title and others indicate (*Le théâtre des paroles, Devant la parole, Le babil des classes dangereuses, Je tu il*). His writing is defined by a proliferation of words, many invented with a linguistic jubilation that situates him somewhere between Rabelais and Joyce, the poet Henri Michaux, and children's books writer Claude Ponti, to the point of near untranslatability (as will become apparent in the next paragraphs, with excerpts from the dialogues). Indeed, his essays have been published in other languages more than have his plays. It should probably come as no surprise that this latest creation of his metaphysical comedy of the Word echoes the recent gender wars in France: is not grammatical gender about nouns, their feminization or masculinization, and rules of agreement?

It is impossible to summarize Novarina's plays; this one is no exception. Characters with names that could have been borrowed from Lewis Carroll (such as "the Unindividual" and "the Delogician"), funny ("Abbot Boom" and "John Too Late") or poetic ("the Woman of the Shade" and "the Parietal Child"), come in and go out, sometimes return and often disappear, shout and run with a flurry of words. While there is constant action, it is hard to say what, if anything, is going on—except absurd questions, grand statements, and endless enumerations. The opening description of the set that first evokes a bourgeois stage soon transforms into a narrative, whereas the first character to enter seems to read stage directions: "They go out. The theatre is empty. Enters Adam." "The Historian" soon proclaims: "[T]he audience requests a new section of action." She then continues: "Enters a dead man. Everyone goes out, except the dead man," who is soon asked to recite a list of verbs and obliges with imaginary verb groups *à la Borges*. All this in the first three pages (7–9).

One important scene explicitly refers to gender. A character approaches another: "I saw you, eight years ago, playing the part of the Logologist in *L'Acte inconnu*." This is the title of another play by Novarina, also presented to great acclaim during the Avignon festival in 2007 in the Papal Palace. "Your performance delighted me so much that I learned your part by heart." "Do you know," responds the other, "that I quickly abandoned that role to play a much more important one—Raymond de la Matière"? The first speaker exclaims in admiration: "[T]he bold inventor of the theory of the jar, the famous philosopher!" (88). Both can now stage a scene supposedly borrowed from the old play, although, as we shall see, it turns out to be radically different as it is updated for the French gender wars of the 2010s.

Raymond's name clearly makes him a materialist philosopher: "Language is not a fragment of the divine Word. Language is a hormone. A chemical substance." The audience is warned by the Logologist in an aside: "'Tis a scoundrel speaking" (92). This is a literal quotation from the play *Tartuffe*: *C'est un scélérat qui parle*. Molière's common sense is, quite explicitly, a constant counterpoint to the mad philosopher—especially in the stage version (with a character sent by "Valère," "Harpagon's son-in-law" in *The Miser* but also the author's unusual first name, and old insults from Molière's final play, *The Imaginary Invalid*). Raymond de la Matière is thus defined in purely negative terms: "Ladies and gentlemen, I must warn you first: I am hostile to things, I am an enemy of nature, an adversary of God, opposed to animals, recalcitrant to human life" (90).

Nevertheless, the enthusiasm of the Logologist remains intact: "I just read in issue number 93666 of *Ideologies Magazine* that you are one of our philosophical heavyweights! As you constantly broaden the range of your thinking, you have moved from philosophy to psychology, from psychology to sociology, from sociology to saucietology, from saucietology to saucieto-globalo-logology, and then to politics." The word "saucietology" is fabricated, probably to mock the neologism "sociétal": in contemporary usage, this intellectual "sauce" vaguely characterizes "new" social issues (other than class)—such as gender. But it is the last word that provokes the philosopher's ire: "Inaccurate! I did not move to *la politique*, I moved to *le politique*. Politically, you suck!" (93–94). In French, grammatical gender helps distinguish between institutional and electoral politics (in the feminine) and power relationships (in the masculine). But of course, once again, "'tis a scoundrel speaking": this novel definition of politics in a Foucaultian mode is meant to seem bizarre. Not surprisingly, it is through grammatical gender that the supposed irrationality of postmodern philosophy is thus revealed.

This distinction initiates the question of gender. "Beware! He is about to launch his Summa against people." The *Somme contre les gens* (echoing Thomas Aquinas's "Summa Contra Gentiles") was part of the 2007 play, *L'Acte inconnu*. In *Le Vivier des noms*, something happens to the words: Raymond de la Matière rectifies this formulation and asks in four different languages that make the new meaning explicit to listen to my "somme Contre les *genrrres*! Sum'-against-Gender'! Adversus-haereses-sexualis-nominibuso-rum! Philologich-zexualoglobichem-Kampf!" The rest of the dialogue makes clear that "against genders" is the opposite of "against gender": Raymond de la Matière starts to "undo gender" (grammatically), thus embodying gender studies from the point of view of Catholic demonstrators against the (so-called) theory-of-gender. The Logologist exults: "This is magnificent! You are truly the enemy of humankind." This echoes a declaration by Molière's *Misanthrope*, though with a pun: in French, *l'ennemi du genre humain* conflates Novarina's two Sums—the earlier one against "people" and the new one against "genders."

"What is the difference between *le musique* and *la musique*; between *le pêche à la ligne* and *la pêche à la ligne*; between *le politique* and *la politique*?" Translation here becomes impossible: in French, both music and angling only exist in the feminine—contrary to politics, which can also be masculine. The strange question provokes a revealing answer by the Logologist, who is clearly at a loss: "I was no good at English." The confusion of genders is explicitly linked to the English language—in which nouns have no grammatical gender. The philosopher then takes pain to explain the meaning of this absurdity: "[W]hen you practice *le cuisine* instead of *la cuisine* [cooking], you need not peel vegetables any longer, you can make an omelet without breaking eggs. In the same way, running *le course à pied* [running, normally a feminine noun] in an armchair saves your sweat, just like *le politique* is pure politics that can be practiced effortlessly. One contemplates *le politique*." The materialist philosopher turns out to be just the opposite: an idealist. These fake gender distinctions are exposed as pure abstractions, devoid of any reality; worse, they justify the denial of the materiality of the body (through sport and food). This is the familiar attack launched by the Vatican against gender studies, and in particular against American philosopher Judith Butler, *Bodies That Matter* notwithstanding.

This play with grammatical gender continues with the feminization (and masculinization) of nouns that could refer to both men and women (97): "Give me the reverse gender inversion of these words": "speakerette" (*locuteresse*), "neighbor" (*riverain*), "neighauthoress" (*écriveraine*). Raymond dismisses all the answers in a Latin reminiscent of Molière's quacks ("falsissimus," "nullissimus"), until the Logologist comes up with the most radical formulation of the problem ("la homme," "le femme"), and with a solution that is no less farcical: *Lu Youmanbing*! The (supposedly) French pronunciation of "human being" once again suggests that neutralization is an American import. But the answer more profoundly modifies the French language through the article: neither *le* nor *la—lu. Lû solution*! (98). The philosopher erupts with enthusiasm: our "plethora of vowels" are but "remnants of the Old Regime" (a phrase reminiscent of Ozouf's argument against American-style feminism). "Let us replace every vowel by the sound û! Let us neutralize language! Let us neutralize thinking!" The examples he chooses resonate with contemporary polemics on the feminization of titles: "Lu ministre, lu secrétaire, lu sénateûre, lu youmanbingue." The irony is explicit: "Since we cannot find a resolution to the contradictions in reality and the disorder of life, let us get our own house in order: let us simplify language!" (99). For Novarina as much as for grammarians of the past, gender is not just about language; it is also about "reality" and "life."

While the scene resonates with recent conservative attacks against the theory-of-gender, *Le Vivier des noms* is not a polemical tract; it is first and foremost a play. This complicates matters, as literature tends to be suffused with ambiguity. The attempt to demonstrate that undermining gender stereotypes is ridiculous can easily backfire, as it did in parodies of the theory-of-gender by its conservative opponents, from the movement *Civitas* to the activists of *Hommen*, from "religious drag" to "closeted homophobia" (Fassin, "Gender"). Let us consider this example: "*lu* mommy reads the paper" ("lit *lu* journal"); *lu* daddy peels the leek" ("pluche *lu* poiru"). Is the silliness of the omnipresence of one vowel reiterated by the inversion of conventional gender roles, or does this inversion question the necessity of the convention, which appears equally silly? Reversing gender stereotypes also reminds the audience of what they are: not a natural order of things, but a collection of stereotypical behaviors.

There is another potential contradiction. What is the problem with Raymond de la Matière and others in French gender studies who are under the influence of American feminists? Is it too much gender (as in the distinction between *le* and *la politique* or the feminization of functions), or not enough (as in the erasure of vowels that mark it grammatically)? This hesitation is not specific to literature, of course: Cardinal Ratzinger's 2004 Letter to Bishops "on the collaboration between men and women in the Church and in the World" denounced two kinds of feminism: one that exacerbates differences, and one that underplays them, "antagonism" and "denial" translating respectively into the war of the sexes and sexual indistinction. But what the play does is stage these contradictions, regardless of, or rather beyond, the ideological intentions of the playwright. Gender is French: its inscription in the language becomes all the more apparent in this theatrical representation, however satirical of gender studies.

The Return of the Repressed

The lesson of the scene (both intentionally and unintentionally) is that, in the French language, you cannot escape gender. What might seem, at first sight, to validate the attacks against gender studies could equally undermine their enemies. *Le Vivier des noms* might very well target the latter as much as the former. In fact, the play itself is not exempt from such ambiguities. One anecdote can be interpreted in this light. After seeing the play in Avignon, I purchased the text that had been published simultaneously in order to be able to quote from this "Sum against Gender." However, to my surprise, it does not appear as such in the book version, which still refers to the "Somme contre les gens"–*people*, not *gender*. This was all the more surprising since the author is also the director of his own play. I wrote to Novarina, who called me (on August 1, 2015). He was not aware that the printed version mistakenly referred to *gens*; he confirmed that, in staging his own play, he had insisted on the word *genderrr*; and he sent me a typewritten version of this scene, in a slightly modified version, dated July 5 (the night of the first performance), announcing that it should be used for the next printing (I have here quoted from both versions).

The play's denial of gender studies in the name of gender is thus denied in the printed play. Perhaps this is no accident; maybe it makes sense—not just as a "mistake" resulting from the haste of publishing the book in time for the festival, but as a Freudian slip. To support this tentative argument, I shall refer to a text that has played an important role in gender studies, despite the absence of the concept of gender. In 1978, Michel Foucault published *Herculine Barbin*, the memoirs of a nineteenth-century (pseudo) hermaphrodite first printed in 1874, after Barbin's death, by Ambroise Tardieu, an important figure of legal medicine of the time. This text is better known through the English translation of 1980, if only because Foucault added an introduction to that volume (only published in French the same year in a homophile magazine, *Arcadie*, as "Le vrai sexe"), which was not included in the French version of the book until my edition of 2014.

Judith Butler contributed to the fame of this document with her critique of the preface in *Gender Trouble*: while Foucault, in contradiction with his argument in the first volume of *History of Sexuality*, celebrates "the happy limbo of non-identity" that defines Barbin's early life in the female world of religious schools (Foucault, Introduction xiii), "the temptations to romanticize Herculine's sexuality as the utopian play of pleasures prior to the imposition and restrictions of 'sex' surely ought to be refused" (Butler 98). This discussion in English makes all the more sense if one goes back to the French formulation by Foucault: *les limbes heureuses d'une non-identité* (17). Uncharacteristically, the philosopher makes a grammatical mistake here: in French, *limbo* (*limbes*) is masculine, not feminine; with the correct gender agreement, the adjective should read *heureux*. As I have pointed out in an afterword to the new edition, Foucault seems to add this noun to the only three in French whose gender switches in the plural: *amours*, *délices*, *orgues*—love, delight, and religion that epitomize, in this narrative, or perhaps in the philosopher's fantasy, the bliss of "monosexuality" that we would call homosociality (232).

There are good reasons to count this "mistake" as yet another Freudian slip. First, Foucault keeps emphasizing the feminine definition of Barbin: the title of the French version not only gives "her" first name Herculine but also adds a female nickname: "called Alexina" (with the feminine agreement: *dite*). What is left out is Barbin's first name as a man, that is, "his" legal name at the time of death: Abel. Second, in his preface, Foucault always refers to Barbin in the feminine—except in one sentence that only confirms that she could not be a man: "[H]e was incapable of adapting himself to a new identity and ultimately committed suicide" (Foucault, Introduction xi). Elsewhere, the philosopher insists that "it is not a man who is speaking" (xiii); and while he does not imply that it is a woman, he only writes about her in the feminine, even when Barbin was identified as a man: "When Alexina composed her memoirs, she was not far from her suicide; for herself, she was still without a definite sex" (xiii).

Third, Foucault does not make a single reference to a striking feature of the text—at least in the French preface. While he points out that "Alexina wrote her memoirs about that life once her new identity had been discovered and established," he maintains, "[S]he did not write them from the point of view of that sex which had at last been brought to light" (Introduction xiii). But the narrator's "point of view" appears throughout the text: whereas the second part of the volume is in the masculine, the first is in the feminine. Moreover, these feminine adjectives and participles are italicized throughout these early years, while there is no equivalent attempt to call the reader's attention to masculine forms in later years. This is only acknowledged in a footnote reserved for the u.s. edition: "In the English translation of the text, it is difficult to render the play of masculine and feminine adjectives which Alexina applies to herself. They are, for the most part, feminine before she possessed Sara and masculine afterward" (xiii, n1).

This acknowledgment necessitated by the exercise of translation is, however, immediately dismissed as insignificant: "But this systematization, which is denoted by the use of italics, does not seem to describe a consciousness of being a woman becoming a consciousness of being a man; rather, it is an ironic reminder of grammatical, medical, and juridical categories that language must utilize but that the content of the narrative contradicts" (Foucault, Introduction xiii–xiv, n1). This comment leaves out the dissymmetry of italics between the first and the second parts—and thus the literary "play" that actually complicates the idea that "language *must* utilize" such categories. Indeed, the fact that the gender of the narrative changes not so much after but just as he (rather than she) "possessed Sara" clearly indicates that Barbin's grammatical use of gender is not dictated by medical or juridical categories; it signifies a definition of social gender by sexuality— indeed, by heterosexuality. In a word, it is anything but insignificant.

Actually, Foucault's own footnote contains one element suggesting that grammatical gender does matter. Since it concerns translation, it is not included in the French preface; but the French version can be found in a typewritten original now available in Foucault's archives purchased from his life partner Daniel Defert by the Bibliothèque Nationale de France in Paris. In English, the first sentence reads: "In the English translation of the text, it is difficult to render *the play of the masculine and feminine adjectives* which Alexina applies to herself" (xiii, my emphases). The French original reads: "le jeu des épithètes féminins et masculins." Remarkably, the philosopher makes another "mistake" here—and again, it is a problem of gender: in French, the word *épithète* is feminine, not masculine. This should read: "le jeu des épithètes féminines et masculines." Actually, the history of the word is worth recalling: according to dictionaries, *épithète* was masculine until the seventeenth century; only then did it become feminine. No wonder that Foucault preferred this term to the more common *adjectif* (as in the English translation). One could say that *épithète* is a linguistic hermaphrodite whose gender changes over time, thus an appropriate word when discussing the symmetrical gender changes, from the feminine to the masculine, within Barbin's narrative (and life).

Foucault's example mirrors that of Novarina. While the former minimizes the importance of grammar to exalt the possibility of nonidentity, the latter maximizes it to denounce ideologies of neutrality. Both illustrate in different ways, however, what might be called the return of the repressed. With the playwright, paradoxically, the critique of gender studies and the defense of grammatical gender erected in reaction end up merging—though perhaps the tension between the two resurfaces with the erasure of the "Summa against gender" in the published version of his play. In the philosopher's case, it is precisely when he denies the importance of gender, whether speaking of "nonidentity" or claiming that the play of grammatical gender is irrelevant, that it comes back with a vengeance through linguistic "mistakes" or Freudian slips.

Such paradoxes play an essential role in matters of gender. What this text has argued is that gender is not American by essence. Gender is French, too. But the point is not to reverse the theoretical nationalism criticized at the beginning of this text; on the contrary, this is a way to displace the question. Shifting to France here implies a move toward French—not "the French": while there is a longer tradition of gender studies in English, the French language helps those who use it, albeit unwittingly (or perhaps all the more efficiently since it is unconsciously), incorporate gender in almost every sentence. This is how "gender is French" should be understood: it is *in French*—inscribed in the language and inscribed through the language in French speakers and writers. History teaches us that the politics of grammatical gender are part and parcel of the politics of gender in society. This is why we must take grammar seriously. When it comes to gender, language matters.

Gender as a Language

Gender is in French, which means that it is French insofar as it is inscribed in the French language. But there is more: gender *is* a language. This actually derives from Scott's classic definition: not only is gender "a constitutive element of social relationships based on perceived differences between the sexes," but it is also "a primary way of signifying relations of power" ("Gender" 42). Not only is gender about sex; it is also a language that says much more: it signifies religion, class, race, and nation. The argument can thus be revised accordingly: gender is French insofar as it speaks of Frenchness. This is what I have tried to analyze in the polemics surrounding "marriage for all" and the so-called theory-of-gender with an emphasis on race and nation. The next paragraphs summarize this argument (Fassin, "Same-Sex").

The starting point of this interpretation is a comparison with the United States: on each side of the Atlantic, what is the issue that matters most to opponents of "gay marriage"? The answer is: while marriage itself is sacralized in the United States, there is a symmetrical sacralization of filiation in France. In each country, one or the other is supposed to be beyond the reach of democratic decision. This national difference has to do with different national models, that is, models of the nation: the contrast is not only among but also *about* nations; and, in both cases, it is about racialized definitions of imagined national communities. In the u.s. context, the racial meaning of marriage has long been most explicit in discussions of out-of-wedlock births, while filiation defines the French "stock" in contrast to immigration, thereby contributing to the racialization of the nation (*Français de souche*). The connection with the politics of same-sex marriage is clear: in the French Civil Code, filiation defines the rules not only of descent but also of citizenship; it prescribes who belongs in the family as well as in the nation, and conversely, who does not. Homophobia and racism can thus be understood as two versions of the same logic of naturalization (and of reaction against denaturalization)—of the family, on the one hand, and of the nation, on the other.

But this is not all. Despite their common logic, race and sex do not always coincide in the various rhetorics mobilized around "marriage for all." Indeed, the nature of their complex articulations becomes a political issue in itself. Let us take but one example. Throughout the aughts, according to homonationalist discourse, homophobia was supposed to belong outside or on the outskirts of the French nation, whether among non-European migrants or among their children, especially if they were Muslims. Opposition to equal rights allegedly defined "them," by contrast to "us"—fresh converts to what I have called "sexual democracy." This racialized reading was turned upside down a decade later, at the time of the "Manif pour tous" and later the "Printemps français."

The people demonstrating in the streets against the Taubira law were clearly not "of foreign origin": they were Catholics from Versailles and other bourgeois parts of France, whether urban or rural—a far cry from the working class, though often unemployed youths from the *banlieues*, France's racialized suburbs. In a word, homophobia turned out to be white: it was still about national identity, though now it was about "us," not "them." The mobilization against the so-called theory-of-gender illustrated the hesitation between the two versions of France: on the one hand, it was initiated by the Vatican and pursued in the streets by conservative Catholics from private schools; on the other hand, it was prolonged in public schools by conservative Muslims. These strange bedfellows created a dilemma for the far Right: was such an unholy alliance an option? Or, to put it differently, should sexual politics be the primary focus, or should racial politics?

This is not just a problem of logic; it becomes a question of rhetoric. It is not simply about naturalization (and denaturalization), that is, the convergence of racial and sexual logics. It has to do with rhetorics, either convergent or divergent, of sex and race. This has theoretical consequences. If Scott's definition of gender as "a primary way of signifying relationships of power" helps us understand that it means much more than just sex (that is, marriage and family, heterosexuality and homosexuality), and implicates, in particular, religion, class, race, and nation, what *signifying* means still needs to be clarified. In fact, it has two different meanings. Saussure's distinction between *langue* (language) and *parole* (speech) helps us understand it. Same-sex marriage speaks about relationships of power; this is why the meaning of the polemic is not just sexual but also racial: it functions as a political *language*. But this is a language spoken by different actors: political *speech* makes sense of the intersections between sex and race; it articulates them. Not only does same-sex marriage *signify* politically; it is also *signified* by political usage. One needs to understand both *what* it signifies (logically), and *how* it is signified (rhetorically).

Approaching gender in this way implies that gender is not just in the language; it is a language. It is French both because it is in French and because it is about Frenchness. One theoretical consequence has to do with an issue that has become central in feminist politics as well as in gender studies, including in France in the last decade: intersectionality (Fassin, "D'un langage"). Legal scholar Kimberlé Crenshaw first conceptualized the term. The point was to be able to take into account the plurality of domination, in particular racial and sexual. This is where gender provides a useful theoretical framework: it signifies not only sexual but also other forms of domination (including racial). It is true that intersectionality has to do with social categories (such as Blacks and women), as well as political identities (such as Black women); it can also define properties that coexist in social actors (such as class, race, sex). But it also works as a language in which the different forms of domination signify one another.

Speaking about gender can be a way to signify racialized class relations in France; conversely, class and race are used to signify gender. This mutual process of signification can be called *translation*. This is why intersectionality is not just a theoretical issue; the reason it remains a vibrant political argument is that translating one form of domination into another is indeed political work. Just like gender, not only does it *signify*; at the same time, it *is signified* by political usage. The difference between *language* and *speech* applies here, too. Intersectionality does not only describe the inevitable logic of plural forms of domination. There is something at play in what social actors do with it, that is, in the rhetorics they mobilize to produce these translations.

The theoretical paradigm of gender thus helps move beyond a substantialist approach to domination, including in its plural form. Thinking about gender as a language does not imply that gender functions as an exception. On the contrary, it can serve as a model to reflect on how domination, whether sexual or not, works by mobilizing various symbolic meanings, such as class, race, and religion, so as to establish a sexual order but also a national one. This is why the question of language is to be taken seriously. The theoretical suggestion that gender not only is in the language but also is a language is not just a metaphor. In fact, it helps understand how power functions metaphorically. The Frenchness of gender is a reminder that gender is also about Frenchness. But beyond this, the argument developed in this paper hopefully helps bridge the gap between theoretical and political approaches to gender. Not only does gender speak about politics; it is also a language of politics, used by social actors to signify sex, of course, but beyond that, domination in its various forms—and thus also to resignify them.

ÉRIC FASSIN is a professor of sociology at the University of Paris 8 Vincennes–Saint-Denis in the departments of political science and of gender studies (which he cochairs). His work focuses on sexual and racial politics, as well as their intersections, especially concerning immigration issues. He recently edited a special issue of *Contemporary French Civilization* (with Daniel Borrillo) called *Au-delà du mariage* (Fall 2014), and one of *Raisons politiques* titled *Les langages de l'intersectionnalité* (May 2015). He is a coauthor of *Discutir Houellebecq: Cinco ensayos críticos entre Buenos Aires y París* (Capital Intelectual, Buenos Aires, 2015) and is currently completing an essay titled *Le genre français* (La Découverte, 2016).

Notes   1   In this text, I try to translate the distinction I have drawn in French between "l'Amérique" and "les États-Unis": while America (and therefore the adjective *American*) is a rhetorical figure, the United States (and therefore the adjective *U.S.*) is an empirical reality.

Nota bene: All translations of untranslated texts are mine (in particular my own texts and Novarina's plays).

Works Cited   Académie française. "La féminisation des noms de métiers, fonctions, grades ou titres—Mise au point." 10 Oct. 2014. http://www.academie-francaise.fr/actualites/la-feminisation-des-noms -de-metiers-fonctions-grades-ou-titres-mise-au-point-de-lacademie.

"Are French Women More Tolerant?" Room for Debate. *New York Times* 18 May 2011. http:// www.nytimes.com/roomfordebate/2011/05/18/are-french-women-more-tolerant.

Bourdieu, Pierre, and Loïc Wacquant. "On the Cunning of Imperialist Reason." *Theory, Culture, and Society* 16.1 (1999): 41–58.

Butler, Judith. *Gender Trouble: Feminism and the Subversion of Identity.* New York: Routledge, 1990.

Chervel, André. *Histoire de la grammaire scolaire. Et il fallut apprendre à écrire à tous les petits Français.* Paris: Payot, 1977.

Cusset, François. *French Theory: Foucault, Derrida, Deleuze, and Cie et les mutations de la vie intellectuelle aux États-Unis.* Paris: La Découverte, 2003.

Derrida, Jacques. "The Time Is Out of Joint." Trans. Peggy Kamuf. *Deconstruction is/in America: A New Sense of the Political.* Ed. Anselm Haverkamp. New York: NYU P, 1995. 14–38.

Ezekiel, Judith. "Anti-féminisme et anti-américanisme: un mariage politiquement réussi." *Nouvelles Questions Féministes* 17 (1995): 59–76.

Fassin, Éric. "Au-delà du consentement: pour une théorie féministe de la séduction." *Raisons politiques* 46 (2012): 47–66.

——————. "D'un langage l'autre: l'intersectionnalité comme traduction." *Les langages de l'intersectionnalité.* Spec. issue of *Raisons politiques* 58 (2015): 9–24.

——————. "Gender and the Problem of Universals: Catholic Mobilizations and Sexual Democracy in France." *Religion and Gender* 6.2 (2016). Forthcoming. https://www.religion andgender.org/.

——————. "The Purloined Gender: American Feminism in a French Mirror." *French Historical Studies* 22.1 (1999): 113–38.

——————. "Same-Sex Marriage, Nation, and Race: French Political Logics and Rhetorics." *Au-delà du mariage.* Spec. issue of *Contemporary French Civilization* 39.3 (2014): 281–301.

Fassin, Éric, and Véronique Margron. *Hommes, femmes: quelle différence?* Paris: Salvator, 2011.

Foucault, Michel. *Herculine Barbin, dite Alexina B.* 1978. Paris: Gallimard, 2014.

——————. *Herculine Barbin.* Trans. Richard McDougall. New York: Pantheon, 1980. vii–xvii.

Novarina, Valère. *Le Vivier des noms.* Paris: P.O.L., 2015.

─────────. "Le Vivier des noms." Unpubl. ms. 5 July 2015.

Ozouf, Mona. *Women's Words: Essay on French Singularity.* Trans. Jane Marie Todd. Chicago: U of Chicago P, 1998.

Scott, Joan Wallach. "Feminism? A Foreign Import." Room for Debate. *New York Times* 18 May 2011. http://www.nytimes.com/roomfordebate/2011/05/18/are-french-women-more-tolerant/feminism-a-foreign-import.

─────────. "Gender: A Useful Category of Historical Analysis." 1986. *Gender and the Politics of History.* New York: Columbia UP, 1988. 28–50.

Smith, Bonnie. "Not a Matter of 'Frenchness.'" Room for Debate. *New York Times* 18 May 2011. http://www.nytimes.com/roomfordebate/2011/05/18/are-french-women-more-tolerant/not-a-matter-of-frenchness.

Viennot, Éliane. *Non, le masculin ne l'emporte pas sur le féminin! Petite histoire des résistances de la langue française.* Paris: Édition iXe, 2014.

Yaguello, Marina. *Le sexe des mots.* Paris: Seuil, 1995.